COUNTRY ROADS

Memoirs from Rural Canada

edited by Pam Chamberlain

D1282061

NIMBUS
PUBLISHING

Nimbus Publishing Limited
3731 Mackintosh Street, Halifax, NS B3K 5A5
(902) 455-4286   nimbus.ca

Printed and bound in Canada
Cover and interior design: Matt Reid
Pam Chamberlain photo: Drew Stolee

Library and Archives Canada Cataloguing in Publication

Chamberlain, Pam, 1970-
Country roads : memoirs from rural Canada / Pam Chamberlain.
ISBN 978-1-55109-759-6

1. Rural men—Canada—Biography. 2. Rural women—Canada—Biography. 3. Country life—Canada. 4. Canada—Biography. I. Title.

S522.C3C53 2010   971'.0097340922   C2009-907318-8

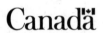 

We acknowledge the financial support of the Government of Canada through the Book Publishing Industry Development Program (BPIDP) and the Canada Council, and of the Province of Nova Scotia through the Department of Tourism, Culture and Heritage for our publishing activities.

We are grateful to the Alberta Foundation for the Arts for providing funding that made this anthology possible.

For my parents, Ralph and Gloria Chamberlain,
who moved us to the farm in 1971

TABLE OF CONTENTS

Part II - Journeys

Part III - Departures

Introduction

I GREW UP in the rolling hills of the North Saskatchewan River Valley, on the northern edge of the aspen parkland. My parents ran a mixed farm, growing wheat, oats, and barley. Over the years, they raised cattle, horses, sheep, pigs, turkeys, chickens, ducks, geese, rabbits, cats, and dogs. Our farm was much like the farms of our neighbours, and my brother, my sister, and I were typical farm kids.

I rode my first horse when I was two. Paddy was a bay gelding that had been my father's horse since Dad was eleven years old. When I turned eleven, Grandma gave me a palomino mare named Brena, and I rode her bareback to help Dad move cows or to visit friends on neighbouring farms. At an auction at the stockyards, I bought a flock of three Suffolk-cross ewes—Julia, Lucy, and Pepper—that I faithfully tended during lambing season. As a member of the Tulliby Lake 4-H Club, I raised Charolais-Hereford calves named after characters in my favourite novels and cried my eyes out each spring when I sold them for slaughter, even when I was seventeen years old and, I was told, far too old to be crying over an animal. I grudgingly helped my mother weed our large vegetable garden, pick saskatoons and chokecherries, and make jams and preserves. I painted fences, picked roots, and mowed the lawn.

I shouldn't pretend it was all work and no play, though. We found plenty of time to ride our bikes, make expeditions into the bush, and build rafts and forts. And, as my parents will surely recall, we spent many

Pam (age 18 months) in the calving pen on the family farm near Tulliby Lake, Alberta, 1972

afternoons lazily flopped on the floor of the living room watching re-runs of *The Flintstones* or *Happy Days* on CBC or CTV, the only TV channels our antennae picked up.

When I was an adolescent, we often visited my city cousins, and I remember recognizing early on that there was a broad gulf between them and us. It wasn't only that we hadn't seen the latest shows on cable TV, that we didn't know how to hang out at a shopping mall, or that we rarely went to a movie theatre. While I did have some interests in common with my cousins, of course, such as my burgeoning interests in fashion and pop music, many of my passions were foreign to them. I spent my spare time training my 4-H steer and grooming my horse. I worried about the plague of tent caterpillars munching their way through the poplar stands on our hill, and about drought, hailstorms, and early frosts. My concerns were no greater than those of my urban cousins, but they certainly weren't the same. I knew I was different.

As I moved away to larger and larger cities for university and work, I found myself—with my rural background—a minority in academic, work, and social settings. What a delight it was, in those environments, to occasionally meet a fellow farm kid with whom I could exchange stories of country schools, long bus rides, and beloved horses. I realized I was likely to have more in common with someone raised on a potato farm in far-off Prince Edward Island than with someone who grew up in the Mill Woods suburb of nearby Edmonton. As years passed, I became more certain that my rural upbringing had significantly moulded me, perhaps more than anything else had.

That belief drove me to compile this anthology. What a delight it was to read submissions from across the country and discover I was right: I have much in common with country kids from across Canada, whether they grew up in Nova Scotia or British Columbia, whether in the 1930s or the 1990s. I wasn't the only one who built forts with straw bales or spent summer days weeding a shelter belt. I wasn't the only one who, in the absence of plentiful human companions, found a best friend in a dog or a horse. I wasn't the only one whose rural background profoundly shaped who I am today.

I don't suggest, though, that all rural people or experiences are the same. The writers in this anthology remind us that there is no one rural experience. After all, rural people, places, and communities vary greatly in a country as geographically vast and culturally diverse as Canada. For some, the country was a place of happiness and belonging; for others, it was a source of hardship and sorrow. For many, it was both. Some contributors loved their homes and never wanted to leave; others couldn't wait to escape to the city. Despite these differences, common themes emerged in the narratives.

I was struck by how powerful the sense of home is for those who grew up in rural settings, and how closely that sense of home is tied to the land. In his memoir, *Lake of the Prairies*, Warren Cariou has written of his home in Meadow Lake, Saskatchewan, "I suspect that most people have a Meadow Lake of their own, a place they can't let go of. … It has taken hold of them and shaped them so irrevocably that they can't imagine who they would be without it." This is clearly the case for many writers who contributed to this anthology. Their senses of self, their views of the world, and perhaps even their creative energies are inextricably linked with their home places.

Although I left when I was seventeen and have been away for over twenty years, Tulliby Lake, Alberta, is the only place I have ever called "home" and perhaps the only place I ever will. In *Inside Memory*, novelist Timothy Findley wrote about his home in Ontario:

> This is what I have that feeds me—both as a person and as a writer: the curve of these hills, the lines of these horizons, the shapes and smells of these trees, the harshness of these stones,

the ghosts within these walls, the harshness of this climate—and
all its weathers—and the sounds which fill my ears.

Home, for a person raised in the country, is only partly related to a house
and the people who live in it. What makes a place home is that particular
shape of the horizon, that particular smell of the soil on a rainy spring
morning, that particular chorus of birdsong at dawn.

The landscape of my family's farm defined not only *home* but also
beauty for me. The enormous evergreens and cedars of British Columbia
are lovely and enchanting, but I could never feel at home among them.
For me, only spindly aspens, saskatoons, and chokecherry bushes will do.
The Rocky Mountains and Atlantic Ocean awe me, but they could never be
home. For me, home means open rolling hills covered in prairie wool and
wildflowers. The sky that says home to me is big and blue—even on the
coldest winter day.

Of course, each of the writers in the collection has his or her particular
vision of home. For Keith Collier, who grew up in the tiny outport of
St. Joseph's Cove on the south coast of Newfoundland, home isn't home
without the ice-cold waves of the Atlantic Ocean. For Luanne Armstrong,
home is the towering mountains, dark forests, and glacial lakes of British
Columbia's Kootenay region.

It is striking that of the thirty-four writers in this anthology, only three
live on the land on which they grew up, and two of those three returned
only after a long absence. Many rural families simply found it too difficult to
make a living off the land, as Janice Acton, Habeeb Salloum, and Rudy Wiebe
reveal. Inexperience, harsh climates, economic challenges, and many other
factors contributed to failures that sent families fleeing to cities in search of
better lives. In many other cases, rural teenagers chose to leave their homes
and families behind—also, they thought, in search of better lives.

A mood of loss and longing threads through many of the narratives.
As Marianne Ackerman demonstrates in "Departure and the Eternal
Return," no matter how far we move from our rural homes, those places
continue to pull us back, and we continue to yearn for them. When I
packed my suitcases and headed off to university at seventeen (and,
of course, most farm kids must move hundreds of kilometres to go to
college), it never occurred to me that I was making a one-way trip. Perhaps

it wouldn't have bothered me, back then, even if I had understood, for I was eager to see and learn new things in bigger and better places. I couldn't have imagined that two decades later I would carry in my heart a homesick ache that strengthens rather than weakens with the passing years. I couldn't have foreseen that the fantasy of going home would become the most desirable and unattainable of my dreams. For complex reasons that are difficult to understand or articulate, it seems heartbreakingly impossible to return to that place. Wes Jackson, an advocate of sustainable agricultural, has written that in North American universities "there is no such thing as a 'homecoming' major." Most of us who trotted off to university in search of greener pastures realized that truth too late. Many of us discovered, as Harvey Walker laments in "Harvest Moon," we never can go home again. For even if we do travel back to visit those places, we often find them changed—the landscape altered, the people gone, the way of life vanished. Eventually, as Jill Sexsmith suggests in "A Country Song Played Backward," country roads can take us home only in our memories.

Many of us who grew up in the country feel urgency in telling our stories. After all, our stories are becoming increasingly extraordinary ones, for there are fewer and fewer people living in those places. In 1910, 60% of Canadians lived in rural communities. This number dropped to 40% in 1950 and to 25% in 1975. Today, only 20% of Canadians live in rural areas and only 2% live on farms. Add to these startling figures the fact that the average age of rural residents is quickly rising, and it is clear there will be fewer and fewer Canadian children who grow up in the country. Many of us who were fortunate enough to do so know our rural upbringings profoundly shaped our sense of ourselves, our world, and our place in it.

These memoirs are like the blocks of a patchwork quilt. Each is distinct, yet together they create a composite image of rural life. Although no individual can hope to tell "the" rural story—for rural people and their experiences vary as much as urban ones do—each of us can tell his or her own story. As Shelley Leedahl insists in "Road Trip," each of us can say, with authority: For *me*, in this place, at that time, it was like *this*.

—PC

Part I
Home

Landing
LUANNE ARMSTRONG

THE PIECE OF land on which I grew up and have lived most of my life was once a creek delta, a cedar swamp, an almost-flat place at the bottom of the Purcell Mountains, before it was cleared by Pierre Longueval, the young Frenchman who, in 1920, bought 160 acres of raw land beside Kootenay Lake and set out to create a farm. Kootenay Lake is a long, broad, deep expanse of clear green-blue water threaded between the Selkirk Mountains on the west and the Purcells on the east. Human inhabitants perch uneasily here, on bits of flat land on the toes of the mountain next to the lake. There are few beaches. The rocks are granite. The forest is dark—mixed fir, larch, pine, and hemlock.

When my parents, my two brothers and baby sister, and I arrived at the farm, it was early spring in 1955. Our parents were excited. The farm was a place of promise and hope.

I was five. We had been living in Riondel, a mining camp toward the northern end of Kootenay Lake. Riondel was a dishevelled place made up mostly of people who had migrated to Canada after World War Two. These people were referred to then, by everyone, simply as DPs, although most of them were Italian. Many of them didn't yet speak English, and they lived in a haphazard collection of shacks, tents, and bunkhouses built by Consolidated Mining and Smelting, called CM & S, or more simply, the Company. Riondel was a tiny place at the end of six miles of rutted twisty

Luanne (age 6) on Lady and her brother Phil (age 8) on Gypsy, 1955

dirt road that led from the main road. Besides the houses and tents, there was a gaping hole in the rocks beside the lake that was simply called "the mine." Every day, my father disappeared into that hole and then came home again at night, dirty and tired, carrying his black lunch bucket.

Before Riondel, we had lived on another small farm, called the Mannerino place after its first owners, just above the south end of the lake. This farm was a cleared piece of steep mountainside beside a creek. The Wilsons, who lived a mile down the dirt road, were our nearest neighbours. I played sometimes with their son Alan, who was three months younger than me. But in Riondel, my mother promised me, there would be lots of children to play with. I was three, my older brother was six and just starting school, my younger brother was only a year old, and my mother was pregnant again. The idea of other children my own age to play with was exciting.

When we first moved to Riondel, we lived in a company bunkhouse on the outskirts of town, but the next spring, we moved to the unfinished basement of the new house our father was building for us. The basement was damp, the walls and floor were concrete; the only heat was from the wood cookstove. This house was right in the middle of a lot of other half-finished houses. Outside the basement door was a dirt yard and, beyond that, enclosed in a picket fence, an expanse that my father had said would be our garden.

I stayed inside a lot, at first, underfoot and unsure of myself in such a new environment. One day my exasperated and exhausted mother said, "Go outside, there's lots of children out there. Go make some friends." Reluctantly, I slumped outside by myself, loitering by the back door, shuffling my feet in the muddy dirt. Finally, I saw a boy coming down the dirt street, and I went towards him. The next thing I saw was a rock spiralling towards my head. I saw it clearly, but I didn't have time to duck—in fact, I was too astonished to duck. Then the rock hit me and shattered my faith in making friends, and I ran wailing back into the house.

My mother found out who the boy was and told me to stay away from him. Gradually, my older brother and I began to find out who the other kids were and to make friends. The Italian family next to us had several children, and we did play with them sometimes, but more often we threw rocks at them over the back fence. The kids in the camp were part of shifting gangs that formed and dissolved, fought and played together, and I learned to wait until my brother Phil came home from school so I had an ally and a protector.

Eventually my mother found me another friend, a girl who lived up the hill above our house. She was the daughter of the mine supervisor, but I didn't know that—I did know I had to climb to her house through the trees and up a long flight of stairs. I was entranced by these trees, by the grey-piped stems of young alders, as well as by the long moss-covered flight of stairs in front of her house. Whenever I went to her house, I would climb slowly up and down the stairs, loving the feeling it gave me, with no ability to understand why. I had no words for beauty—and since I was alone, there was no one to ask. But something about that place, something about the slender lines of trees next to the grey wooden stairs, the broad yellow flowers of skunk cabbage among the trees, the brilliant multi-shades of green, called me, and I responded.

———◆———

I also learned to fight in Riondel, a skill that stood me in good stead in later school years. One spring morning, I stood outside on the road with my dad and a bunch of other men—the mine was on strike and the men had nothing much to do. Junie Munro was there with her dad, Hughie, who was big and red faced and English. Soon the men egged Junie and me into fighting. Junie was older than me; I was four and she was five. We were little kids, but it remains in my mind a fight between giants. I knew that my mom and dad didn't like Hughie, so even though Junie was older and heavier, I fought for my family and my dad. As we yelled and tore at each other and rolled around on the gravel road, I felt her give in, and I rolled on top of her and began pounding her head into the gravel. One of the men, maybe Junie's dad, pulled me off and made us apologize to each other, but I knew my triumph. I knew from that moment that I could win a fight if I had to.

There were a few other bright moments. In the summer, some days my father would come home, stooped and dirty from the mine, and we would take our supper to the beach north of town and play in the shallow water while the sun bent the light over the mountains on the other side of the lake.

But the winters were long and dark and damp. My mother was unhappy. She couldn't make friends since most of the women in Riondel didn't speak much English. She didn't want this new baby. We three small children always seemed to have colds from living in the damp basement. We sat inside and stared out the window while rain dripped off the lumber scaffolding on the makeshift roof and leaked in under the front door.

Winters in the Kootenays are always dark. The long narrow north-south valleys sock in with clouds in November, a ceiling that doesn't lift until March, and the snow that comes is usually wet slush. But occasionally it would snow a deep rug of powdery snow, and usually after that the sun would come out. On one occasion this happened on a Sunday, and the whole town turned out with cardboard boxes, toboggans, and sleighs. Everyone spent an afternoon sliding down one of the hilly streets. Someone made a fire and someone else donated hot chocolate.

When evening came, I didn't want to quit. My mother grabbed my hand and towed me reluctantly home, but while she was making dinner I slipped out, took my small red sleigh, and went back to the hill. In the darkness, I slid and swooped until my father came to find me.

One Sunday afternoon, the tent on the lot next to us burned. The people got out and the neighbours came running, but a canvas tent only takes a few minutes to burn. The ruins of the tent smoked for days while the camp kids, including my brother and I, raked through the warm ashes for the pennies that we heard had been in a jar in the tent. But the fire upset my mother. The parents and their five children had barely made it of the tent alive.

My mother began to hate Riondel. She could never get warm. She stuffed wood into the stove and shivered anyway. She was still in her early twenties and pregnant with her fourth child. When my father came home, she would rage at him, and he would rage back. They had moved to Riondel to try to earn enough to money to build up a stake so they could go back to farming. But now they were too young and exhausted, and the mine didn't pay enough to get them out of the trap of poverty and endless work into which they had fallen.

When my sister, Robin, was born, the cord was twisted around her neck and she was blue from lack of oxygen. When my mother came home, my small sister cried and cried. One night a few months later, my mother began crying and crying as well and couldn't stop—finally some men came, and she went away with them. A few days later my grandmother, my mother's mother, came to look after us. My grandmother and my father were never friends—I don't think they ever even liked each other, but there were four small children to be cared for.

Then my father got sick as well. In the mornings, when he got up, he coughed and coughed and hacked up black mucous. He got headaches and occasionally blacked out at work, but the company doctor didn't know what was wrong. At that time, both of my parents chain-smoked, as did almost everyone they knew. My father had managed to get himself out of the black depths of the mine, work which he hated and for which he was too tall, and reassigned to loading cyanide-laced mine slag on the dock; he hand-rolled his own cigarettes and smoked a toxic combination of lead, cyanide, and tobacco. My mother had come home again, but she was still far from well. She was exhausted all the time.

My grandfather decided to retire from farming and move into the nearby small town of Creston. He offered to sell the farm to my parents. They were both homesick for farming, for land, and for distance from other people and so, finally, we left Riondel behind. We arrived, late one night with all our stuff crammed into the back of our green Dodge pickup, at a cabin on the edge of the farm that was called Shelackie's cabin after the man who had built it. It had been sitting empty for years. It smelled of damp plywood from the always-leaking toilet, of creosote from the bridge timbers that Louis Shelackie had used to build it, and of pack rats.

In Riondel, I had become used to being on my own. I liked to wander, and no one had the time or energy to worry about it much. The farm invited wandering; I didn't know where anything was and now my father disappeared each day across the pasture towards my grandfather's house. One morning, I set out to follow him, but it was hard going. The grass was tall, there was a wide brown creek which meandered between humps of mud, and beyond that, a jungle of thistles and ferns with thin trails winding through into darkness. I could see my grandparents' house, but not how to get there. I started into the thistle jungle, where the paths were so narrow the thistles reached out to catch and scratch my bare arms. It was dark in the thistle patch, and I could no longer see the house. I heard crashing behind me; it was Tiny the Jersey cow, the one my dad called muley because she had no horns, and the other cow, Bossy, the black and white Holstein, following me through the thistles. I'd met them before; my father had taken us out to the barn and squirted milk in our faces out of their glistening huge bags and thick teats, but my father was far away and the cows were close. I ran as fast as I could, twisting and turning down the many tangled aisles of this enormous jungle, until I spotted the page-wire fence, sagging under its burden of brush. I made it over the fence and into the yard.

My father had seen me coming. He was standing there, laughing at someone so foolish as to be afraid of a couple of cows.

"Cows won't hurt you," he said. "Turn around, stand up to them. Yell at them."

I believed whatever my father said. I stared back at the cows, triumphant now on the right side of the fence and beside my powerful father.

Since I was around, my father did what was most natural to him and found some work for me to do. He said from now on I would have to feed the chickens. If I forgot, he said, the chickens would go hungry and it would be my fault. Bantam chickens dusted themselves and scratched and squatted under every bush. He showed me where the grain was and threw some on the ground. The chickens came running.

From then on, when I went to the shed and got a bucket of grain, chickens came running from all over the yard. They crowded around me and ate what I gave them. I loved their colours, their magnificent glowing iridescent feathers, their red combs, and their wise, golden eyes. But mostly I was proud of how they came running, that they followed me and trusted me to feed them. One evening, I stood with my small tin can of wheat at the edge of the yard, staring across the pasture, where the sunlight was slanting over the emerald grass, and I fell into belonging. My feet sank into the grass, my head swam in the warm air while the chickens pecked and scratched at my feet. I was home now, and I knew it, knew that wherever I roamed, from now on, on this land, it would belong to me and me to it.

———◆———

My grandfather and his wife, whom we called Grantie because she was the sister of our real grandmother who had died, were still living in the old green farmhouse. Every day, my mother made lunch for all of us and loaded it into my older brother's wagon, and we all trudged down the dirt road to the farmhouse, where my grandfather and Grantie were slowly packing and getting ready to move. One day my brother tried to tow the wagon with his tricycle, and, going down the hill, he went too fast and the pot of stew that was in the wagon turned over and spilled. My mother raged at him. It had taken her all morning to make the stew, and she had no other food.

That spring, my father began ploughing ground and setting out tomato seedlings, thousands of them. My baby sister was now a year old; my youngest brother was two. When my mother wasn't cleaning or cooking or washing the milk things or doing laundry with the wringer washer, she went to help. I was alone with a new universe to explore on my own.

In Riondel, I'd been on my own a lot as well, but there were other kids, other houses, other adults always around. In Riondel, my oldest brother, Phil, and I usually played together. But at the farm, I was often alone. Phil had to work with my dad; my younger brother, Bill, and my sister, Robin, were in the house with my mother.

I got into the habit of following my father around. The farm work fascinated me. There was a lot to learn. That first summer, I stood beside my father on top of the hay wagon as the labouring horses pulled the wagon up the hill towards the barn. He shouted and slapped the horses; even I could see it was too hard for them. They puffed blasts of air out of their red nostrils; sweat ran in dark streams down their necks and legs. They went slowly, their heads down, heaving the wagon in little jerks, until it was below the square hole in the back of the top of the log barn. From there, my father hoisted the hay up a forkful at a time and stuffed it in that hole, where it piled up and up until the whole top of the barn was bulging with hay. My job was to stomp on the hay as it came up in scratchy flying forkfuls into the barn. My father stood below, his shirt off, the long muscles in his back working and bulging as he lifted and bent again for another load.

———————◆———————

And after the work was done, our reward was a trip to the beach, a golden curving crescent of sand surrounded by water-worn granite on the south edge of the farm. To get to the beach, we followed a rutted grassy road that went out of the yard and past the end of the chicken shed where a mysterious black pool of water hid in a fringe of elderberry bushes. Here the creek that trickled through the yard made a wide sandy spot in the road that we splashed through in our bare feet. Then we ran under the dark cedar trees where clouds of mosquitoes waited to attack and down the long hill to the narrow path above the beach.

Because we went to the beach by ourselves, my mother wanted to make sure we knew how to swim. She didn't have time to come with us every day, although she loved the beach and came when she could. At least she knew if we could swim, we wouldn't drown. But I had a yellow inflated duck that I loved to float on, staring down at my peculiar angular feet in the green water, or drifting from place to place, paddling my feet and pretending to be a boat.

One afternoon, when I put on my pink bathing suit and grabbed the duck, my mother took the duck away. "You have to learn to swim," she said.

I stared at her. I knew perfectly well I could swim. I'd already figured it out. Swimming was simple. It wasn't something anyone had to learn; all you had to do was run into the water and kick hard. Dog paddling, we called it. Except our small black dog Willy wouldn't go in the water at all unless our father picked him up and threw him in. Then he swam frantically for shore, his head high and his front feet splashing in desperation.

"I can swim already," I told her, but she held my yellow duck over my head. Disgusted, I left the house and went down the long path to the beach. No one else was there. I waded into the water, swam a few strokes and went back up to the house.

"I can so swim," I said. Defeated, my mother handed me the yellow duck, and I went back to the beach. I spent the next few weeks paddling around on the duck, but my father found out and made fun of me. Toy ducks were for little kids, for babies. I knew my father must be right and, reluctantly, I left it behind on the next trip to the beach.

We had to run to the beach through the clouds of mosquitoes that hovered under the trees. We learned to whip towels around our ears and shoulders to keep them away. But there were no mosquitoes at the beach. Instead there was the hot sun smouldering onto the layered folds of granite. The same stream that ran through our yard ran here over the rocks and then gullied the sand into layers, smoothing it into long sandbars at the edge of the water. There were sun- and water-worn giant tree stumps— which could be turned into pirate ships or elephants or spaceships—and piles of driftwood left from high water. We leapt and raced on the long ropes of logs, sure-footed as mountain goats.

In the forest above the beach were small secret rooms, carpeted with moss, in the midst of huge leaning fir trees. One day, I went into one of these rooms and took off all my clothes. I lay on the moss, excited and guilty, looking up through the trees. Coming into such a place always made me catch my breath and hesitate; I knew it was beautiful, although I had no words for it, and magical, although I had no concept of magic. I only knew that this kind of place drew me in; when I was inside it I fell inside a kind of dream. Such places went somewhere inside me, made me wonder, made me happy. When I lay down on the moss, I found myself in the middle of a perfect room, a room of silent green happiness. It was a kind of worship, an amazement that there could be such a place and that I could be in it, rolling on the moss, prying it apart to watch a tiny miniature world of bugs and ants and dust.

<hr />

The first summer flew by; I made friends with the cows. My father's solution of turning around to yell at them worked. I followed them around and let them lick my hands and face with their long gooey tongues. I followed my father around, as well, out to the barn to milk, into the house, stride, stride; if I tried, I could stretch out my legs to match his steps. When I marched behind him, from place to place around the farm, everything obeyed him, everything was ours, except inside the house, where my mother was always working.

Until we moved to the farm, my father had been a distant figure, someone who went to work and came home and caused trouble. Back then, on weekends or occasionally on hot weekday evenings in the summer, he had taken us to the beach. Or sometimes we played outside beside him while he worked in the garden he had made or on the tall picket fence he built to enclose it. But my mother was the centre of the house, the centre of our lives.

Now, at the farm, everything interesting, joyous, unexpected, magical, or mysterious belonged to my father—the chickens, the enormous horses, the cows, the endless trees, the tall grass-and-thistle fields were my father's, and the rules were my father's as well. My mother seemed as trapped as a flightless bird; her children came and went from the house, but she stayed in it. I tried to bring her gifts from my new world by telling her stories or bringing in flowers or gifts from the gardens or the fruit trees. But more and more I ran after my father, who didn't care what I did as long as I didn't get in the way. And when he was busy or gone, I ran by myself.

Initially, my mother tried to make me responsible for my younger brother and sister. One day she ordered me to take my sister outside. I stood around for a bit, watching my one-and-a-half-year-old sister tottering around the muddy yard. I didn't like my sister, who cried a lot and annoyed me. My father was lying on his back under a tractor, taking it apart. I thought Robin would go back inside to our mother if I ignored her, so as soon as no one was looking, I trotted off to find something more interesting to do. An hour or so later, a car stopped. A neighbour had found my sister heading down the gravel road.

"I thought Dad was watching her," I said. My mother knew I was lying, but she didn't ask me to look after Robin again.

———◆———

My brother and sister were my mother's problem and none of mine. Mine was this new kingdom of fields and green glowing rooms under trees and golden water where fish swam and clams full of pearls waited to be opened. Mine was the garden, the new peas and carrots, the apple and cherry trees that could be climbed to the top. My mother tried to catch me, comb my hair, wash my face, but more and more each morning I escaped her, out to the barn or the garden or the beach.

For that first summer, the farm was a place of hope and sunshine, a place where my mother sang at her endless work. That August, my father took us out to the tomato field and handed us enormous tomatoes to eat, full and dripping with juice.

And finally, late that first summer, we moved out of Shelackie's cabin and into the farmhouse. The man who had founded our farm, Pierre Longueval, had been in the process of building the house when he drowned in the lake, and my grandfather had done little to finish it. Pierre had built it one room at a time, so each of the rooms had a door. And for the first time, I finally had a room of my own. Every night, I climbed the long stairs in the dark to my room, with its two small windows facing north, where I could look out over the cow pasture. I had a big double bed and a rug on the floor, a hairy rug backed with green felt, which my mother told me had once been the hide of my grandfather's favourite horse. I wasn't sure how I felt having a dead horse on my floor, but I both loved and was terrified of my room. Each night I undressed in the middle of the dead horse rug and then leapt for the bed, where I tucked in the blankets to keep myself safe.

The house was dark and spooky. We didn't yet have electricity, so our light came from kerosene lanterns that my father lit every evening. I had to find my way to my room in the dark. My mother and father both joked about Pierre's ghost, and indeed doors opened and shut at odd moments. At night, after we all went to bed, the house creaked and snapped as it settled into itself. The tin chimney in the corner of my room that went down to the wood cookstove whispered and rattled as it cooled or as the wind outside hit it. I could hear my brother and sister breathing in the next room. I could hear the cows lowing in the pasture. And when the windows were open, I could hear the wind coming over the fir trees; I could hear the night birds trilling as they went after mosquitoes, and the creek eternally murmuring in its muddy ditch. I thought perhaps the house and the wind and the land were all having a conversation, voices I could almost hear and understand. The house was spooky, but I wasn't afraid because I was part of this land as well, and the sounds I heard were the sounds of home.

In the early dawn, I would always wake when my father got up at five o'clock to milk the cows. He slammed the stove lids as he lit the fire in the cookstove, then the back door creaked, and the milk buckets rattled together as he went across the yard to the barn. And I would turn over in the warmth of my bed and go back to sleep.

The Place I Call Home

LAURA BEST

Evening red, morning grey
Will help the traveller on his way,
Evening grey and morning red
Will bring down showers upon his head.

WHEN I SEE a bright red sunset I'm reminded of this little poem my father taught me when I was young. I've always been curious as to where this traveller was going and *why* he was travelling in the first place. After all, I've lived in the same small community all my life.

My earliest memory is of being lost in the woods behind our house in East Dalhousie, Nova Scotia. I was four years old and had big plans that day of going with my father and two older sisters, Tina and Wanda, in search of some hollow wood for building birdhouses—big plans that came to a standstill the moment Dad said I was too young to go. I have no doubt that when I took the cookie Mum offered me with the promise that I'd stay in the dooryard and play, I intended to keep that promise, but the woods were calling me. If I ran fast enough, I might catch up. The day was hot, my legs were short, and no matter how quickly I hurried back Dad's old hauling road, I couldn't catch sight of them. I wasn't frightened,

Laura (right) with her sisters Tina (left) and Wanda (middle) and their dog, Tilly, outside their home in East Dalhousie, Nova Scotia, 1964

for I was busy trying to cross the large chopping that spread before me. Unfortunately, I became tangled amongst the gnarly dead branches of trees in the chopping. Our next-door neighbour found me fast asleep and sunburned in an old pile of brush. I cried out as he started to carry me away, for my boots were caught up in the brush pile, and I didn't want them left behind. My fingers clamped tightly to my red rubber boots as we made the trip back home.

That fall, not quite five years old, I begged to be allowed to go to school even though Mum and Dad had their reservations. Would I be able to walk the mile and a half every day to and from school? Back then it was not uncommon to keep children home from school an extra year. Tina did not start school until she was six, and Wanda's October birthday meant she was nearing six when she started. Did I want to wait an extra year? Not on your life! This was one time that I was not about to be left behind. As I hurried up the schoolhouse steps that first day and stood in the doorway, I was scarcely able to contain the excitement that stirred inside me. I had finally made it to school.

"The little Legge girls may put on their coats and go home." How many times I heard those words my first year of school I cannot say. Of all the students, my sisters and I lived the greatest distance from the school, and the teacher often dismissed us early because of it. There were eleven pupils in the school during the 1965–1966 school year. A mere five miles down the road was another schoolhouse, but it may as well have been on the other side of the world, for I knew nothing about those students even though we lived in the same area.

By the time I started school, the school bus was already transporting some of the students in the community to the Annapolis Valley about thirty miles away. Eventually my parents decided it was time for us to board the bus and make the hour-long trip to school even though the "little school" in the community remained open for at least another year. Although the ride to school was a long one, Mum and Dad knew that the larger school had much more to offer us.

The road to the Valley was rough and muddy in the spring. In winter it was not unusual for the bus driver to put steel chains on the back tires to get us through a particular stretch of the road. It was always fun when our bus was sent home early on account of a snowstorm that might have missed the Valley altogether. Since we lived in what some called the snow belt, it seemed we were always on the worst end of things when a storm hit.

Going from a one-room schoolhouse with fewer than twelve students to the new school in Aylesford with thirty-five students in one class was overwhelming. In the beginning, I was always afraid of getting on the wrong school bus after school. Fortunately, I had two older sisters to watch out for me and a small white tag with a big number seven printed on it that was pinned to my coat the first day of school. As the weeks went by, the tag became worn and eventually I felt confident enough to have it removed altogether.

The new school offered us music and gym classes and a library filled with books. Once I discovered the library, a whole new world opened up for me. I brought home the Bobbsey Twins, Nancy Drew, and the Hardy Boys, and Mum read to Randy and me every night although she was only able to see the words by removing her glasses and holding the book very close to her eyes. Each evening brought a new chapter of suspense, and the expression in Mum's voice brought the stories to life.

Mum is visually impaired and spent several years at the School for the Blind in Halifax when she was growing up. However, limited eyesight never stopped her from doing the things other mothers did. She canned fruits and vegetables and made pickles every year. Every other day she mixed a batch of bread that she baked in the wood-fired oven, and there was always an ample supply of cookies and cake in the cookie can. No one baked bread like Mum, but Dad took credit for this, and often mentioned that he was the one who taught Mum to bake bread when they were newly married. In the summer we grew a vegetable garden, and Mum prepared things like Swiss chard, lettuce and cream, hodgepodge, and potato hash. Potatoes were a staple. In the winter we ate pork and sauerkraut, pickled beans, stew, and corned beef and cabbage. For many years, the Saturday night meal was baked beans and brown bread.

Dad worked as a woodsman most of his life and, like so many, in his younger years he worked in the lumber camps. I recall when he browned gingersnaps in a cast-iron frying pan and perked them in the coffee percolator to show us what they did in the lumber camps years ago when they ran out of coffee. It made a pretty good substitute. Dad was also the community handyman and was often hired to do odd carpentry jobs. I suppose he was what one would call a jack of all trades. It amazes me how many things he knew about: farming, carpentry, mechanics, plumbing, electrical wiring, and logging. He encouraged us to learn the older ways of doing things, ways that I suppose he recognized were quickly disappearing.

In the sixties and early seventies, the Grocery Truck came out from the Annapolis Valley on Thursday afternoons to deliver groceries to the houses along its route. A large box-style truck, it had two doors that swung open at the back, and inside it smelled of cardboard and dust. The truck did not carry perishable items, but it had a little bit of everything else stocked on its shelves. It was exciting to hear the truck come rumbling down the road on Thursday afternoon toward suppertime. Tina, Wanda, Randy, and I eagerly waited for the driver to open the big doors in back and set a small wooden step on the ground. Then we scrambled into the truck to buy treats for the week. At the front of the truck, on a shelf, sat a cardboard box filled with chocolate bars, and we searched for our favourites. Kit Kat, Smarties, Coffee Crisp—they had them all. We never knew what lay hidden beneath the pile, but if we rummaged around enough we might find a treasure.

In the spring our neighbour—one of only a few in the community who still owned a workhorse—arrived with his horse and plough, and we used to follow behind and pull worms from the newly furrowed earth. Dad cut alder bushes and made us each a fishing pole and away we went with five homemade fishing rods sticking out the back window of the car, bobbing up and down over the dirt road. How brave Dad must have been to take all four of us fishing! It seemed no fishing trip was complete without someone getting his line tangled or her feet wet. Sometimes in the spring we'd set our lines overnight and go back in the morning to see whose bobber was still afloat and who might have been lucky enough to have a trout dangling on the end of the line.

Around the time of the full moon in May we went dipping kiacks at Indian Falls. These fish were called gaspereau in the Valley, but to us they were always kiacks. Kiacks resemble herring, but as my father often said with a smile, "A kiack has one more bone." Dad attached a chicken-wire dip net to a round metal hoop. The net had a long wooden handle so that the person standing on the bank of the river could reach into the water and dip out the fish that were swimming up the falls for spawning. Because of its long handle, Dad had to tie the net to the outside of the car on the passenger's side in order to get it to our destination.

The road to the falls was narrow and rough, and we would reach out the window and grab fast to the alder bushes that grew at the sides of the road. The drive was worth it, for when we eventually reached our destination, a most beautiful sight awaited us. The river was not tremendously wide, but the water was fast and alive with fish jumping up the falls. When Dad brought the net out of the water, it was jam-packed with silver bodies trying to flip and flop their way to freedom. We filled burlap feedbags with kiacks and took them home to be salted and smoked.

One of my favourite things was exploring the stonewalls of old abandoned farms in the area. Stonewalls were the places people threw their garbage years ago, and we searched for coloured bottles with corks, sunken bottoms, or round air bubbles in the glass—all indications that the glass was antique. Sometimes we had to dig into the ground to uncover a broken bottle that was barely visible, nestled among the fallen leaves and dirt. These bottles were not worth the fortune I imagined, but whenever I found a beautiful old bottle unscathed by time, I felt as though I was holding something truly precious in my hands.

During the summer, my sisters and I became well acquainted with the chickens, as it fell to us to feed and water them and collect the eggs from the nests. Come hatching day, we'd go to the chick hatchery in Barss Corner and pick up day-old chicks to raise for butchering. The entire building was filled with the high-pitched chirps of thousands of newly hatched chicks. Only the pullets were kept by the hennery. The rooster chicks were tossed into a huge barrel to be disposed of. It was obvious to us that the ones on the bottom would suffocate long before they could be euthanized. We arrived with a cardboard box, and we picked the chicks right out the barrel and placed them inside the box to take home.

An important part of my summers for many years included Red Cross swimming lessons. Sometimes we'd get a ride to the lake with the mail driver, but many times we walked. After my first year of lessons, I moved up into the same class as Tina and Wanda. By the time I was thirteen, and we had gained what we thought was enough strength and experience, we decided to swim to the island in the lake, which was a mile-long swim. Dad led the way in a rowboat with Mum and Randy on board, and we swam our way stroke by stroke across Lake Torment. What a fitting name it seemed once we had nearly reached the far shore and stepped out onto that little island in the middle of the lake! On the way back we sat in the little row boat, towels draped across our shoulders shivering in the late August evening, and pleased that we had been the first to make such a swim. We received recognition in a local paper.

There were pie sales at the community hall in the spring and summer. Sometimes a pie sale was held to help out someone in the community who was suffering from a lengthy illness or injury, but more often it was to raise money for the one of the churches. In our tiny community, there were three churches all within a few miles of each other. We always looked forward to the pie sales because we got to see people we might otherwise not see. The ladies baked pies and cakes to be auctioned off. The pie sale put on by the Catholic Church was something special because not only did they auction off pies, but they also sold homemade fudge, set up a chocolate wheel inside the hall, and brought around grab bags. This all went on before the pie auction began. When the bags of grabs made their rounds, we paid either a dime or a quarter depending on which sack we chose from, then reached in and hoped for good luck. The grabs were little things like pencils, spools of thread, or plastic rain bonnets, each one wrapped in a piece of brown paper. It didn't seem to matter what we got. Unwrapping those little prizes was almost as much fun as opening presents on Christmas morning.

When the pies were brought out, we'd listen for the auctioneer to begin: "How much am I offered for this lovely blueberry (or apple or coconut cream) pie?" And the bidding would begin. One gentleman bought pies only to send them back to be sold again. He rarely took one home. How we'd all laugh as the bidding went up, up, up, knowing we'd see that same pie come out again! After a pie sale, there was a square dance, and a local lady from the community played her fiddle while one of the gentlemen accompanied her on guitar. Music played, skirts flared, the floor thumped, and on hot August nights the door to the hall was opened wide, letting loose squeals of laughter from the ladies as the men lifted their partners clear off the floor. We arrived home, tired from being up late, the night air filled with the tiny sparks from fireflies flickering in the dark.

The biggest event of the year was the community fair in early September. We entered our school work to be judged. There were categories for pretty much anything—vegetables, flowers, sewing, pickling, and baking. One year Dad made cages and we entered some roosters. There was musical entertainment in the afternoon, and two meals cooked on a wood stove and served in the basement of the hall. People lined up outside the door waiting to be let in. Tina, Wanda, and I waited on tables. There was also a small street parade, a fish-pond game, a dunk tank, and a horse and ox pull that usually did not end until after dark.

In late October, Dad began to cut Christmas trees, and we helped drag the trees out of the woods. Early on a Saturday morning we'd gear up for the woods: boots, mitts, hats, and coats. The autumn woods had a flavour like no other time of year. The last remaining leaves clung stiff and frost laden to the hardwood branches, and every breath released a cloud of white air. As the sun brought everything to life, the woods warmed with the fresh sweet scent of balsam fir.

The trees Dad cut grew in the wild. Once the trees were dragged out to the main road, a buyer came along with a truck, and the trees were tied by hand for shipping. What little money we earned was spent the next week when the Grocery Truck came rumbling along. Sometimes we pooled our money to buy Christmas presents for Mum and Dad. We'd sit on the bed with the Sears Wish Book spread before us trying to find something we could afford.

Coming from a community that relied not only on family farms but also on forestry, I grew up knowing a bit about both worlds. For so many years in East Dalhousie we lived in our own little world until we began to slowly branch outward. Many traditions we grew up with came to an abrupt end as everyone clamoured for the new and modern ways of doing things. In a world that was quickly changing, the older ways suddenly were no more.

The experience of growing up in East Dalhousie will never leave me. It will be a part of who I am and what I do no matter what new experiences come my way. A red sunset means tomorrow will be fine, and a red sunrise means rain. My heart is filled with these small reminders of my youth.

When I drive through the community just as the sun is rising and the smoke from my neighbours' chimneys is drifting high into the clear morning air, I have this knowing in me that this community's history is embedded deep inside me where it cannot be erased or forgotten. I am reminded once again that this is the place I will always call home.

The Centre of the Universe

PAMELA WALLIN

To thine own self be true.
—William Shakespeare

FOR ME, THE centre of the universe will always be Wadena, Saskatchewan. And even though I live in Toronto and New York, cities that claim that title for themselves, I will always see the world through the prairie lens. I never read between the lines of a breaking news story without looking at the facts and the feelings involved from that born-and-bred prairie perspective. And when the inevitable question arises, "Would they care about that in Wadena?" I never hesitate to make a phone call.

My parents are still there, and so is my sister, Bonnie, and one of her daughters, Meaghan, and her husband, who are raising their family there. They are my touchstones. I always test my thinking against theirs, my instincts against their reality. And it's not just about their take on the prime minister's latest gaffe or some bureaucratic bungle. It's about what matters. I may not live in Wadena, but it'll always be home. It's where I go for Christmas.

If all the residents of Wadena, man, woman, and child, went to a baseball game together at Toronto's SkyDome, they would barely fill the first two rows. It's certainly not true that the most important thing about Wadena is its smallness; but its size, or lack of it, allowed my childhood to unfold in a manner unknown to most city kids. It was a little like the *Leave*

It to Beaver years some of us look back on with nostalgia. As children in Wadena, we walked in a cloak of security.

That's not to say we didn't resent the "know it all, see it all" town busybodies who never hesitated to call our parents if they saw us riding our bikes hands-free or cruising Main Street with the wrong kind of boy. Bonnie always laughingly concedes that all the nosiness that drove us crazy back then is exactly the reason she decided to move back to Wadena to raise her children.

In the booming fifties, suburbs, strip malls, and television antennas were dramatically changing North American landscapes. But you could hardly tell in Wadena that the post-war future had arrived.

As kids, we would run errands without any concern for our well-being. We'd be sent off to the Red and White store to pick up groceries because Bob and Mary Somers, the owners, were neighbours who'd make sure we left with the right goods. Mina and Hartley Graham did the same at their grocery store at the other end of the street. Wes Ottmann, a friend of Dad's and fellow legionnaire, ran the meat market. He loved kids and always let us sneak a peek into his big cooler at the back of the shop. Of course, this was long before *Rocky* made such scenes famous, but my sister and I were horrified and fascinated by the animal carcasses suspended on vicious-looking hooks.

We didn't need the pagers or cell phones that seem a must, especially for urban kids, these days. If Mom was in search of a tardy child or husband, she would simply call any of the shopkeepers on Main Street, and he'd stick his head out the door, spot us, and tell us to come on inside and call home. Wadena was one big Neighbourhood Watch.

Displayed on the wall above my desk today is a framed piece of prose about the Wadena we grew up in, written and cross-stitched for me by my sister. It says in part:

> *You know you're in Wadena when…*
> *you don't have to signal at Wesa's because everybody knows that's*
> *where you turn;*
> *you can't walk for exercise because every car offers you a ride;*
> *Third Street is on the edge of town;*
> *you can dial a wrong number and still talk for fifteen minutes.*

By the mid-fifties, Wadena was home to about a thousand and a half souls, and there was a good chance that anybody I passed on the street would be a friend or neighbour. It was a place where adults and children had little to fear. And if you were ever in need, you could count on someone being there for you. At the time, I didn't particularly value the town's enfolding community because I had no real understanding that life was different anywhere else. But that implicit security allowed me to grow up with a sense of self and place and confidence that has been invaluable to me.

I'm not about to start a movement, literal or figurative, to herd us back to rural towns as a means of making our own lives, or our children's, richer and safer. It would be difficult to be entirely convincing, since I now live in the centres of two of the continent's largest cities, and, at least for now, I like it that way—despite the wailing sirens and pollution and lack of space.

But I do believe that the values of small-town Saskatchewan had much to do with the fact that in places like Wadena there are few strangers and, as a result, fewer dangers. It's hard to think of a better place to be a child. If I'm looking for formative influences, then one is my hometown—Wadena, Saskatchewan. The other, of course, is my family.

Though I believe very strongly that each of us must take responsibility for our own path, I never forget that in the catalogue of life's blessings, at the top of the list is a fortunate birth, and I was very fortunate.

———◆———

Wadena is in the middle third, top to bottom, of a province most people know only from side to side. The name Saskatchewan usually calls to mind the view from the Trans-Canada Highway, which cuts straight through the southern part of the province, with dozens of little towns and hamlets and grain elevators on either side that you'll miss if you blink as you speed along.

In the summer, I still marvel at the physical beauty of the place. From the air, it looks like an elaborate patchwork quilt. From the ground, the quilt has depth and colour. Blue flax fields against the yellow of the canola or the gold of the wheat. The black patches of summer fallow that allow the land a season to breathe. When I go home there is no better feeling than jumping behind the wheel of a car and spending a couple of hours just soaking up the scenery. Sometimes I can drive for an hour and never see another human being.

One of the many things I miss about Saskatchewan, now that I'm an urban dweller, is the big sky and the sound you can hear only when all others are silent. W. O. Mitchell described it as the "hum and twang of the prairie harp"—the music of the wind as it glides along the miles of telephone wires.

There's plenty of good farming around Wadena, but there's little of the bald prairie about it. It's known as the Parkland. The top third of the province is almost unpopulated except for trees and lakes and remote native communities. In the south where my uncle Don Macfarlane farms, there is more of a sense of that *Jake and the Kid*-type prairie that's so well known, but that is a very different place from where I lived.

Even in my earliest memories, the sun is always shining from a bright blue sky. That's because Wadena is blessed with an incredible amount of sunshine, winter and summer. It can also have relentless weeks of brutally cold days and nights, but if the sun shines, somehow you can cope.

The town of Wadena had nine churches and a Jehovah's Witnesses' Kingdom Hall, two railways stations, two schools, a curling rink, a skating rink, a movie house, a Legion hall, and three Chinese restaurants. It still has no traffic lights. Nothing was really missing for me as I grew up, though whenever I visited my grandparents in Moose Jaw, I rode the one-floor escalator at Eaton's like a ride at Disneyland.

———◆———

Our first home, a tiny two-bedroom house that my father did much of the work on himself, eventually had running water but no plumbing. It sounds somewhat nineteenth century, dragging the slop pail out to the honey wagon twice a week, but, like everything else in a contented child's life, the lack of modern conveniences wasn't a particular hardship.

Much of what my parents taught me was about the core values that shape how you see the world. One virtue my mother instilled in me, by example mostly, was despising the sin and not the sinner, and least when the sinner is a child.

Many children from the surrounding area were bussed into town for school. Often I would hear my mother's regrets about the farm kids who would appear only after harvesting in the fall and would disappear again at seeding time in the spring, often failing school because of their absences, cutting off their options and pinning themselves for life. She lamented the perpetual absence from class of many of the native kids from the nearby reserve who were supposed to come into town for school but who never seemed to arrive. The few who came were often badly fed, and Bonnie and I were always given an extra sandwich in case someone at lunch needed one.

My mother never let us forget that there were obstacles in place that made these kids' lives harder than our own. And if they were rough or angry, she reminded us, their behaviour was only a small bit of a story, with its biggest part hidden.

Many of these insights I gleaned by osmosis or indirectly from casual conversation. Most Saturdays, after we cleaned our rooms and finished household chores, Bonnie and I spent time in the kitchen, helping Mom with the baking. I learned a lot of culinary skills in that kitchen, and I still love to prepare meals. Like my mother, I seldom glance at a cookbook.

I also learned a little about life. Bonnie and I would ask about teachers or parents or rumours that were going around the town and share our opinions and theories. And through our mother's responses, we always learned the intended lessons.

◆

In terms of spending time alone together, I was often with my dad, just the two of us. I think that's why I have always felt so at ease with men and have so many good male friends. Dad liked to hunt and fish and putter around. He had no sons, and Bonnie was totally uninterested in outdoorsy pursuits, so I would hang around with him, and we'd go off to the lumberyard or the hardware store for whatever was needed.

He taught me how to play crib, and I even became a sometime hunting companion. I'm not talking about shooting moose or even geese, but gophers and other small things generally agreed to be a pain in the pasture.

There was a small shed in our backyard where my dad had once tried to raise chinchillas as a source of extra income. When the project proved to cost more than he could make, he soundproofed the walls and converted the space into a room of his own where he stored his guns and practised his aim.

We spent long hours out there together and, in a warm privacy that contained (in a way I later learned to think of as very male) few words, I learned to load bullets. I may be the only person I know in my current social circle who can make that claim, although the skill appears to be no more useful than algebra.

My father hunted to fill our deep-freeze with meat for the winter, and since he kept guns around, he believed we should know about them, largely for our own protection. And I do. I know enough about guns to know I don't ever want one in my house as long as I live in a city. But I'm not sorry to have felt the heft of a rifle or to have felt it explode against my shoulder, if only to have a clearer idea of why the idea of them touches me so viscerally.

I feel fortunate to have had the opportunity to experience an aspect of the rural life that's usually restricted to male children. And that sensibility informs my views today on issues like gun control. As my father is quick to point out, the laws for city folk simply don't make sense on a farm. He's right.

———————◆———————

The anchors and centres of activity of town life were the church, the Legion hall, and, from fall to spring, the curling rink. Our own church was the United, and besides the usual Sunday business there were potluck suppers, teas to serve at, various charity events, rummage sales, and, of course, the weekly meetings of CGIT—Canadian Girls in Training—our town's answer to Brownies and Girl Guides. The church basement, or rather the many church basements, provided a lot of what passed for entertainment in the town. Bake sales, post-funeral wakes, even bridal and baby showers, were often held there.

But it was the curling rink, conveniently located at the end of our street, where we could have plain fun with no pretence of seriousness. Becoming a curler was a rite of passage into adulthood, but before that the rink was simply a place where a young girl might be sure that the guy she had her eye on would likely appear. Bonspiel time was like a holiday. For two or three days over a weekend the rink was filled with kids running around or grabbing a hot dog or each other while Mom and Dad were otherwise cheerfully engaged.

The Legion hall was also an important place of community. Of course, the Remembrance Day service was the big event, but most wedding suppers and dances were held there and the New Year's Eve dance was such an event that my Uncle Don—then a bachelor and generally considered a "good catch"—would drive up from his farm south of Moose Jaw just to survey the local scene.

———————◆———————

So, was it a perfect childhood in a perfect place? To me, Wadena was friendly and safe, a wonderfully protective cocoon from which I could later emerge to confidently fly off to Moose Jaw, Regina, and beyond. It wasn't so, however, for every child in town. But our response to the darker aspects of life did help define some of the issues that all kids have to confront: tolerance, difference, and the idea that life isn't fair.

Can you learn tolerance, or teach it to your children, in a place where everyone seems the same? There's more diversity to the small community than might appear to a big-city eye, and my parents never let us forget how privileged some people, ourselves included, were compared with so many others.

So yes, I still find a tolerance there that amazes me.

Take my sister, Bonnie. I see in her life and in her work the kind of values we were taught as kids. Against the odds and those old notions about difference, she has integrated a real workplace, not a workshop, for the mentally and physically challenged into the community, along with the group homes where clients live and learn life skills. They don't just make baskets. They run, among many other projects, a catering service for weddings and banquets, a shoe repair, the dry cleaners and a furniture shop, and manage the town's recycling efforts. It wasn't always an easy battle, but Bonnie made her converts, one at a time, by proving the mentally challenged could be contributing members of the community. Despite their own disabilities, they willingly lend a helping hand to the elderly or those less fortunate or more vulnerable than themselves.

Bonnie does more real and valuable work in a day than most and gets less credit than her more famous sister. But Bonnie believes in making a difference, or at least trying to. And she is the proof that a caring community is not just a possibility but a must.

When the *Globe and Mail* asked me to write a brief article on my thoughts on Canada as we approached the millennium, what I wound up writing about was my fear that we might lose the values that my sister lives and practises. With the decline of community, we may not have much reason left to actually like and care for one another in the future. I sometimes feel part of a society in which civility is eroding and tolerance is fading. Urbanization is creating a kind of social amnesia in which no one is anyone's keeper. Our "gated" lifestyle has broken our faith, loyalties, and trust in one another.

Individual values and shared practices collectively equal a community. But those values and those practices are harder to share in these more driven, self-centred times. And the situation is exacerbated by government funding cuts to services that many have come to expect and certainly need. We may have balanced the books, but have we rebalanced the social contract to sort out who will be responsible for filling the void and meeting the needs of the needy?

Small towns are not perfect communities. They are flawed and not spared the petty politics that you inevitably find at the office or in the cabinet room or permeating the bureaucracies we've set up supposedly to help those in need. But at least it is still possible to extend a helping hand in the Wadenas of the world.

There are no homeless, because everybody has somebody or at least somewhere to go. And personal needs and foibles are more easily accommodated. If you know that Mrs. Smith doesn't drive quite as well as she used to, then you make a point of giving her a lift more often or a clear berth when you see her car coming down Main Street. And if you know the recently widowed Mr. Jones could starve to death before he figures out how to use the microwave, then you, and all the others, will be at his door with dinner until he learns.

In the city, it's so much easier to just send a cheque to some charitable organization fronted by a celebrity than to help your neighbours, especially when the celebrity is sending you his or her message in well-produced, thirty-second bursts several times a night and your neighbour is silent and invisible.

Caring, I know, can't be legislated. But it bothers me that when we send that cheque, the government recognizes the act and even pays us back some of it in the form of a tax refund, but when my father builds a wetlands bird sanctuary, or my mother makes and delivers a meal for a neighbour, or my friend Grace answers a midnight call from someone who has fallen off the wagon, or my sister takes a lonely client into her home because his or her family won't, the government gives them neither recognition nor compensation. This is the behaviour that should be recognized and rewarded.

Wadena was not perfect, but it gave me safety, self-confidence, and a wide-enough range of experience to fill my growing lust for knowledge and newness. From my parents I learned, among much else, curiosity, an appreciation for hard work, and the habit of concern for others' lives.

I learned a lot growing up in Wadena, Saskatchewan, and I'm glad the town is still there, at the centre of my universe, as a reminder of what really matters most.

A Solid Foundation

KAY PARLEY

MY YEARS ON the farm stretched from 1923 to 1933, and then I spent each two-month summer vacation there until 1941. My earliest years gave me an experience so close to pioneering that I actually knew, personally, some two dozen pioneers— men and women who settled in my corner of Saskatchewan in the 1880s and 1890s. They named their settlement Moffat. My grandparents were among them, my grandpa arriving in 1883, and my grandmother in 1884.

In the beginning, the community of Moffat consisted of about forty families. The majority were Scots, and there were well-educated people among them. They established a Presbyterian church in 1884 and, through it, developed a debating club, a book club, a community newspaper, musical concerts, plays, and organizations for all age groups. In 1891, the congregation replaced their framed church with one built of fieldstone. By the early nineteenth century, a cracking good soccer team helped put the community on the map.

There was never a town or village at Moffat. The church and cemetery stood alone until 1910, when a community barn was built. In 1929 the locals added a community hall. The church had been used for fowl suppers and concerts and plays, but, as a sanctified building, it was never used for dancing. With the opening of the hall, dances could be held at a central location for the first time. The hall was also the social centre for card parties.

Kay in front of her grandparents' stone house, 1926

Farms were no larger than a half section then, so there were usually neighbours within half a mile in at least two directions. We really weren't isolated. Probably the chief difference between Moffat in the twenties, when I was small, and Moffat in pioneering days at the end of the nineteenth century, was one of transportation. When I was a child, we still used horse-drawn sleighs or cutters in winter, and sometimes had to resort to wagon or buggy when roads were very muddy, but much of the time we got around in cars. It had taken the pioneers an hour to get to the church, but we could get there in twenty minutes.

Moffat had a sense of permanence. It always gave me a feeling of security and a comforting sense of the familiar to know who lived on

A Solid Foundation

every farm we passed, to know if their dog was hostile and if there were children there to play with. Once a week, the trip to church brought the whole community together, and we would find out if everyone was well or if there was trouble anywhere. Small communities have a reputation for being gossipy. Of course, everyone knew everything about everybody— that is crucial to survival in a small place—but private matters were never mentioned in public. That is the rural way, and it assures the peace and harmony necessary for a community to function. Since I have become urbanized, the stubborn way in which rural people hang on to secrets maddens me, but I still understand the purpose of it. As a growing child, I learned that community was an expansion of home, and, like family, the members had to get along with each other.

Between 1886 and the mid-1890s, the Moffat area established four country schools. I began school at Wolf Creek, the school my father had attended and the school at which my mother had taught. Such continuity is the rural community. In the little white one-room schoolhouse, the children were all from families I knew, and there was a feeling of mutual support. When I was in grades one and two, I listened to senior classes reading Pauline Johnson or studying Trinidad, and I couldn't wait to find out what lay ahead. When I was forcibly moved to a town school at the age of ten, closed up in year-tight compartments in which we didn't play with children unless they were in our narrow age bracket, I felt as if my mind was put in prison.

In Moffat, we walked to school in decent weather, sometimes two miles or more. There were no wild animals and certainly no wild humans to frighten us. The only time I recall being warned of strangers was in the thirties, when hobos were riding the rails and occasionally walking through farm areas looking for work. They were suspect because they were sometimes desperate with hunger, but they were also suspect because we didn't know them. Familiarity was the keystone of the rural community.

Whether walking to school, playing in the bluffs, or driving along the country roads, we saw beauty in every season. Southeastern Saskatchewan was a paradise in the 1920s. Poplar trees flourished. Farmers were doing mixed farming, so half the land was in pasture. That provided space for nature, so we had carpets of wild flowers. We picked saskatoons, chokecherries, dewberries, and raspberries. Wild strawberries grew in profusion in the ditches. We heard what sounded like millions of birds, carolling in the mornings and cooing in the evenings, and their songs accompanied us wherever we walked. Bluffs buzzed with insects. Squirrels and chipmunks scampered. Pussy willows delighted us in springtime. To this day, Moffat bluffs are ringed with wild roses in June.

We got used to death. Gophers, considered pests, were killed by the hundreds. Cattle and pigs were slaughtered right on the farm, hung on tripods, and butchered for preserving and freezing. We had no running water, no electricity. We learned to chop wood and kindle a fire in a cookstove, to get water from a well, to care for poultry, and to prepare them for the table. We learned to can meat, fruit, and vegetables because, along with the henhouse and the garden, the cellar shelves were the supermarket. Most of the children could milk cows. They could all ride horseback. We learned to expect to work for a living, and we learned to take responsibility. We treated animals with respect, and we were cautious around machinery. We learned to recognize every plant, whether useful or a weed, and we weeded endless garden rows, over and over again.

At the same time that we were learning to work, we were learning the old culture, especially the Scots songs. We played table games from whist to ping pong to crokinole, and group games like Kingdoms (Twenty Questions). Many young people took music lessons. Radio was in its infancy and no one had records. We were responsible for our entertainment. Local musicians played hymns in church on a pump organ. Having visitors at home meant spending part of the evening gathered around the parlour organ for a sing-song. Once in a while we would hear of a neighbour actually going to Wolseley to attend a play or concert, but nine or ten miles was a long way, so people didn't go often.

We did go to town to shop on Saturday nights, weather permitting, to buy what we couldn't produce on the farm. That trip felt like one more community affair, for it was always fun to greet the neighbours when we ran into them in town. I am sure Wolseley residents thought of Moffat as a kind of suburb that incidentally supplied them with butter, eggs, and beef, but to us Wolseley was the annex. After all, Moffat dated from 1882. We had a very distinct identity, and we managed to hold on to that identity for a very long time.

The Scots pioneers had worked to achieve a comfortable lifestyle. Because several were stonemasons, our community had the greatest number of fieldstone buildings of any community in Saskatchewan. The founders built two churches, one schoolhouse, and twelve homes of fieldstone, together with a number of barns, milk houses, granaries, and sheds—this in an area about ten miles square! That is one of the reasons Moffat flaunted itself as a proud and permanent community. Who could forget the dignity of the stone houses, in harmony with their natural surroundings? Cozy and unpretentious, they gave the impression they would be there forever. They cemented my early world view that the only authentic community was one consisting of fieldstone houses.

Not even the weight of stone could hold a rural community together, though. The thirties disillusioned us. The war showed our young men a bigger world and made them discontent. As in every part of Western Canada, cars and modernization drained the countryside. Farms grew larger, country schools closed, populations declined. Moffat hung on to its identity by keeping up sporting events and social activities and by holding regular anniversaries every five years.

My mother would say what impressed her most about Moffat was the good manners of the Old Scotch. Those manners were often passed on to their offspring. For a young person to be saucy to an elder was literally a sin, and the decency with which boys treated girls was outstanding. Years later, a friend of mine who, like me, had never married, remarked, "The men of Moffat spoiled me for other men." I knew exactly what she meant.

The unquestioning faith of those days accounts for much of the dignity I remember about Moffat. Sunday afternoons at Moffat Church always revealed the heart of the community. There were Sunday school classes for all ages, including one for "young people." Often there were more than twenty young men and women in that class. At the end of that hour, there would be a break, followed by a church service. Although Moffat joined the United Church in 1925, some of the Presbyterian discipline remained. Church was impressive and the stone building was packed. Although I recognized early that I had the makings of a good agnostic, I always appreciated Moffat Church, and I recognized that it helped to maintain the standards of the community. Moffat was not only hard-working and hard-playing; it was, above all, respectable.

Did belonging to a rural community demand a price? It did. Our Presbyterian background made people intolerant of laziness or any breach of a strict moral code. Horizons were narrow. There was never a wide circle from which to choose friends, which may have been just as well. We learned to appreciate people for what they were, despite differences, but some people were *too* different and, unfortunately, I was one of them. I knew from childhood I wanted to be a writer and painter, and no one I knew was interested in creativity. Art was unrealistic, a waste of time, and, besides, all artists were dead. In school, we learned about the works of Rembrandt and Rosa Bonheur, but we weren't aware that anyone had been painting since. I recognized my marginal status, too, when I became aware of the clearly defined sex roles in the community. Men had fun at community picnics, playing games and supervising sporting events for the children. Women spent the day behind tables, serving food. I recognized the importance of the contribution they made, but I did not want to have to make it myself.

Perhaps it was lucky, in a way, that my dad took ill and we had to leave the farm. My mother, an ex-teacher, saw to it that I got to Regina to study art. I furthered my education at every opportunity. It would not have been so easy had we stayed on the farm.

Moffat had a clear definition of who belonged and who did not. I have been away from Moffat for many years, but I have continuing membership, not because I have written extensively about the community, but because my dad and his siblings were born in Moffat of a founding pioneer family. I simply belong. Rural communities are like that. As a descendant of pioneers, I will have permanent membership in Moffat as long as there are those to remember. I still go back for every jubilee. I still write about Moffat, and I still go to Wolseley to visit a friend I went to school with in the little one-room schoolhouse. I love the permanence, the feeling of having a place in the sun. Urban memories are short. Rural memories are long.

Valley Girl

Shirlee Smith Matheson

I AM SURROUNDED by ghosts. As I drive down the narrow dirt road speckled with yellow and brown fallen leaves, phantoms swirl about me. I hear chatter and laughter as the figures flash, unchanged in thirty years. It's hard to believe these people are all gone.

I steer my car into the Rossburn Cemetery grounds, my visit not complete until I have stopped by every gravestone. I try to recall all the names, some nearly obliterated by moss that creeps across the granite tombs. I find our family plot, the resting place of my grandparents and their daughter Nellie, my father's sister, who died from meningitis just after her thirteenth birthday. I never met her, but her photo was always on our bookcase, and the events of her life are chiseled into my childhood as deeply as the inscriptions on her headstone.

I was born at a time when most of the men had deserted Manitoba's Birdtail Valley to fight in World War Two. *Hospital* and *war* were the first words I can remember. I used to say them over and over to myself: *hospital, war*. They sounded grown-up.

We on the farm did not suffer as much as some city people did from the Depression of the thirties and the gap in normality caused by the war. Although there was no cash, there was always enough to eat. I was born after the Depression, but the subject was still new: "In the thirties you could buy a young calf for a dollar—but who had the dollar?" My mother's

Shirlee with her brother, Ken Smith, and horses Dot and Min, returning
from a day in the fields on their farm on the Birdtail River near
Rossburn, Manitoba, 1940s

voice: "I used to shine the floor with skim milk. We couldn't afford wax."
I'd missed it all. I'd missed being included in the family legends: the day
my father walked across the kitchen floor carrying a precious five-pound
pail of syrup and suddenly dropped it. The family seated around the table
watched in amazement as the impact sent the syrup flying straight to the
ceiling, where it dripped in a solid amber line from ceiling to floor. They
talk about that yet. And I wasn't around.

I was not aware of my peculiar place in the family. I did not
understand the tremendous sadness our family had suffered before I came.
Like the legend of the syrup pail, I accepted the stories: I once had a sister,
Helen, who had died. It was her grave we went to visit each spring, to clean
out the peony beds and plant pansies. I knew only that I was born on her
nineteenth birthday and had come to replace her in some mystical way.

There had been so much illness. Somehow, I connected it all with
the Depression. There had been five children, and only my older brother
Ken and I survived. Two boys, the first dead at birth, the second dying
when only a few days old, were both buried by our father. He made his
sons' coffins by hand and laid out the bodies. Their unmarked graves are
somewhere in the family plot.

I am eighteen years younger than my brother Ken. "Just a little Helen,"
the well-meaning neighbours used to say, and I felt proud. She had left

me her things: knitted sweaters, jewellery, lovely gold lockets containing photos of her and her boyfriend Jim, who kept hoping to marry her even when they knew she would never recover from polio. I wore those lockets all through my school years, carrying the pictures of these people unknown to me. She left me her Evening in Paris toiletry set, her scented embroidered handkerchiefs, and little high-heeled shoes that fit me when I was twelve years old. I got her room, the two matching black and white dogs that sat on the dresser, and the jewellery box with the tasselled handles. I got her eyes, her personality—and even her birthday.

———◆———

I return to my car and slowly drive north along the one-lane country road, unchanged since my youth. I cross the narrow bridge over the brown, slow-moving Birdtail River, still smelling of swamp, holding its mysteries under a cover of leaning willows. I pull into a field and turn off the engine. I stroll along a tractor track into waves of heavy-headed grain. The wind sighs, carrying the smell of oncoming autumn. The silent years close in.

———◆———

My brother made his spending money selling gopher tails. He bought his bicycle with gopher-tail bounties. Sometimes I would accompany him to check the traps. We would carry the dead gophers back home to the chopping block if he had forgotten his knife. One day I set out by myself, accompanied by the dog. In the farthest corner of the field I spotted his newest trap, glinting silver in the sun. It had been sprung and now lay useless. I would reset it. He'd be so proud of me. Kneeling down, I grabbed the strong steel jaws with my small five-year-old hands. Snap! The trap sprung to life, slapping my two hands back to back in its jaws. I pulled, but I couldn't get the chain off the stake that had been pounded deep into the ground. I yanked uselessly, sobbing. My hands were blue and bulging, bleeding where the teeth bit into my skin.

I sat down beside the gopher hole. Was something moving down there? Was I to be trapped here forever? Would the gophers run over me in the night if no one came to get me? I sobbed aloud. Then, losing all control, I wailed until tears flooded my throat. The wind pushed my cries back, dried my tears, and reprimanded me for breaking the prairie silence. The dog circled me, nervous, whining. Then, with one guilty backward glance, he slunk away over the rise, belly to the ground, tail between his retreating legs.

I lay down on the prickly stubble, burrowed into the warm earth, and eventually fell asleep. I dreamed I saw a waving endless field and, somewhere in the middle, two black moving specks. Closer and closer they came, their shapes wavering in the horizon. The gophers were silenced, the prairie still and timeless. The forms took shape: my dog and, behind him, my mother, running.

———————◆———————

Now, as I stand in this field of silken yellow, I see again the little girl who sat awaiting her fate, feel again the fear and fury of abandonment. I pick off a stalk and brush the full barley beard against my face. It rasps against my skin.

In my car again, I drive farther, past the old farmhouses whose owners are now gone…to the seniors' home in Rossburn or to live with family members in Brandon or Winnipeg. I imagine them staring out the windows onto the prairie that changes only with the seasons.

I drive north. The road twists and turns, following the Birdtail River. The brush becomes taller, and willows from the riverbank are replaced by poplars and spruce as I enter Riding Mountain National Park. I never knew it was so close, just six miles from the farm, but in the days of my childhood it would have been a trip that required planning, taking a full day from the farm labours. I have never been here before.

I park the car, climb up onto a bluff, and look back over the Birdtail Valley. It shimmers in the heat. In the far distance is the Ukrainian cemetery with its ornate stones that I once viewed from my swing behind the buggy shed. I see our old farmhouse with its high, pointed, four-sided cottage-style roof that sheltered me so many years ago. My gaze sweeps over the brown river, the yellow fields, and the green haze of trees that shade the lush valley. Here, I'm still somebody's child.

Wave Riders

NJ BROWN

seek wander
and be born again beyond
the sun setting lustwandering
no time for rest...
—Jon Whyte, "Homage, Henry Kelsey"

MEMORY:

"How old are *you*, Grandma?"

As the blown-out candles on my brother's birthday cake send little puffy waves of smoke up toward the ceiling, I try to trick my grandma into telling me her age. Maybe if she's not ready for the question, she'll say a number instead of making me do math.

But it doesn't work. Her answer is exactly the same as the last time: "Figure it out—I'm exactly the same age as Alberta."

1905: Etta May Cook (1905–2002), paternal grandmother

A province is born to Canada. Named for a princess, Alberta raises her hand in a royal wave, beckoning: *Come. Be born again, here in this land of mountains and rivers and wind and sky and wild open spaces. This land of new beginnings.*

NJ (right, age 3) with her siblings Shane (left)
and Dawna (middle) shucking corn, 1967

Her hand casts a shadow that reaches across three provinces, to where a family of German heritage celebrates the birth of a daughter. Etta is not named for a princess, and there is little connection to royalty discernible here in the sparse surroundings of the little home in Ontario's interior. But her family is beginning to feel the first pulls of the wave.

When my grandmother is seven, they answer Alberta's call and claim a homestead on her southern prairies.

And another new life begins.

1907: Thomas (Tom) Noel Wood (1904–1994), maternal grandfather

The pull of the wave reaches out, across the ocean, to the Liverpool Harbour, where a British family boards the *Virginian*. Thomas is three years old, young enough that he still wears a dress in the custom of his motherland, old enough that he is able to reconstruct vague impressions—formed of the view from his mother's arms—into memories. Years later, he writes of this beginning that will shape the rest of his life:

Slowly the land disappeared from view and we were surrounded by the rolling surf of the great Atlantic. Day turned to dusk, dusk turned to darkness, but we still steamed on—into the waves—into the night. Hours went by, days, almost a week, as this beautiful palace ploughed on through the dark green water that rolled and heaved as far as the eye could see.

Later we boarded a Canadian train, and for days and nights we roared into the beckoning west, always toward the setting sun. Then this steel giant came to rest in Medicine Hat, Alberta....In and near Medicine Hat I've made my home. Many times I've wandered, but I always come back to this remaining bit of the west.

1911: Frances (Frank) Joseph Rubbelke (1885–1972), paternal grandfather

Across the border, a young bachelor of twenty-six feels the pull, abandons his newly acquired homestead in North Dakota, and rides the wave to Alberta to stake a claim. To supplement his farming income, Frank tries his hand at hunting coyotes. For the princely sum of five hundred dollars apiece, he imports two greyhounds from the States and rounds out his team with a wolfhound. As luck—or skill—would have it, the gamble soon pays off in coyote pelts.

I consider what my grandfather left behind, try to calculate the sacks of flour and bags of sugar he could have bought for a thousand dollars. I'm baffled. What brought him here? Where did the money come from? What compelled him to take such risks? When I ask my father these questions, he laughs. "I don't know. I think he was a glutton for punishment."

In the absence of answers, I give my risk-taking grandfather over to my imagination where he becomes, under different circumstances, a prospector panning for gold, an explorer discovering distant lands, or (my favourite) a gun-slinging cowboy, living off wits and poker winnings, riding into town on his palomino paint, propelled by wind and waves of fortune, daring any yellow-bellied, sap-sucking snake-in-the-grass to stand in his way. Pushing his way through the swinging doors of the saloon, dust rising from the heels of his boots, he swaggers up to the barkeep: "Whiskey. Straight up. Make it a double."

Wave rider. Wave maker.

Memory:

"I'm a plane."

The heads of the wheat brush against my brother's outstretched arms. His running feet stomp out a runway and the wind gives him lift.

"I'm a bunny."

My sister crouches down, and the wheat bends low in the wind, over her head, tucking her into her bunny burrow.

We are commandos, creeping low in the jungle, bare skin tickled and scratched by the thick foliage we must push through to reach our destination undetected. We are foxes and hounds, running in wild circles, with wind-blown hair and sun-burned shoulders. We are pirates on the open seas, listening to the whispers of the wheat for clues to the location of the sunken treasure.

Here, in this whiskey-coloured sea of wind-pushed waves, we are whatever we want to be.

1915: Ida Bechtold (1915–2003), maternal grandmother

On the wide expanse of open prairie and rolling hills, on the homestead of Russian immigrants, sits a tiny shiplap cabin with a ridgepole roof. Here, Ida, the first of my native-Albertan ancestors, is born. For my grandmother, the journey to Alberta is no longer than the length of the birth canal.

As the family expands, so does the cabin. My grandmother's father, forgetting that his height is not that of the average adult male, builds the doorways too short and hangs the stovepipe too low. When neighbour men come to visit, they invariably bang their heads. The craftsman offers no apologies, no excuses for this flaw in his design. "Let them duck," he shrugs. This, after all, is *his* home, *his* dream.

He will shape for himself and his family a world in which they fit.

1930s: Tom and Ida Wood

The wind blows hard across the prairies. Unforgiving, unrelenting, it pushes a wave of dust and despair across the land, leaving in its wake a steady supply of buried dreams and abandoned aspirations.

Against this backdrop, Tom and Ida meet. They move slowly, with a caution born of the doubt and disillusionment that is the order of the day.

Determined that they will not fall victim to the devastation the landscape hands out so liberally, they count their pennies. Tom earns thirty-five dollars a month working as a farmhand, and Ida works as a domestic, making a top monthly wage of fifteen dollars.

On July 10, 1938, four years after they met, they marry. This has not been a whirlwind romance, but it is a love story nonetheless.

Even here, even now, stories of new beginnings await those who are willing to write them.

Memory:

"Who moved the farm, Grandma?"

I point out the window to the farm that is usually a speck in the distance, the old house now so close I can almost see through its windows. Grandma joins me at the window and smiles as she leans closer.

"No one moved it, honey. It's a mirage. The heat waves are magnifying it and making it look closer than it really is."

I squint my eyes and focus on the air between me and the farm. Sure enough, there they are—see-through waves with shimmery edges dancing up and down above the ground.

"Don't squint. And don't stare so hard," Grandma warns. "You'll ruin your eyes."

She sends me to empty the slop pail, and by the time I return to the window the farm has turned back into a faraway speck.

1942: Frank and Etta Rubbelke

The Canadian government appropriates Frank and Etta's land in Little Sweden[1]; the army needs a site for chemical and biological defence trials, and this sparsely populated area of southeastern Alberta fits the bill. As compensation, my grandparents receive 50 cents an acre for grassland, 75 cents an acre for cultivated, unseeded land, and $1.25 an acre for seeded land.

---

(1) Little Sweden (as it is still called by the old-timers), approximately eighty kilometres north of Medicine Hat, is now part of the Suffield Range. The range covers more than 2,690 square kilometres, and the army continues to conduct live-fire training in this severely restricted area.

I imagine them standing together in front of their home, surveying their land, knowing that the edges of their dream are becoming fuzzy, drifting away as dreams often do. Counting the money and calculating the price per vision.

But they are wave riders—their boat has been rocked before. Alberta is a big place, with room for more than just one new beginning. On little more than gumption and a gamble, they move fifteen miles further north, to the Buffalo area, and begin again on a piece of unclaimed land. Faith and fortitude keep them there until they are able to claim title under squatters' rights.[2]

Memory:

Almost every weekend, we travel to Alberta from our home just barely over the Saskatchewan border to visit aunts and uncles and cousins and grandparents.

"Close your eyes," my father says when we are just a few miles from the border. "See if you can guess when we get to Alberta."

We have played this game before, so we already know what clues we are waiting for. We squeeze our eyes shut and concentrate until the road smoothes out and the car stops bouncing over bumps. My mother laughs when we say "now."

"Okay," she says. "Smooth sailing ahead."

1988: Norma Jean Brown (1964–), Story gatherer

My own move from Saskatchewan to Alberta is waveless, marked by calm. Crossing the border is as simple as hiking through the hills of the South Saskatchewan River valley, where there are no green welcome signs to indicate a change in location, and the passage from one place to another occurs in a single step. If not for the annoyance of packing boxes, filling out change-of-address cards, and updating my driver's licence, I would hardly know the difference.

---

(2) The legal term for squatters' rights is "adverse possession." It is not clear exactly how long Etta and Frances lived on this particular piece of land before they were able to claim title; however, the current requirement for "actual, continuous, open, visible, notorious and exclusive possession" is between ten and twenty years.

For me, this blurring of borders between places and sentiments remains a reality. Saskatchewan is the land of my childhood, but Alberta is the land of my roots: my grandparent's children, their children's children, my own children, all born here. The wave riders—Tom and Ida and Frank and Etta—and my mother, all buried here.

With Saskatchewan, I have an ongoing love affair. With Alberta, an ongoing life affair.

2007:

A city-dweller for five years now, I find myself craving the sight of open land stretching out endlessly before me. Frequent road trips feed that craving. Alone in the car, I welcome the silence and the growing distance between towns and buildings as I once again become aware of my connection with the world around me. From time to time, I catch sight of old barns or abandoned farmhouses—sometimes right there in the fields beside the road, sometimes in the distance, far-off specks dotting the horizon.

I entertain myself by creating lives and stories for the people who put them there—beginnings and endings and continuations. It fascinates me to be here in this place, the place the wave riders came to. The place they still come to—crossing borders, crossing countries, crossing oceans— sometimes in small ripples, one at a time, sometimes in great torrents of answered opportunity. Their stories of dream building and new beginnings written all around us.

Written in this land of mountains and rivers and wind and sky and wild open spaces, where the princess raises her hand, waving…always waving…

Welcome.

Marlborough Township

Joyce Glasner

THE FARM HAD been in my mother's family for two generations. It was a small, isolated place in Marlborough Township, a flat, fertile region where substantial agricultural operations and dirt-poor subsistence farms sat side by side. Long, straight stretches of two-lane blacktop cut across country between endless fields of wheat and corn. And the gleaming domes of silos rose majestically above the treetops, visible for miles around. The white, century-old farmhouse, without so much as a veranda for embellishment, was perched on the edge of a narrow dirt road. Out front, two ancient maples flanked the driveway like sentinels. Scattered around back were a garage, a chicken coop, and a ramshackle log barn with a rusted tin roof. The cedar rail fences were kept up, the yard and house immaculate, but the threadbare look of rural poverty was unmistakable. The only hint of extravagance about the place was a lavish bed of vivid pink peonies on the front lawn.

My great-grandparents, Hugh and Elizabeth Lyons, had settled on the farm shortly after they were married in 1884. They'd carved the place out of the wilderness, clearing fields and fencing in pastures, planting an orchard and cultivating a large vegetable garden. My grandfather, Alvan, was born and raised on the farm. In his twenties his hunger for adventure drove him out west. After a stint with the Royal North West Mounted Police, he went to work building bridges for the Canadian Pacific Railway.

Joyce (age 2) and her father stand by as Joyce's sister
Judith takes her first horseback ride, 1959

Around that time he fell in love and got engaged, but shortly before the
wedding his fiancée contracted the Spanish flu and died, leaving him
heartbroken. After her death, he moved on to Brandon, Manitoba, where
he got a job managing a pool hall and barbershop for a fellow named
Cecil Bradford. Cecil had a pretty, dark-haired sister named Ethel, who
caught Alvan's eye. She was eighteen and he thirty-four when they married
in 1924. Two years later, he received a letter from his mother informing
him that his father's health was failing. Since the old man could no longer
manage the farm on his own, my grandfather decided it was time to
return home. After saying their goodbyes, he and Ethel packed their few
belongings and their one-year-old daughter, Anna, into his Model T Ford
and headed east.

Forty years later, we were living in a cramped two-bedroom apartment
in London, Ontario, when Mom received a letter from my grandmother.
Grandpa was becoming forgetful, she said. He was in his seventies then,

and having difficulty keeping up with the demands of running a farm. Mom's younger sister, Patsy, was only seventeen and too young to take on the responsibility; her older sister, Anna, had died just shy of her twenty-ninth birthday. Since Dad had recently received his discharge from the military, there was nothing to keep us in London. So in June of 1963, we packed all our possessions into a U-Haul, piled into the Meteor Rideau 500, and left the city to begin our new life on the farm.

My mother's childhood on the farm had been idyllic, so after several years of city living she was once again in her element. She loved the self-sufficiency of farm life and was happiest gardening, berry picking, or canning, pickling, and preserving the fruits of her labour.

Despite my ancestral connection to the place, it didn't feel like home to me. Having spent my first five years in the city, adapting to the isolation of rural life wasn't easy. Our nearest neighbours lived a mile down the road. Between our place and the Wilsons', there was nothing but fields, forest, and a gravel pit. To make matters worse, electricity and telephone lines hadn't yet been installed along our road. Being so completely cut off from the rest of civilization made me anxious. But then, so did a lot of things. I had just turned six and was pathologically timid. I was afraid of just about everything, but topping my list of fears was the dark. And with no electricity, nights on the farm were darker than anything I'd ever experienced. Once the lights went out, each floorboard creak would send me burrowing deeper beneath the covers, praying for daybreak.

I wasn't the only one having difficulty adapting to country living. Dad, too, was out of his element. He'd grown up on Laurier Avenue in downtown Ottawa. After surviving a childhood marked by grinding poverty during the Depression, he was struck with paralytic polio at seventeen. The doctors told him he would never walk again, but he was determined to beat the odds. The Depression years had taught him how to live by his wits, how to scavenge, improvise, and adapt. These qualities, combined with a mulish streak and a powerful will, pulled him through. A few years after walking out of the hospital, he celebrated his twenty-first birthday on the front lines in Korea. Just before his tour was over, he contracted malaria and shipped home in a feverish delirium. Farming, he must have believed, would be simple compared to the trials he'd already endured.

While Dad struggled to grasp the basics of husbandry that first summer, my brother, sister, and I ran wild in that extraordinary new world. Having spent my entire life in cookie-cutter dwellings with straight white walls and all the modern conveniences, everything on the farm struck me as remarkable. The faded floral wallpaper, ornate tin ceiling, and worn linoleum flooring seemed like artifacts from some distant place and time. Even the names of the odd nooks and crannies sounded exotic. We didn't have a living room but a front parlour—a sunny room with lace curtains on the windows and doilies on the overstuffed horsehair furniture—which was only used on Sundays or when company called. There was also a summer kitchen, a root cellar, a pantry, and a room my mother called the darkroom.

This shadowy, narrow space tucked beneath the eaves of the house had only one small north-facing window, so even on brilliant summer afternoons, the room was shrouded in gloom. I'm not certain if it got its name because it was suspended in a perpetual state of dusk, or if it had once served as the room in which my grandfather—an amateur photographer—developed his photographs. Whatever its original purpose, the darkroom was now a musty archive. Boxes, suitcases, and trunks stuffed with papers, diaries, photographs, postcards, books, toys, games, and clothes were crammed in along the waist-high outer wall. Large, hand-tinted photographs of grim-looking ancestors hung along the inside wall. Their piercing stares seemed to follow us no matter where we went in that room.

The darkroom was off limits, we were told. But the fact that it was forbidden (and I was terrified of it) didn't deter us. We'd sneak in there on rainy afternoons and spend hours sifting through its treasures—quill baskets and other curiosities Grandpa had brought home from his travels, a gramophone and a stack of thick vinyl records, his Kodak Brownie camera and tripod, and dozens of photographs depicting life in the Wild West. We fiddled with the camera and pored over the photographs, marvelling at how young and handsome Grandpa looked in his scarlet uniform.

Without a doubt the most peculiar item in the darkroom was a large shadow box containing a hair wreath. My great-grandmother, Elizabeth, had made the wreath with locks shorn from her dead sons' heads, Mom told us. Elizabeth was thirty years old when she married my great-grandfather. By the time she was forty-two, she had given birth to seven boys. Only four of them survived. Two died within the first two months. The third, a month after his first birthday. The thought of my great-uncles dying so young (possibly in the very room where I slept) haunted me. The wreath both repelled and intrigued me. I'd often peer into the shadow box, admiring the tiny rosettes and intricate knots and flourishes. I imagined my poor great-grandmother sitting by the fire, tears streaming down her face as she twisted her babies' auburn curls into this elaborate work of art to commemorate their brief lives.

We followed our grandparents everywhere that summer, getting underfoot while Grandma did the laundry in her old green wringer washer and watching in awe as Grandpa milked the cows. When the first thin streams of milk zinged against the inside of the stainless steel pail, the barn cats slinked in and hovered on the periphery, waiting for him to direct a squirt their way. I was crazy about cats and longed to stroke and cuddle them, but learned the hard way that they weren't pets. My brother and I spent hours chasing them around the hayloft until one day we finally managed to corner a kitten. I could hardly wait to hold that tiny ball of fur, but when I picked her up and began petting her, rather than purring contentedly, she hissed and raked her razor-sharp claws across my face. After that I kept my distance.

When we weren't hanging out in the barn, we tramped through the fields and forests, surveying the terrain and getting a feel for the land. We engineered an astonishing array of forts all over the farm. And when we whined about being bored, Mom handed each of us a plastic container and dragged us out to pick raspberries, promising that if we picked enough there'd be pie for dessert that evening. For the first half hour or so, it was fun. There was something satisfying about discovering a heavily loaded thicket of brambles and hearing the hollow *plunk, plunk, plunk* of the first few ruby-red berries hitting the bottom of the pail. Mom could pick berries all day long, but by the time my container was half full I'd lose interest. My arms and legs would be pricked and scratched, and I'd be fed up with swatting at mosquitoes and horseflies. But once the tantalizing aroma of the pies began drifting through the house, I'd forget all about the misery I'd endured to get those berries.

By the time that first summer came to an end, the farm seemed a little less intimidating but still far from comfortable. In my brief time there, the city had gotten under my skin. I missed the closeness, the cheek-by-jowlness that made you feel you were never really alone. In the country, I felt like a transplant struggling to survive—a feeling I would never completely shake. It was only during our weekly Sunday visits to my paternal grandmother's place in downtown Ottawa that I felt at one with my surroundings. The sound of wailing sirens and roaring engines seemed far more natural to me than wind sighing in the wheat fields and wolves howling in the distance.

◆

That fall, things began to change. In September, my grandparents moved to a house in North Gower, leaving us to our own devices. My sister and I started classes at our new school. Mom started work at the bank in town, and Dad, at the Ford dealer. Raising three young children while working full time and running the farm was an enormous challenge. Mom and Dad would often spend half the night cleaning and grading eggs, tending to a sick animal, or playing midwife to a farrowing sow. But they still had to be up before dawn the next morning to milk the cows, feed and water the animals, and get us kids fed and dressed before rushing off to work. The lack of electricity meant we had none of the modern conveniences that made life much simpler and more comfortable. The house was lit with a combination of propane and coal oil lamps; cooking was done on a wood stove; laundry was washed in the propane wringer washer and hung on the line to dry, summer and winter. Since the nearest power lines were miles away, acquiring electricity or telephone wasn't simply a matter of having the house and barn wired and hooked up. Ontario Hydro said they'd be happy to put in the poles and run the wires down our road—if we agreed to cover the cost. At thousands of dollars per pole, this proposition was out of the question.

Dad knew that in order to make a go of farming, it was essential to modernize the place. To do that, electricity was necessary. Although he couldn't afford it, he was bent on finding a way to get the power installed. For the next few years, he haggled with the power company, updated rusty old equipment, and invested in new livestock.

What my father hadn't foreseen when he decided to take over the farm was the drudgery, danger, and disappointment inherent in the life of a subsistence farmer—the crop failures, litter losses, and accidents that whittle away at body and spirit year after year. One wet summer we lost an entire crop of potatoes. An unexpected cold snap one spring killed off a few hundred chicks. Living on the edge as we were, losses like these cut deep. But being resourceful, Dad always managed to find a way to survive. And it seemed that neighbours were often willing to lend a hand, without being asked. They'd show up unexpectedly and pitch in with threshing or haying. If there was no money for feed or seed, the Co-op owner would give it to Dad on credit. "I know you're good for it, Ron," he'd say as he helped load the bags onto the back of the truck.

———————◆———————

Three years after my father began his campaign to get electricity, he finally succeeded. With the flick of a switch, life on the farm suddenly became brighter, easier, and far more comfortable. By then, it was the late 60s. Change was in the air. That summer the whole world watched as the Apollo 11 mission got underway. Up 'til then, my parents had resisted buying a television. But they finally broke down and rented one that July so we could watch the historic lunar landing. The day the astronauts were scheduled to walk on the moon, we crowded around the tiny black-and-white set, filled with anticipation. When Neil Armstrong stepped onto the dusty surface of the Sea of Tranquility and stated, "That's one small step for man, one giant leap for mankind," I knew things would never be the same again. For the first time since moving to the farm, I felt connected to the world beyond Marlborough Township.

Not long after that, subdivisions began springing up along our road. I was overjoyed to see rows of identical little bungalows invading the surrounding farmland. It meant that for the first time we had kids our age to hang out with. Nights didn't seem as dark and lonely anymore. However, in spite of all the changes occurring in the township, part of me continued to yearn for the liveliness and lustre of the city.

What I didn't realize then was that no matter where I went in the world, that farm in Marlborough Township would always possess me. Decades after moving to a city on the east coast, I still miss the sound of whippoorwills singing in the fragrant darkness outside my bedroom window. The taste of ice cold well water quaffed from an enamel dipper on hot summer days. And the feeling of driving down those long, straight county lines at dusk, windows rolled all the way down to catch the sweet smell of freshly mown hay.

The Goulds

Wayne Johnston

I WAS BORN in St. John's, but my parents moved to my mother's hometown, the Goulds, when I was one.

My mother's people, the Everards, were from Petty Harbour, which is now the postcard outport of Newfoundland, primarily because of its close proximity to St. John's. You can drive to Petty Harbour from St. John's in fifteen minutes by way of a coastal road that wasn't there when my mother was growing up.

The Everards took pride in the fact that from nowhere in the Goulds could you see the town of Petty Harbour or the ocean.

My mother's people were not of the water, very much not of the water, though their most recent ancestors were. They were very much of the land, such as it was, sea-scorners, sea-fearers, one rung up the social ladder of the lower classes by dint of their non-association with the sea, with merchants and the truck system and because what they harvested they had themselves created and so they did not have to depend for their livelihood on the whims of such a lowly, bottom-feeding creature as the cod.

The Everards had moved inland from Petty Harbour in the late nineteenth century, when the fishing grounds became too crowded. The first of them to move still fished part-time, maintaining summer shacks in Petty Harbour or nearby Shoal Bay, at the same time farming in the Goulds.

Wayne (age 3) in front of the family home in the Goulds, 1961

My grandfather and some other settlers cleared the wilderness of trees and rocks. My grandfather must have been either a late migrant or an indiscriminate one, for although there was much flatland in the Goulds, he situated his farm on the side of a hill. The angle of the furrows to the vertical was more than forty-five degrees on the steepest meadow, which had to be ploughed from the bottom up because a horse going downhill could not keep its feet.

The labour that went into clearing this land I could not, did not, begin to imagine. It never occurred to me as a child that the farm had not always been there, never occurred to me to wonder why there was a meandering wall of stones along each cartroad, or how what we called "the stump meadow," a bog in which hundreds of uprooted stumps lay slowly rotting or ossified by age, had come to be.

The Goulds was much younger than Ferryland. It had no historic sites or plaques, no stone churches from another century, had not grown from a colony founded by some aristocrat from England, had no founding heroes at all that were commemorated in books, no town museum. The Goulds, in New World terms, was anomalously new and anomalously agricultural.

But although it was not as old as Ferryland, the Goulds felt and looked older, because the remnants of its first generation lay not, as they are in

Ferryland, so deeply buried that the place is now a favourite digging site for archaeologists, but above ground, in plain view—the empty shells of long-abandoned barns and cellars that you could see straight through still stood at angles to the ground, as did fences built for some forgotten purpose, their posts supported by the grey-washed stones that, within someone's living memory, had been uprooted from the ground. There were already by my time farms that looked the way my grandfather's does now, failed, long-abandoned farms, open fields where hay and fodder that no one bothered with grew wild, fallen fence posts still joined by wire, stands of stunted, wind-bent junipers along the road, grown up since the levelling of spruce and birch. In one place, criss-crossed by paths where we played and took shortcuts to school, a mature forest had arisen on land that must have been among the first to be cleared a hundred years ago. The rocks pried from the earth were piled in heaps that now were all but overgrown by moss.

We wandered my grandfather's farm on Sunday afternoons when he was sleeping, played among trucks left for good where they had broken down and been deemed beyond repair, among discarded farm implements, ploughshares without handles, handles without blades, tires complete with rims from some early version of the tractor. There were old hubcaps nailed to trees. Rain-greyed lengths of rope that had been used to tether livestock hung from branches. Upside-down paint cans had been stuck on fence posts for target practice. On the ground lay rusting coils of chains. We were on orders from my grandfather not to move any of these things, as if they had been placed with a purpose. His history in the Goulds was commemorated haphazardly throughout the farm by unculled artifacts.

The only constant in the Goulds was the contour of the land: the land as it looked in winter, shorn of most of its vegetation, shorn down to bedrock; the hills beyond the farms that bound the town on every side but west, where lay one leg of the bog of Avalon. The hills were so far above the town they were merely dark green shapes, at night bald silhouettes against the sky.

My grandfather's farm seemed to me a vast place. To go to the uppermost hayfield, beyond the pound, beyond the grazing field, beyond the crops, beyond the fodder, was a great, rarely embarked upon adventure.

But the last time I was there, a few years ago, it took me less than ten minutes to climb to the top of the hill. As I looked down at the site of the old house and barn, it seemed impossible that a man and a woman had supported themselves and their seven children on the annual yield of that barely arable few acres and the milk produced by a dozen cows.

It was into this farming family that my father married, in this farming town he eventually settled, among farmers-in-law who held forever in reserve the trump card of irony that a man of his particular field of specialization—he was an agricultural technologist—ended up working for the fisheries while they were growing crops and raising cows without the benefit of a diploma in anything.

Awakened
by Stars
SHARON BUTALA

I WAS A rural child from my birth in Saskatchewan in 1940, first in
the wilderness of the bush country to the north and then in a series
of small towns, each slightly larger and more southerly than the last,
until the summer of 1953. Confronted with the question, *What was it
like growing up rural?*, I find that I cannot answer, *It was like this*, because
what it was like was so interwoven with what it was like to be alive, to be a
person in the only world I had ever seen, that I can answer only by writing
about the life I began to live the year I turned thirteen and came to the city.
It was, in fact, the very day of my thirteenth birthday that I arrived with
my family in Saskatoon. Saskatoon—the only believable city in the breadth
of stories I had heard—had fewer than fifty thousand people then, but still
was unimaginably urban to me.

I don't think that, before I arrived there, I had any notion of what
people did in cities. I had mostly seen only cowboy movies, and even
those rarely, until I was perhaps ten years old; nobody talked to me about
life in cities because we were all country people and hadn't lived in them.
The exodus then was from the country to the city and never the other way
around—going to the city was like sailing off the edge of the earth. We had
no television—nobody did then—and I have no memory of the books I
read giving me any sense of urban life, other than, maybe, that of London,
England, in the nineteenth century. The result was that I had a hard time

Sharon (age 2) in her father's arms, with her mother beside him, in front
of her grandparents' log house north of Garrick, Saskatchewan, 1942

seeing how the things that seemed simply *life* to me would have seemed to
anyone else. When finally I was old enough to recall details about that past
on the land, I would never speak of them because that life was tainted, it was
something of which I could be only ashamed. Because, in that pioneering
era in Saskatchewan, it certainly meant that I had been poor (and, also, one
of the certifiably ignorant). People did not then routinely value whatever it
was I had learned in that childhood, whatever it was that I had experienced,
things of which I wouldn't have known how to speak anyway.

Here I must pause to point out that in those years and in that place
virtually anyone—anyone at all, and especially anyone who tried to settle
in the north—who was rural was, by definition, some variation of poor.
And when we moved to the city, we moved, naturally, to the part of town
where the immigrants lived alongside the small population of misfits and
the shiftless and hopeless, in the midst of the city's large working class
that planned, by dint of every effort, to move somewhere better as soon
as possible. So my experience changed from that of the rural poor to that
of the urban poor. *Poor*, although omnipresent, wasn't quite the issue in
either place, at least not until I began university and, looking back, saw

Awakened by Stars

how my personality, my character, my beliefs, and my hopes had all been formed, saturated—*drenched*—with the limitations of familial poverty in a poor society. But that is another story. I don't think that anyone not poor lived in the places we lived. Why would they, if they didn't have to?

Nonetheless, people who lived in Saskatoon during the years I was a rural child and didn't know it existed tell me stories that suggest how very rural even that city was then, with its lack of plumbing in the houses on the poorer side of town where I would one day live, its "honey wagons," its communal water pump on a street corner in each neighbourhood, its outdoor skating rinks, its gravel streets. (Of course, it would have been different in the prosperous parts of town, but few rural immigrants got to live in them immediately.) By the time I moved there, there were no more outhouses—at least, not that the city knew about. All the houses were plumbed and had telephones, and even the horse-drawn milk wagons were mostly gone.

My earliest childhood memories are of unsteady, richly coloured lantern light, of the patient, easy power—the very *people-ness*—of the workhorses, of the biting cold and mountains of snow, the howling of timber wolves and the constant worry about bears. They include the first time I remember seeing the northern lights when, in a small town, just at twilight, a bunch of us were playing kick-the-can on the gravel street in front of our houses when one of us gazing into the northern sky, shouted, "Look!" We followed his pointing finger, and then, at first only one, and then two and three, and then all of us, ran shrieking like maniacs, in terror that was either pretend or real or a mixture of both, for the safety of our houses. *It's only the northern lights*, my mother would have said, amused. I must have said, *But what are they?* but she could not have told me. I'm not sure that in 1948 anyone knew, and I always knew that *what* wasn't the question anyway.

My memories include all the long spring one year when my cousin and a friend built a raft, and we spent all the time we weren't in school or in bed rafting on a big slough on the edge of town. Or before that, in those unimaginably cold and snow-buried winters, riding in what we called a caboose, a small house-like structure on wheels pulled by a team of horses and which had a cast-iron heater inside it that our fathers would feed wood to as we moved—the strangeness of having a stove in a moving vehicle delighting us children, giving us a sense that wonders would, indeed, never cease. Or the way the pine logs of our house oozed sap, so that sometimes, if I forgot and leaned against the wall as I sat on the rough, home-made bench spooning up my porridge, my hair would be caught in it and my mother would have to come and rescue me.

When we moved to the city, I was too young to actually miss the life from which I had come, or to feel any sense of loss, and in the midst of a true awakening to a different, immensely exciting life, far from ready to say, *I want to go back*, if I had even thought such a thought. One of the biggest differences once I moved to Saskatoon was that the other kids knew a thousand times more about Catholicism than I did, because there had been no exclusively Catholic schools where I'd lived, and even the churches were few and far between. I don't suppose I went to church before I was four, and then only once a month or so when the circuit priest came to the little log church in a clearing, so cold inside that I could see my breath. In Saskatoon, the church was huge and painted with pictures on the inside and decorated with gold, and afterward I remembered the sermon, the choir's single soaring voice, the clouds of heady incense, instead of just how very cold I had been or how pale and sickly looking the priest was. And the kids, whose lives had come complete from the moment of their births with nuns and priests, thought nothing of making fun of them behind their backs, although in confrontations they said politely, primly, "Yes, Sister," "No, Sister," or "Yes, Father. I'm sorry, Father," while I gaped, quaking at their easy perfidy.

I did not know not to put my clasped hands on the starched white cloth at the altar rail until my friend nudged me to show me; I did not know what the Sodality was, hadn't even heard of it—I'd been forced, in my Catholic-less rural past, to belong to CGIT even though I'd hated it— until a priest who looked after the Sodality told my friends, who belonged, that they should ask me to join, and they did not, a rebuff that stings to this day. Or, more accurately, I still carry the memory of the sting. In that long search for news of oneself is the memory of not being wanted and the puzzlement as to why not. Who was I then? What had I done? Or did they just not like my bumpkin ignorance?

How tough the city kids were, or we thought they were tough, and how much more they knew about life than little girls from the country did—and what they knew about life was mostly not good. Not good at all. The boys, coming into their sexuality, had no sense of tenderness, or of the possibility of love as something beautiful, having seen so little gentleness and beauty in their young city lives on the wrong side of town. These—how to be a Catholic child, how to negotiate in a less gentle world—were two of the things that I had to learn very fast once I began school in the city. But, just as poverty was omnipresent but was not the issue, so was the harshness of the society I moved in not the issue.

In the city we did not have a social group the whole family could be part of as we had had in the country. We children went to different schools; each of my sisters had her own friends not even known by the rest of us, and we did not know each others' friends' families; when our parents went out socially, rarely, they went their own way, usually leaving us at home. In the end, I think the move to the city had a lot to do with breaking apart our family. Not that it was destroyed, nothing like that, but that our intimacy was dissolved; our intentions, in which we were once united, grew disparate and secret, and a disharmony, never spoken of and that was never there before, crept in to our family life as we began to establish ourselves, individually and together, in the city, as we became, slowly, misstep after misstep, city people.

Our past had been filled with hardship. Our parents knew that it was hardship, but we children didn't know it until we were grown and, looking back, remembered when we had to light kerosene lamps because the only other light was from the stars and the moon; when we had to carry water every day, or in winter to fill pails or basins with snow to fill the cast-iron stove's reservoir for our water supply; and when we had to run out to the outhouse at every hour of the day or night, in all seasons and weather. Our fathers chopped down trees and built houses and sheds. They built our roads—such as they were—and chased away the wild animals, or hunted them, and found ways to wrest a niggardly living out of the forest and the grass and the dirt so that we might eat, grow, and carry on. *It was brutal*, a friend says, as the visceral memory of it assails her, and she hugs herself and shivers.

So when, in the seventies, hippies, those soft and privileged city kids, began to move from middle-class homes out into the wilderness—going *back to the land*, they said—I was one of those who, remembering all too well how hard that life was and how we'd have given anything for the amenities they so readily spurned, thought they were all crazy. I said not one word, so in shock was I at the madness of such a notion. Back to outhouses, to being eaten alive by mosquitoes and black flies, back to an opportunity-less poverty—no films, no dance, no theatre or concerts, no learned conversation, barely even any books. I, who had had only books, and few of them, as a child, yearned for all of them, clung to them, as the very best there would ever be in life, while those who had had them all were turning away, as if they were nothing, had no value.

I was angered by them, and bitter about their folly. If I knew I would meet them socially, they wearing their moccasins, suspenders, long cotton dresses, and long hair or braids, I would put on makeup, curl my hair extravagantly, and wear my fanciest city clothes. I wanted to laugh at them, but they were so sure they were right that I didn't dare. They seemed to think that my family and I and our feckless neighbours just hadn't known what we were doing. They never seemed to think that we did what we did without a nearby community or a nice house in the city to which we could retreat if things didn't work out. They didn't know about, or else found romantic, the miscarriages our mothers suffered, often all alone in the bush cabin, or with only their husbands, or the child taken seriously ill in the night and no phones, no decent roads, no proper transportation to the nearest doctor, usually miles away through the bush. I guess they thought it would be fun to be chased by a wolf or to fight off a bear. Or else, and I think this is the key, they thought that we simply weren't thinking about our hardscrabble lives in the bush in the *right* way, the way which they somehow—but how?—knew.

As the years have passed since their exodus back to the land, I've rethought my anger, or maybe it's just the effect of getting old (to be more forgiving of folly), but I suspect that I have been too hard on them. Maybe they wanted something else, something they couldn't name or describe, but that, for its acquisition, they were willing merely to endure—or thought they were—all the rest of their lives. They'd grown up with everything set out before them on the proverbial silver platter; they didn't have to struggle for anything, from flicking a switch for light, to turning a thermostat for heat, to walking to the corner to buy fruit from California and vegetables from Mexico and meat trimmed neat in plastic trays. It was all too easy; they wanted a little challenge, not knowing how ill prepared they were for a real challenge, or worse, how desperately hard it would be. Perhaps they wanted, too, to be free of all the middle-class authority in their lives, all that class's rigidity, and also, its superficiality. They wanted, above all, a little *freedom* and a chance to make their own world, one that had true meaning.

I think now, too, that they must have known at some level that the reason the city lives they were facing were so unsatisfactory had something to do with disconnection from natural things. That was what those young people, behind all the posturing—the costumes, banjos, and fiddles—and the foolishness, or what seemed to people brought up as I had been like foolishness, were really yearning for: a chance to live in nature. Because nature was *real*, or smacked of something real, as nothing else in their lives did.

That is what my rural upbringing gave me: a connection with the earth. Had I not had those thirteen years of life in wilderness and then on its edge, my first experience and knowledge of life being of life in nature, I think perhaps even with the last thirty years I have lived back in rural life, I wouldn't have come as far as I think I have—as I *feel* I have—in understanding something about what I can only call the meaning of land. So much so that, eventually, I began to see my life on the land in almost purely spiritual terms—that is, that life is itself spiritual, first and foremost, and nature (not sidewalks and telephone poles and high rises) is imbued with spirit, waiting patiently for the solitary wanderer to come in silent supplication, to come without remedy, without hard-edged knowledge, even—or especially—without belief. I came to see nature as not only beautiful and peaceful, but also as solace for the cruelty of life. Nature as more than all of these things, and something else besides.

I could not write about how it was to be a rural child because any time I tried to think of nature—of living as a child in nature—my brain would shut down. This, because my childhood experience was that nature was so huge, so powerful, so unalterable, and, above all, so filled with mystery that it couldn't be thought about. It just was. We lived in the midst of nature. Every night we had only the moon and stars for light, we were utterly governed by the seasons, and the weather was our eternal foe. Our parents fought nature every single day for our very lives. And, although I cannot know what they thought then, I believe they tried never to conceive concretely of what nature might be, because she was just too big, too implacable, too utterly overwhelming.

My first contact with the world was with the Great Mystery that is nature. That is why, I think, twenty-six years later when I came to live on the southern prairie, on a cattle ranch, back in a settler's shack without an indoor bathroom, in the middle of miles of un-peopled grass, that I began to be acquainted with nature. I found an intermediary out of that great force that seemed to be directed toward, seeking a link with, my own puny human consciousness. I had already been awakened to the appropriate, indeed insuppressible, wonder, awakened by the stars and the snow, by the howling winds and the green summer meadows sparkling with dew, by the shifting, pale dance of the aurora borealis and the light-filled, rustling forests of fall. I had no silly notions of conquering, owning, or managing nature; I wanted only to smell and see and hear her, and thus, overcome by awe, to find my way, ecstatically, into her heart.

Awakened by Stars

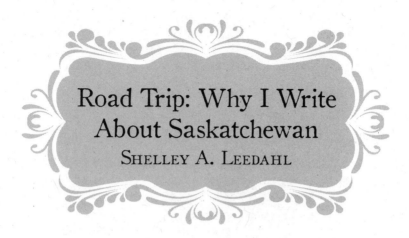

Road Trip: Why I Write About Saskatchewan

Shelley A. Leedahl

WE'RE ON **HIGHWAY** 16. Troy's driving. The kids are quiet and behaving in the back. The radio's playing "In the House of Stone and Light"—or "In the House of Stone and Love"—I can't quite make it out, but I like it. On this highway it's not hard to imagine why Columbus believed the world was flat; I feel we could drive right off the edge.

We're on our way to Meadow Lake where I'll do readings and workshops. I'm nervous about facing the hometown crowd. Will my old friends show? Will anyone? At Carpenter High, where I stumbled off the stage at my graduation, someone, perhaps the joker in the back row whose hair curls over his denim collar, will ask: *Why would anyone want to write about Saskatchewan?*

I have an answer.

◆

Because in another town, the town where I was born, the boy who lived above the meat market had two turtles, big as badgers, and we used to tear barefoot down the back alley over all the stones and it never hurt, it really never hurt, not like it did when I saw my first motorcycle, chased after it, then fell and sliced my knee so badly I still have the scar to prove it and there were plagues of grasshoppers on a white picket fence and Father

Shelley (age 8) ice-skating near Turtleford, Saskatchewan, 1971

fell off a roof and Sam Wong from Wong's Cafe on Main Street made milkshakes so thick you couldn't suck 'em up a straw and always, at night, the sound of soldiers, marching in my head.

◆

I love this section of the highway. I can see the valley and the wide blue sash of the North Saskatchewan River running through it like a vein. In summer, when everything's green as garden peas, this area reminds me of Scotland. Not that I've ever been there, but I've seen it often enough in movies to have a pretty good idea. Troy must have switched stations. "In the House of Stone and Light" (or "Love") is on again. We're coming up to Borden. I know someone who grew up there. She's a painter. We pass the sign for Redberry Bible Camp.

◆

Why write about Saskatchewan? Because when I was twelve I went to summer camp and all the girls had a crush on Counsellor Bob and we slept in sleeping bags beneath the stars and Thursday night at the group campfire we were talking about religious stuff and this really weird thing happened—one camper started crying, then someone else and I thought, *It's not going to happen to me, whatever the hell it is*, and soon just about everyone was bawling and hugging each other, even the guys, and I couldn't help it, my tears snuck up like a prairie storm and years later I saw Counsellor Bob in Saskatoon, even met his wife, who was substitute teaching at my kids' school, and no one ever talked about that night at the campfire again.

———◆———

Not even in Radisson yet, and I have to pee. Serves me right, all the Diet Coke I knock back. I'll see if I can hold it until North Battleford. In the far right-hand corner of the sky: a breath of blue. *This is Saskatchewan*, they say. *Cold enough for you? Wet enough? Dry enough? Hot enough?*

———◆———

Why Saskatchewan? Because when I was twenty, I crossed a picket line to work at the Westview Co-op on 33rd Street and my boyfriend had the best tan of his life walking that picket line and we had no idea I was pregnant and that summer there was a major flood in the city and I thought, *Oh, boy…God's pissed off now*, and everyone got to leave work early and I saw a Dickie Dee cart fall right over on its side like a big cow and the rain was coming down in walls and the Dickie Dee boy's goodies spilled across the wet cement like manna and he just stood there with the rain pinging off his head, he just stood there.

———◆———

They're twinning the highway between Saskatoon and North Battleford. About time. Too many accidents. Phone lines: we hold our breath between them, see how many we can pass while humming one long note. Railroad tracks. That superstition: lift your feet for good luck. I lift mine now and will forever. Just past Maymont we pass a yellow school bus.

Why this place? Because that first snowfall each year makes you gasp, part of you glad that it's finally come after all the cold weather and wind and you know how happy all the little kids are because you can see them in the schoolyards sticking their tongues out to catch the candy of flakes, and the other half with that sinking feeling that this is the beginning of it, this is the long haul, the lugging out of boots and pairing of gloves, the frosted windshields and battery cables…Why write about this? Here?

Because I remember watching that first snowfall from a friend's bedroom window. Bev's family lived in the country. We took the bus. It had a funny name—Clover Bell, or something. There were loads of kids in her family and it was loud in that house but there, by the window, just then, it was quiet and the snow was confetti and I would never have guessed that years later I would read that Bev died in a freak accident—electrocuted while vacuuming her van—and I heard her mother was going to raise Bev's son and I was sorry for it all, the orphaned little boy, the grieving mother, and my friend, who never knew what it meant to me, that first snowfall through her bedroom window.

54-40. "Ocean Pearl." I like this song. The landscape has no colour now, but it's a sly chameleon, this prairie. In a few months, another season and a new palette. New textures, too. Coarse crops. Powdery dust. And those big fat cumulous clouds we imagine into sheep and fellow animals. Speaking of animals, there is a pasture full of horses, not knowing they are beautiful.

Why write? Because I had the fourteen-year-old's fling with horses—Prince, Candy, Black—and was lucky enough to have friends who owned them. That summer at Lerene's when we were all riding bareback and then the night, when we met up with the boys and we were still kids but we were swinging our legs over the edge of night and knowing and knowledge and never looking back and we saw a UFO and we were all pinned there, underneath a white, blipping light that two-stepped around the stars and likely no one believes us but we were there and as sure as a cocktail of dirt and manure was caked beneath our runners there was an unidentified object, flying.

———◆———

Now we're on the oldies station. "Hot Child in the City." I remember when this song came out. Nick Gilder. Trooper. Supertramp. My God: *I'm* an oldie! Troy hasn't spoken for several minutes. We get like this on road trips. Hushed. The sign for the Denholm Hotel says *Rooms*. Troy blurts, *There's the sun*, like it's a long-lost friend, and it is. It's also still snowing. Pools of water sit like flattened sapphires upon the still-blank faces of fields. Give it a few days. Saskatchewan is the sunshine capital of North America.

———◆———

Why? Because we are children of the sun and I will never regret my teenage years, all those nights at the lake, on the lake, in it. I don't regret the parties, the concerts, the trips to the neon cities that were another world I was desperate to explore, knew it from the time I was a little kid and my father brought us to Saskatoon. It used to wake the butterflies in my stomach when I saw the first grey outline of skyscrapers, or better, the thin long line of lights in the night that spelled a word on the tip of my tongue.

Why would anyone want to write about Saskatchewan? Because of the boy with pet turtles and Bev of the first snowfall. Because of the sun and the coldest damn rinks you could imagine. Because I've never been to Scotland. Because, as the song goes, "I can see for miles and miles." Because of thick vanilla milkshakes in metal containers at Wong's Cafe, Main Street, Kyle, Saskatchewan. Because of the ghosts of elevators that are fondly remembered dreams and the wheat-like stalks that are power poles. Because in Lucky Lake, everyone still says hello to strangers. Because there's a lighthouse on a hill in Cochin, where few ships ever come in. Because of haunted houses and hollyhocks. Because all across this province there are cemeteries and, beside them, there used to be drive-in theatres where on Sunday nights kids lined up for hours for the triple feature. They snuck beer in, and maybe a friend or two in the trunk, and when I was a little kid Dad took me to *Tales from the Crypt* at the drive-in beside the cemetery where Grandma was sleeping and it scarred me for life.

Because I was born here. Learned to read and write here. Caught my first butterfly here. My first fish. Chicken pox. This is where I learned to do the one-foot spin and play spin the bottle. Because of the sunsets and skyscrapers, small-town parades and fathers who are Kinsmen and Elks. Because of riverbanks, ball diamonds, and beaches. Because thirty years ago I wrote a little song:

> *I am prairie, through and through,*
> *My hair is wheat, my eyes sky blue.*

Because there are still almost a million people here whose stories deserve to be told, and most will never put pen to paper. Because around here we weave ourselves through good times and bad, through love and desire, just like everyone anywhere else. We stumble, dust ourselves off, and get back on the grid-road trail. Because of all of these things but, especially, because some day someone might want to know what it was like to live in this particular part of the country, the world, the universe, at this particular point in time, and I want to be able to say, *Listen, it was like this.*

Part II
Journeys

Fargo, North Dakota

Ruth Latta

DADDY WAS GOING away. We stared, saucer-eyed, when he told us the news. He had just come back from his brothers' farm and was sitting with Mum at the table having a cup of tea. We had been outside playing, enjoying the newfound freedom of summer holidays. It was early July, green as far as the eye could see, whether I looked up the road a mile to the end of our property or down the road, which led to school, town, and faraway cities. The northeastern Ontario woods had come alive once again a few months earlier, and the poplars and birches were in full leaf, the leaves rubbing against each other in the wind with a gentle, shushing sound.

Was Daddy really going on a trip, just when the garden was coming along nicely, just two weeks before the hay would be ready? Incredible, since Daddy never went anywhere. Years earlier he had come to Canada with his parents from England. Once settled onto the farm, he never wanted to budge. We two girls, with Mummy, were the travellers, spending a week each summer with her family in Sturgeon Falls, a sawmill town a hundred miles south. Daddy always drove us there and returned to bring us home, but claimed he couldn't stay away from our farm for a whole week.

Was he leaving for good? Sometimes, when our parents fought, Dad would threaten to leave and would stride out of the house, get into the green International pickup truck and go for a drive. Though he always came back within an hour, we always felt afraid and sad. There was always the chance that, this time, he meant business.

He was mentioning a place. Fargo, North Dakota. Uncle Gil was going, too. My uncles had been clearing land to grow more grain, not only for themselves, but for the neighbours and for us, too. Now, in the 1950s, thirty years after the first settlement of these lands, some areas were going back to scrub forest. The tag alders and shrubs on our back acres had been pushed up into a long windrow beside the bush. The field was ploughed and planted with oats. To us, with my mother teaching school, it was not vital to have more land in production, but to other farm families whose entire living came from the soil, it was crucial.

My uncles were the only farmers in the area who owned the bulldozer necessary for this work. The machine was also a wonder for winter snow clearing, so it paid for itself when my uncles were hired out to clear brush or snow for other farmers. Until the bulldozer broke down, that is. A key part of the machine kept breaking. My uncles kept patching it together, only to have it break again, usually in the middle of a job. The parts they ordered were never quite right. My uncles talked it over and decided they would have to go straight to the manufacturer.

The only trouble was the machine had been made in Fargo, North Dakota, in the United States, over a thousand miles away. They calculated that they could get there in two days if they drove eight hours a day. All told, they might be away a week. But there was another problem. Someone had to stay home and look after their farm. Uncle Bob was married and had a family. He would stay behind, but who could go with Uncle Gil to share the driving?

My dad could. The truth was that his farming operation was not that big. Our cows could graze, the garden grow on its own.

"I think you should go," Mum said. "See something of the United States. We'll manage."

She got out an old school atlas, and we all peered at it, finding the dot on the map that said "Fargo," trying to figure out what route they would take. There were a couple of possibilities, but Uncle Gil planned to go to Sault Ste Marie, Ontario, cross over into Michigan, drive through

Wisconsin and Minnesota, then into North Dakota. I gazed at the scale of the map, at the provinces and states, all different colours. Daddy was going very far away.

Uncle Gil wanted to leave in a day or two, as he was losing money every day the bulldozer was laid up. There was a flurry of discussion. What should Daddy take with him? How much money would he need?

We drove into town the next day to get American currency from the bank, and stared at it in wonder. Instead of Queen Elizabeth, the notes featured presidents. Daddy was going to another country!

Back home, Mum got down the brown suitcase, which we girls took on our summer trips. Now Daddy was taking it.

"Will you write us a letter?" my sister asked wistfully. She was only seven.

"I'll be home before a letter would," he told her. "Besides, we'll be driving all day except for meals, then stopping only to sleep at night."

Where would they sleep? Motels. He didn't know exactly where—wherever seemed a good place to stop after a day's driving.

He was going off into the unknown.

One rainy morning, my uncles' black sedan, freshly washed, glided down our driveway. Uncle Gil was at the wheel. Daddy kissed us all goodbye, and my sister's eyes filled with tears. The three of us stood outside and waved as the car went down the hill, up another, and out of sight behind the trees.

We were alone. We had no telephone, no neighbours within three miles. True, the truck was parked in the yard, for emergencies. Mum could drive it, or claimed she could, but didn't have a licence. All three of us could drive the tractor (even my sister had steered it with Daddy sitting behind her), but it was for work, not for travel. The forest across the road and the grove behind the barn seemed closer and darker than before.

Reading and games didn't seem fun any more; I felt the need to help out, so I offered to pick peas and beans in the garden. The dog seemed on edge. He lay on the back doorstep, facing the road where the car and Daddy had disappeared. The mail came three times a week, and on those days, around 11:00 A.M., my sister and I waited for the mailman, mostly to have contact with the outside world, but also on the off chance that Daddy had written. Most days the mail carrier just waved to us and drove on.

Every day the three of us walked up the field and around the grove to see how the cattle were doing in the back pasture. Cows that got loose might wander through the crops, getting bloated on clover. They could trample our vegetable gardens and flower beds or take to the bush where they might never be heard from again. The fence, though it was only a single strand of barbed wire, kept them in by giving them a mild electric shock. We had to check that the fence was not grounded by a fallen branch. But the cows were fine. They had ample grass to eat, and a pond for drinking water.

When Daddy took us to check the cattle, we always gathered daisies, paintbrush, and buttercups growing wild by the grove. The only wild animals to be seen in daylight were field mice and rabbits. Yet with Daddy away, we did not pick flowers but walked along smartly, keeping close to one another.

After sunset, I felt especially lonely. True, we were free to listen to whatever we wanted on the radio, rather than baseball, boxing, or the news, but we missed Daddy being there, with the smoke curling up from his cigarette. When the moon came out, I realized that it was also shining on him in Michigan or Minnesota or wherever he was. In the big bed with Mummy, we wondered aloud where he was now.

"Halfway there, in some nice comfortable motel," she would say. Or, "They must be in Fargo by now."

One morning a rattletrap truck roared into our yard. It was Uncle Bob and our cousin Ian, on a gas and grocery run to the store, stopping to see how we were. We ran out in alarm, fearing bad news. With a grin, Uncle Bob told us that Gil had phoned their house the previous evening. He and Daddy were safe in Fargo and were buying the bulldozer part today.

Hurrah! Daddy still existed. From then on, we counted the days until his return. Mummy baked. We helped her clean the house and weed the garden. My sister joined the dog on the step, looking down the road for the first glimpse of the car.

"It may be tomorrow," Mummy reminded us. "We don't know exactly when they'll be back."

In mid-afternoon, the dog's ears stood up. He bounded, barking, to the road. The black car purred down the hill, then turned into our lane.

There they were! We hugged Daddy. He looked proud, yet glad to be home. Uncle Gil looked pleased with himself, too. They'd had no trouble. The entire trip had been fine. My uncle couldn't stop for a snack but wanted to get home. Maybe he and Bob could fix the bulldozer before dark.

Holding Daddy's hands, we led him inside. Mummy carried his suitcase. We poured his tea and put his cake on a plate, all the while plying him with questions. He had no souvenirs, and his description of the farm equipment factory left us cold, but we were glad to have him back.

We pressed him for details. What was it like in the United States?

Dad said it was wonderful, driving along a smooth four-lane highway, so unlike our gravel road. Uncle Gil drove in the cities, but Dad did his share of the highway driving. The northern states near the Canadian border were beautiful. Wisconsin had many lakes, trees, and dairy cattle. Minnesota was prairie: great green fields glistening in the morning dew, with the sky a clear blue with white fluffy clouds. They stopped for meals at restaurants by the highway, smart, modern places staffed by pretty blonde waitresses of Nordic descent who smiled at the customers and filled Dad's coffee cup as many times as he wanted without charge. Mummy sniffed at this part of the story.

"But I never saw anyone as pretty as you girls," Daddy said, taking my sister on his knee. "I wish you could've seen it, too. Someday we'll all go on a trip."

The next day we were back to our normal routines. Our trip—for we had all journeyed—had an uplifting effect on all of us, though. Fate seemed to be smiling on us. The big outside world could have swallowed up our father, but it hadn't. He'd had an adventure and had returned back safe and sound. Something might happen to him many years down the road, when I was a grown woman and could handle it, but for the time being, he was back.

Burning
the Fields
LAURIE ELMQUIST

MY FATHER, IN coveralls and work boots, handed my sister an empty burlap bag. "Get it good and soaked," he said, indicating toward the plastic trash can sitting on the dune buggy.

Shoving the sleeve of her jacket up to her elbow, Grace leaned over the trash can and pushed the potato sack in the water. Bubbles of air rose as it sank. "What now?" she asked.

My father lit his blow torch. He bent down to the edge of the field, pulled some dry grass into a loose pile, and set it on fire, taking a step back as the flames caught. We watched it spread. The fire was sneaky, the way it travelled low to the ground. It seemed to move underneath the grass, burning from the inside out, widening its path as it went and leaving a smouldering black patch behind.

I'd never done anything like this before, but I knew I was expected to help. Seven years old, said my father, was old enough to use a shovel or a rake. It was old enough to make myself useful around the farm, picking up fallen apples or mowing around the trees. It was old enough to do a lot of chores, he said, although it was painfully slow.

Slow wasn't so bad, my sister told me. Slow was the way we liked it some afternoons in the rock piles in the fields behind our house. We'd go out there and dig among the boulders, pulling out old bottles, purple ones with bubbles floating to the lip or square ones with raised lettering along the side. We went to the fields when we didn't want to be found, where we couldn't hear my father calling our names.

———◆———

Dad had announced his plans at lunch. "Today, we're going to burn the fields."

Grace looked up from her bowl of chili. "What do you mean?"

"Set them on fire."

"Cool," said my twelve-year-old brother, tearing into his hot dog.

Grace, who was thirteen, and would rather have spent the afternoon reading *Seventeen*, looked to my mother for support.

"You'll have to wear your old boots," she said, getting up from the table.

My sister stared after her. "What about Laurie?"

"I'm going to need everyone," said my father. "Laurie, too."

Sometimes Grace tried to get me out of things. She'd tell Dad that Mom needed me inside to help with dinner or that there was a ton of vacuuming to do. My mother's bad back, broken in a car accident a couple of years earlier, made it hard for her to do housework. Her need for my help was something my sister could usually count on if she thought I'd be safer inside the house with her than outside with my father. "He thinks we're as strong as he is," Grace would complain to my mother. "Wayne's cutting down trees, and I'm hauling them into the trailer, and I look over and there's Dad getting Laurie to hold some log for him so he can cut it with the chainsaw. He doesn't realize she's only seven."

I didn't hear what my mother said in return, but I don't think she really wanted to know what went on outside. She rarely disagreed with my father on anything. She probably just said what she always said, "Your father needs your help on the farm, and that's all there is to it."

"Why do the fields have to be burned?" asked Grace.

"It's April," said my father, as if that explained everything.

He was not burning the fields, as our neighbour Lad Shaw might have done, to get rid of the dead grass and prepare the ground for ploughing and planting. He was burning them to build a nine-hole golf course.

"A golf course?" asked Lad, the night he and Cheryl came over for a game of euchre.

I sat on the carpeted landing at the top of the stairs, listening to the conversation below. Our house, built by my father when we first moved to the Bruce Peninsula, was an open-concept design with a vaulted ceiling and one big room across the front. It was kitchen, dining room, and living room combined. The landing jutted out like the top deck of a ship. Once in a while someone would look up, but mostly I could sit there unnoticed.

"How long you figure it's going to take you to build a golf course?" asked Lad.

"Not long," said my father, dealing out the cards.

"They've been building that course out in Hepworth, must be three years now."

"Pass," said Cheryl.

"Pass," said my mother.

"Had the backhoe out there for months," said Lad.

"They spend a lot of time moving dirt around," said my father, "and watching the grass grow."

"I hear they're growing Kentucky blue grass," said Lad. "Takes time to get it right."

"You passing or what?" asked Cheryl.

"Pick it up," said Lad, startled into the game.

"I don't need Kentucky blue grass. I've got plenty of grass," said my father.

"You got hay," said Lad, scooping up the cards, "and ant hills."

"Hon, could you get the sandwiches?" asked my mother, looking up at me.

She always made salmon sandwiches before our neighbours arrived, taking care to remove all the bones and skin from the tinned salmon. She said some people just mashed it all up, but she couldn't eat it that way: crunching the bones made her teeth shiver. I thought salmon smelled like cat food and was surprised that adults ate it at all.

I offered the plate to Lad and watched him pick up the small triangles with his big farmer hands. "Don't go to no trouble for us." He shoved a sandwich into his mouth, and then washed it down with a mouthful of beer. "Best I tasted." He made the best maple syrup in the township and liked to give credit where credit was due.

My father looked out the window at the fields in front of the house. "It's hay now, but when I mow it, it's going to be a golf course."

"That's a lot of mowing," said Lad.

My father smiled, almost as if he'd been waiting for him to bring it up. "I got a gang mower," he said. "Bought it at an auction: twelve rollers. I'm going to pull it behind the dune buggy."

"That so?" Lad and my father shared a love of all things mechanical.

"You can burn ant hills, right?" asked my father.

"Burn the whole damn field," said Lad. "Clear it right out and save yourself a lot of work."

"That's two points for us," said Cheryl, who seemed to be the only one paying attention to the game.

———◆———

My father lit a clump of grass, and then another. Satisfied, he turned back to Grace. "Hand me the sack."

"Watch," he said, including Wayne and I in his glance. He beat the wet bag against the ground, putting out flames wherever it touched.

"You can control how it burns," he said. "If the fire's not moving in the direction you want, or if it's getting out of hand, put it out."

He made it sound easy, as if this fire were no different from the ones he lit every couple of weeks to burn the household garbage. We'd drag the bags down to the old stone foundation at the end of the driveway, and when the pile got good and high, he'd chuck in a couple of oil tins and empty paint cans just to make it pop and burn with fury. He liked a good fire.

My father dunked the burlap bag into the water and handed it back to my sister. "Don't look so serious," he said. "Just make sure the fire doesn't get too close to the apple trees."

He took another burlap bag from the seat of the dune buggy and handed it to me.

I pushed the sack into the water, the way I'd seen my sister do it.

"You're going to help us, right, Dad?" asked Grace. She had that scowl she wore whenever she was worried. A face like a thundercloud, Dad called it.

"Wayne and I are going behind the barn to burn the back field," he said, filling a watering can and handing it to Grace. "We're going to have a sweet little green right by the old well down there." The fire was already working its way across the front field in long curls of smoke.

"Maybe we should stay together for a while," said my brother. "Just until we know everything's going okay." He could read Grace's face as well as I could and knew that if he didn't take her side now, he'd pay for it later.

But my father ignored his words. "You and me got work to do." He turned to my sister. "Just get it to burn. There won't be any problem. It's going to take a while before it reaches the apple trees. By then, I'll be back." He slid behind the wheel and turned the ignition key. As the engine came to life, my brother jumped into the passenger seat. Water splashed out of big trash can between Wayne's legs as the vehicle turned away.

Grace glanced at the watering can and the damp burlap bags at our feet. "I don't care what he says about getting the fire to burn. We're putting out every flame we see."

I dragged my wet bag behind as I followed my sister's hurried steps. As soon as she got near the fire, she started to beat her burlap sack against the ground. She worked fast, putting out the flames around her. When her sack got too dry, she poured water on it and attacked the ground again, but the wind fed the flames faster than Grace could put them out.

I dropped my sack to the ground and stomped on it, feeling the heat beneath the soles of my rubber boots. Smoke stung my eyes. I pulled up the sack, but underneath it, the fire was still burning, feeding on dry twigs in the grass. "Try again," my sister said, looking over her shoulder. With her straight brown hair hanging in her face, she looked like a witch, but I knew better than to tell her that.

I followed slowly behind as she worked her way toward the old apple trees. The watering can was soon empty. When her bag was completely dry from the heat of the flames, she threw it to the ground and grabbed mine. Her face was smeared with soot.

"Go behind me and step out any flames you see," she said. "You can do that, right?"

Winter storms had brought limbs down around the apple trees, and by the time we reached them, the fallen branches were engulfed in flame.

I kicked a limb with the toe of my boot and sent up a shower of sparks. A couple of them landed on my jacket where they burned small round holes in the nylon.

"You're not doing it right," my sister said, frustration growing in her voice. "You shouldn't even be doing this. What if you get hurt? Then it's my fault."

"I can do it. You don't have to watch over me." I walked away from her and stomped on the edges of the grass like she'd told me to do. I could feel her watching me, but I was making headway and giving her nothing to complain about. She turned around and went back to work, slamming her sack against the ground.

I kept walking, putting out the flames in front of me and moving in whatever direction would keep me out of the smoke. It was like being at a campfire and the wind always changing so that no matter which way I moved, I got a big lungful. I was circling back to Grace when I took a step and stumbled against a rock in the grass. I put my hands out to break my fall.

My palm struck a smouldering branch and I cried out in pain.

"Laurie," my sister yelled. She ran toward me and yanked me to my feet. "Let me see." My hand had curled in on itself like a wounded animal.

I wasn't afraid until I saw my sister's white face, and then my knees buckled.

"We've got to get you to the house," she said.

I couldn't answer because I knew I would cry, and I didn't want to cry.

"It's okay," Grace said, her voice sounding stronger. "Cold water's all we need. Remember what Mom always does. Just runs her hand under the tap if she gets a burn from the stove."

I cradled my hand against my jacket. The house seemed too far away.

Grace raised her head. "Listen. That's Dad coming. He's got cold water on the dune buggy."

She was right. I could hear the engine approaching. "He's going to be mad," I said. "He's going to say I never do—" I swallowed hard against a lump rising in my throat, "—anything right."

"Don't you ever believe that, Laurie," she said.

"I always do everything wrong."

"No, that's not true."

We thought the dune buggy was coming for us, but then we heard the engine quit and realized my father and brother had stopped at the apple trees to put out the fire.

"Come on," said my sister, taking my arm. "We'll be there in a second."

Wayne was using an axe to break up the branches. My father was sloshing water at the base of the trees. "Where did you get to?" he said. "You were supposed to keep the fire away from the trees."

Grace ignored him, walking me over to the bucket. "Put your hand in."

It felt cool and it hurt at the same time. I looked up at my father's angry face. I knew I'd done it again. Gotten careless and now my sister was going to get into trouble.

But it wasn't my father who spoke next. It was Grace, turning on him with all her fury. "You said you were coming right back. Laurie burned her hand and we didn't have any water. And it's all for a stupid golf course. It's always for something stupid, something you want."

I gasped. I expected an explosion, my father's anger cruel and punishing, like paint cans going off in a bonfire. But it never came. Instead, his boots were big and clumsy as he walked over. He knelt down, pulled his work gloves off, and turned my palm up. A purple blister had begun to form. "We better get to the house, put something on that burn."

My sister climbed into the passenger seat and sat me between her legs, her arms encircling my waist. My brother crouched at our feet, one hand holding onto the empty trash can, the other on the bar that ran up the side of the dune buggy. As my father drove back through the fields, the vehicle bounced in and out of the ruts. "Hold on," he said. Grace tightened her grip around my waist. She leaned forward, her hair soft against my cheek. "There's nobody seven years old who can do the things you do," she said. "Remember that."

For the first time that day, I didn't feel a burden to her. I felt like I'd done something right. Up ahead, the sun was a ball of fire slipping behind the trees. The smell of smoke hung in the air. When my father turned off the engine, we ran for the safety of the house.

Joining
the Workforce
ANDREW BEATTIE

WHEN I WAS seven, I went with my brothers to pick rocks on a neighbour's field. Our equipment consisted of a rusty Massey-Ferguson with an unhealthy knock, a hay trailer covered with grey sheets of plywood, and plastic five-gallon pails that were scarred from years of carrying rocks. The field had been ploughed the day before. From afar it looked like a flawless sheet of dark black glass. Once we got down to work, I realized it was littered with roots, rocks, and the occasional rubber boot that the field had claimed in wetter times.

Being nearly ten years younger than my brothers, I was given the worst job. My brothers chose to work in the areas that had large concentrations of rocks, and I was given the job of running behind the hay wagon picking up the stray rocks that littered the wasteland in between. This meant that while my brothers were sitting on the wagon searching for the next rock cluster or taking turns revving the tractor in a fruitless attempt to spin the tires, I was running after the wagon carrying a full pail of stones, attempting to empty it before being left behind once more. I spent five hours of my Saturday running and sweating rather than swimming, biking, watching cartoons, or any of a thousand other things I would have preferred to be doing. When it came time to be paid for five hours of rock picking, my brothers received cheques and I got a five-dollar bill.

Three years later, my father shared some words of wisdom. We were in the midst of a blizzard trying to finish a tin shed for orphan lambs. I kept

Andrew (age 3) at Miquelon Lake, Alberta, 1984

dropping the wrench that I was supposed to use to hold the nut while my father ran the electric drill on the bolt. My knuckles were bleeding inside my gloves from the wrench repeatedly slipping from my frozen hands and whipping around to hit me. Out of frustration, I asked why Troy or Jay weren't helping build the "damned" thing. It was the first curse I'd used in front of my father, and I expected trouble. My father simply wiped the crust of ice from the mouth of his ski mask and said, "Shit runs downhill."

In spite of my previous experiences and my father's dire warning, I started my first regular job at the age of thirteen. Fortunately, the gods of labour were gracious, and my first boss was both kind and generous. Glen and his family owned a cattle operation less than a quarter mile down the highway from our patchwork farm. While our farm was a jumble of veering fences, broken Soviet cars, and ragged goats, Glen's farm was a registered business with two tractors that started on the first crank and a liquid-nitrogen storage tank for bull sperm imported from Sweden. While my father owned eighty acres (neither farm nor acreage, according to Revenue Canada), Glen owned over two sections. Most importantly, Glen's farm had well-manicured lawns and a bush line that needed to be mowed.

Mowing was my primary job at Glen's, but there were also gophers to trap, fences to mend, rocks to pick, cows to feed, stalls to clean, trees to trim, hay to rake, and, best of all, silage to pack. In the summers, I spent most of the week at Glen's. I showed up at seven and mowed under the bush line until noon; then Glen or Marion cooked me lunch, and I headed out to help feed the cows or weed whip around the barns.

I think my parents' primary concern whenever one of their six children found a job was not that we be paid fairly, but that whoever was hiring would agree to feed us as well. Any reduction in the food bill was a bonus for Mom and Dad. Although the food was great, the nicest thing about working for Glen was that there was always work to do. I didn't appreciate it then, but now I realize there is nothing worse than a job that doesn't keep you busy. Idle time scrapes by like a kidney stone. One hitch of a busy first job, however, was that I had to do a lot of things for the first time. Since everything was new, I was bound to make a few mistakes.

When I drove my first standard, Glen sat patiently beside me (or at least tried to sit), as the Ford lurched violently while I tried stomping on clutch, brake, and gas in what I thought was proper order. My first time herding cows down the handling chute was also my first time getting kicked by a cow—and my second, third, and fourth times as well. When it came time for insemination, I prepared for herding by wearing my hockey equipment to work.

It was also at Glen's that I broke my first piece of farm machinery. I was raking hay on the quarter section west of Glen's place, diligently swerving around the rock piles and sloughs that dotted the field. As time passed, however, I became less and less watchful of the moist depressions in the land. After the Allis-Chalmers, the smaller of Glen's two tractors, bulled through the centre of one wet spot without a problem, cleanly turning the green hay as it went, I quit worrying about the sloughs altogether. Besides, the rows of raked hay looked much nicer without interruptions in their straight lines.

I continued on like that for hours, slowly closing in on the lowest point at the centre of the field, where standing water was visible. As my corners tightened, and I reached the point where there were only a few rows of browning hay trapped in an expanding maze of green, the warning signs began. The tractor tires, which had ridden high over the land for most of the day, now began to dig deep black furrows through each slough they conquered. I had to increase the revs to get through the middle of the small sloughs without lugging down. Chunks of mud flew free of the treads and landed on the fenders with loud plopping sounds. Anyone but a thirteen-year-old boy would have known to quit tempting fate.

Nearly finished, I came to a slough at the centre of the field in which the water was so deep that the hay actually floated on top of it instead of lying in a row. I didn't know how Glen had managed to cut it without trouble, but the Deutz-Allis was twice as large as the Allis-Chalmers. Even in my state of seeming invincibility, I avoided the centre of the slough. The edge, however, seemed shallower, and the hay even had some semblance of rows amongst the reeds sprouting there. I knew the slough grass would never be baled up, raked or not, but I wanted to see if I could get through it.

I revved the small tractor to 2,500 and held the cracked plastic wheel straight. The hay coming out of the rakes wasn't merely rolled over, but flipped violently into the air before landing beside the next row. I entered the slough with a splash, and huge columns of mud and water sprayed up and out from either side. I was in and out before I knew it, and the hay rakes sprayed fans of mud, water, and slough grass. I smiled triumphantly as I adjusted the revs back to 1,500 and prepared to go on. The smile vanished as the Allis-Chalmers rolled to a stop, engine revving happily, but going nowhere.

I turned the tractor on and off several times—something meant for computers, not tractors. The engine roared to life immediately each time, but still the tractor didn't move. I then tried shifting the gears while revving the unperturbed engine up and down. After that failed, I walked around the tractor wishing I knew more about vehicles than only how to change oil. Eventually, I knew I was doomed. I turned off the tractor and began the long walk back to the house where I hoped to find Glen taking a break from baling the rented section with the Deutz.

As I trudged through the field, slightly dazed by how quickly my life had all come unravelled, I couldn't help noticing each slough I had charged through on the way to my destruction—each one I would pass with Glen on the way back—their surfaces scarred with deep black ruts that seemed to scream, "Guilty, guilty, guilty!"

I found Glen, or at least his boots, sticking out from beneath the baler in front of the tractor shed, accompanied by banging and the occasional, "Sonofawhore," coming from beneath.

"Glen?" I called.

"Oh, is that Handy Andy?" he replied cheerfully. "I didn't hear the tractor. Finished? Hand me the pipe wrench."

I bent over and placed the wrench in the grease-stained hand that popped out from underneath. It vanished into the void, and metallic grinding rang out with a half-grunting, half-whispered, "Sonofawhore."

"Glen, I think I broke the tractor." I didn't know I was going to say it, but it left my lips in a spurt before I could stop it.

From beneath the baler there was the sound of a wrench being laid on the gravel, then the screech, screech as Glen wiggled out, legs, waist, chest, and finally head, from underneath. The sun caught him in the eyes, and he had to squint up at me. He stared at me for a few seconds without speaking, as if I might be a mirage cast in the heat.

"You walked back here?" he asked.

"Yes. The tractor won't move."

His lips flattened just short of a grimace, and then he was up and searching his pockets.

"Let's take the truck and see what happened."

The ride seemed even longer than the walk back had been. We were both silent as, left and right, the gouges in the sloughs gave uncontested testimony to the kind of job I had been doing. We reached the tractor parked a few yards past its pyrrhic victory. It was spotted with clumps of drying mud, and the deep furrows in the mud behind it had already filled in with water.

"You have to be careful of the sloughs," he said as we got out of the truck.

"I know," I replied lamely.

Glen looked at me and smiled. It was a sympathetic smile, but I could see the worry lines creeping in at the edges. The chances of getting all the hay baled up in time with just one tractor were on the wayside of slim to none.

Glen climbed onto the tractor and tried all the things I had—shifting, revving, restarting—and then climbed back down and rubbed the lower half of his face with his hand while considering the dead steel hulk. He walked around the tractor twice, bent over and looked underneath, and started to walk around it a third time. Suddenly, he stopped and ran back to the centre and looked underneath.

"The drive shaft's gone," he said with a sense of triumph. "It must have fallen off."

Both of us turned to look at the deep, water-filled ruts in the slough.

"I'll go in and check," I said. I untied my father's old steel-toed work boots, set them to the side, and then slipped out of my coveralls. It was a hot day, so I only had boxers and socks beneath. I carefully balled up each sock and put it in the corresponding boot to keep it dry.

"Don't bother," Glen said. "I'll go back to the shed and get the metal detector."

But I was already on my knees in the slough squeezing lumps of mud through my fingers and trying to see through the cool murky water. Of course it wasn't necessary, but I think he understood that this was my act of atonement. He left me to it.

Glen turned to walk back to the truck. He was walking up the nicely turned row of hay leading to my wallowing place when his boot struck something with a dull clang. We both looked up. Glen reached down and lifted a greasy steel bar encased in a cracked plastic sleeve for me to see. The laughter came upon us hard and heavy, and I accidentally wiped my eyes with a muddy hand, streaking my cheeks like a CFL lineman.

Glen got a rag from the back of the truck and wiped some of the mud off my face, and I got dressed in my coveralls and boots again. He put the drive shaft in the back of the pickup and turned back to look at the slough, the tractor, the unraked hay, and the field. The sigh seemed to start from his eyes, swell in his chest, and travel through his torn brown work boots into the land beneath. He turned his head left and right, seeming to take in the freshly turned hay, the newly mended fences, and all the work yet to begin. He smiled like it was all telling him a friendly inside joke that he could never explain.

Glen put his arm around my shoulders and said, "Andy, never become a farmer." But his face and his smile seemed to tell an entirely different story.

Section 29

GEORGE FOX

"**WELL. I GUESS.**" Dad rose from the breakfast table. There was no point waiting for him to finish; it was just a signal to himself, as much as anybody I suppose, that work was about to begin.

He whistled an old Wilf Carter tune as he pulled on his boots in the back porch. I tipped the old kitchen chair back down on all fours and made to follow his lead. "Yep. Well, we'll see you later, Mom."

"Good luck in the hills," she replied.

"I don't imagine we'll be back in time for lunch, that's for sure," I said, cranky at having to tackle this job at all today.

As far as I was concerned, we were really putting ourselves to the test, trying to drive a hundred or so head of yearling cattle up to the top of one of the highest of the Wildcat Hills. Its bald knob rose west of our little farm—not only was it farther away than it appeared, but it was also a heck of a lot steeper than it looked, too. And if I knew one thing about chasing cattle, it was that the path of least resistance was always for them. Once we had them close to the bottom of the hill, tired as they'd be and with that good grass down on the flats in their sniffers, it would take a small miracle to push them up top.

Although I had a lot of faith in my dad's judgment, I was wondering if we shouldn't have tried to get a few more riders out to help.

"No, we'd better not bother. We might end up in a real jackpot," he'd said when I had broached the subject a few nights earlier. "What if somebody gets lost or all tangled in the bush? Not everybody understands cows, y'know."

Well, both Mom and I knew if there was one thing Dad could understand it was those old cows. Who else but him would comment, "Boy, that would sure be a tasty mouthful for a cow, wouldn't it?" after inspecting some exotic legumes in my aunt's backyard in town?

The front lawn, that morning, had been touched by a bit of frost—not too much, but that nip in the air helped me to come to life. In those days, I wasn't a coffee drinker in the mornings. The work for the day tended to come upon me in a hurry, and once I got moving around in the fresh air, I became about as awake as I was going to get.

That particular morning was shaping up to be nice and sunny, but we had other problems. Neither Dad nor I had remembered to shut our saddle horses up in the corral the night before. Valuable time (not to mention patience) slipped away as we tried to get our two mares, Jenny and Dixie, out of the willows and up to the barnyard.

"Hi! Hi! Hi!" I yelled as I slipped and tripped in the bog, getting my boots wet in pursuit of the two. I looked over and saw Dad shaking a rusty old pail full of oats at Dixie. "Whoa, girl…That's it…That's it…Eeeaassy." He was a real horse expert and damned if he didn't manage to get the bridle around her neck. That old horse never even saw it coming. The two horses always stuck together, so Jenny followed Dixie up to the corral, and I caught her easily then.

Before long the sun was hot, and we had about one hundred head of yearling cattle strung out in front of us. Dad wasn't whistling anymore. "Crowd 'em up," he'd shout at me once in a while. That ticked me off because I thought I knew pretty good how to move cattle, and I thought I was keeping things going about right. Sometimes there was just no pleasing Dad. Whenever I tried my best and succeeded at something I was excited about, like getting a hat trick in hockey or making a new friend at school, he would give me a patronizing "Oh, yeah, good…Yep, really good!" I didn't feel all that special after getting his reaction. I imagine he thought I was in a hurry to grow up, and until I could perform what he recognized as worthwhile in his world, he felt some responsibility not to give me any false encouragement. He probably figured it wise not to take any grown-up posturing of mine too seriously.

We were on a government grazing lease my dad had secured back in the fifties. Dad was granted custody of two sections of country that was too rocky to farm; yet it provided decent pasture along the creek bed and the odd flat where clover, timothy, and other native grasses grew. It had been logged off ten years earlier, and all the new growth was coming up thick as hair on a dog, which made it pretty hard travelling once we headed off the beaten trail.

"Hi! Hi! Hi!" My gawd! Those yearlings had no clue what direction to travel. Through heavy poplar growth, they went crashing down toward the creek, and I could barely keep up. I rode along through the young trees until I figured old Jenny and I had been stung enough by those branches. Then I tied the lines up to the saddle horn, jumped off, and hoped Jenny would either follow along or graze while I lit out afoot to monitor the progress of the herd.

"Ho! Ho! Yaaah!" We reached the beaver dam. Now it was critical to stay to the west of them—if even a few head got on the trail going west toward the creek bottom, we'd lose them all. It was definitely the path of least resistance, and thinking like a cow, or just like my dad, I knew they could be awfully stubborn when they got it in their heads to go somewhere. I knew I'd better not slip too far behind.

The whole event reminds me of that old proverb: "You should never confuse movement with action." Like a sailboat tacking into a headwind, we zigged and zagged across the face of the slope. The cattle trail I'd cut out last summer obviously didn't appeal to their bovine instincts. My trail-blazing idea had come from getting the buggers within a hundred yards of the gate last year—just to see them get confused and run back down the hill. We then had to give up and we spent every morning of the next week riding around getting a few at a time up that big hill and into the destination pasture, which we referred to by its legal land description: Section 29.

"Let 'em go! Let 'em go!" Dad was bellowing. I stopped my yelling and stick-swinging performance long enough to realize he was shouting at me and not the yearlings. I could hear him, but I couldn't see him, and he couldn't see me.

"All right! All right!" I shouted back toward his voice. But something inside me didn't want to give up just yet. I was not the kind of kid who was belligerent, but I wasn't going to be back here tomorrow riding around trying to find these bunch-quitters if I could help it. Damn! I wanted to pull this off.

Berserk is a word of Norwegian origin. I learned this from a Swedish farmer who told me that the Vikings ate a certain variety of mushroom before going into battle. The spectacular bravery and savage attacks were apparently due to some chemical in the mushroom. Well, I momentarily became a Viking. I lunged into the bush, creating as big a commotion as I could, whistling, screaming, yelling, and pounding the backs of those poor cattle the likes of which they'd never experienced. They responded by bucking up in the air to pull themselves through the tangled brush and deadfall in that thickest part of the bush. Then with one final bellow, I sent them scattering in every direction.

"What the heck am I doing? Calm down," I told myself. Completely hoarse, I scrambled back behind the heavy brush to push what was left of the main bunch uphill.

Along the creek bed was a beautiful flowering weed called larkspur. About that time of year, before it flowered, it contained enough methyllcaconitine—which acted like strychnine—to entirely shut down the nervous system of any large mammal, cows included. Dad had become familiar with this killer weed the hard way, finding a dozen dead steers in the willows one July. Like they say, cows are always finding new ways to die—if they weren't catching the latest virus, they were drowning in water holes, or even being electrocuted by barbed wire fences during lightning storms.

Because of that larkspur threat, it was life or death that those young cattle of ours made it up that hill into safe grazing territory on Section 29. Like all the other ranchers we knew, we were just trying to do what was best for the animals. In spite of what those less familiar with the profession (or, for that matter, the cattle themselves) might think, the mission at hand was in all our best interests. If only they could see that lush clover on top of the hill!

When you're holding a hammer, everything can start to look like a nail. In this case, instead of a hammer, I held a nice long willow stick. Whack! Whoosh! I became an expert over the next hour or two at stinging the stragglers of the bunch with my new persuader. My voice played out and only a good crack on the backside could get these tired critters to move along—and at this point, we were all into our second (or even third!) wind. Slowly but surely, the cattle and I made our way up that big hill.

When I spotted Dad again, he was making for the lead to open the gate into Section 29. This could be it! I hoped they wouldn't make one last attempt to turn back on me, like last year. At that stage, I didn't have the energy to battle their retreat.

Once they caught a glimpse of some nice long grass on the other side of that open gate, we seemed to have them beat. With a sudden burst of energy, they ran through the gate into the pasture, reaching down to grab mouthfuls of grass as they went.

"Well, I guess we're about thirty short," Dad said as he pencilled a number into the gatepost. I could tell by the tone of his voice that he thought we'd done a pretty good job.

I was just about to reply that getting over half the herd in there wasn't too bad for a day's work, when I saw, just on the other side of the east fence, looking confused and anxious, those thirty missing head!

I made a beeline for the fencing pliers Dad always kept tied to his saddle. Dixie was still puffing. I tugged at the leather knots holding the pliers, glancing nervously over my shoulder until I finally got them. I walked, slow and deliberate, toward the east fence.

In a few minutes, I had the wire down, and Dad jumped aboard Dixie to coax them through the gate with the others. It was clear they had heard, and now seen, the fate of the main gang munching on the rich clover of Section 29, and they wanted to be with them in the worst way.

"Well, for gosh sakes! I guess we got lucky today," Dad said with a satisfied grin. He got down off Dixie. "It's a mystery why they'd climb that hill all on their own. They couldn't have gone through that jungle where we left them, could they?" he asked.

I wondered if he had heard me raging like a wild man after he told me to give up on them a few hours earlier. Dad continued. "I had visions of us riding for the next three or four days before we'd get them all captured."

"Yeah, I guess you're pretty disappointed at that, eh?" I joshed him.

We both lay back on the grass and had a chuckle at our good fortune. "They'll be all right now," Dad said happily. "We'll just have to come up and put out salt in the next day or two."

I suppose if we were real, old-time cowboys, we'd have pulled out the makin's and rolled a couple of smokes, but instead we rested a while, enjoying the rewards of a job well done.

A hummingbird appeared for a few seconds and hovered between us as it checked the buttercups and shooting stars. "Isn't that something!" I said, as it flicked, whirling this way and that before it was sucked back up into the big blue sky.

I felt the sun warm against my face, and something inside told me that this was a special moment. We were both proud of what we'd been able to do. Neither of us would ever say it, but to me that really didn't matter.

Some dramatic show of affection is supposed to demonstrate the breaking down of barriers between father and son. Back out there on the pine and poplar slope, I was probably going to get more affection from my sweaty old horse Jenny, when I finally located her on the trail, than I would from my dad. He knew, and I learned, that a real father-son bond is built through shared experience.

I knew I'd never be an equal to Dad when it came to ranching, but that didn't mean he couldn't make me feel good about accomplishing something on his terms. Using the hard work ethic he'd taught me, I later proved myself through accomplishments at school, at sports, and at making music. Looking back on that special day, I realize both Dad and I got to feel like we'd proved a point. We took our time as we made for home—Dad in the lead.

The Outhouse Affair

Betty Howatt

AFTER THE **B**LITZ in London during the Second World War, the British government sent about two hundred thousand British children to Canada, Australia, New Zealand, and South Africa. Twenty-five of these children came to Prince Edward Island. One of them, a girl named Brenda, lived on the farm of relatives with whom I spent most of my summer holidays when I was a girl. Brenda was several years older than I, and, coming from a crowded area near a big city, much wiser in the ways of the world, particularly where boys were concerned.

The term "culture shock" wasn't in vogue then, but I think she must have experienced it, in spades. To leave the lights, the hustle and bustle, and end up in rural PEI must have been a shock. No electricity, no running water, no cars, and, because of the lay of the land, few other farmsteads to be seen—that was the situation when she arrived. However, she was quite prepared to work, and learned how to do many things around the farm, even how to milk cows. The big problem, for her, was evening entertainment—or the lack thereof. She was not accustomed to going to bed as early as the farm family did. For her, evening was the time for playing in the streets with her friends. On the farm, on the other hand, we rarely left home in the evening, and never after 7:00 P.M. Our family had to rise early to bring the cows from the pasture, milk them, and carry the milk cans to the gate by 7:00 A.M., before the milk hauler arrived to

Betty (age 15) on her uncle's farm in eastern PEI, with
cousins Gordon MacBeth and Nell MacBeth, 1944

take the milk to the cheese factory. As a general rule, we went to bed
around 8:30 P.M., unless we were going to a church-related affair. Other
events in the community, such as "times"—parties where there might be
dancing—were not approved. In the only autograph book I have, my uncle
wrote one summer:

May your life be filled with sunshine,
And gladdened by romances,
But take advice from one who knows
And avoid the country dances!

I loved that uncle dearly, and heeded his advice. Most of the time.

During those years, a group of travelling evangelists from the United
States, known locally as the "Go Preachers," set up a large tent—the
Gospel tent—every summer in the next district. The evangelists held a

series of evening meetings, which we were allowed to attend. Actually, the services were more in the line of entertainment for the young people who gathered there. Certainly there was lots of preaching, mostly of the hellfire-and-damnation variety, but it was the singing we enjoyed. It was accompanied by a small, portable pump organ, usually drowned out by the enthusiastic—but not necessarily musical—voices from the crowd.

One night when there was no "preaching," Brenda and I went to bed at 8:30 P.M., but couldn't settle down. Our yammering annoyed the folks in bed in the adjoining room. "Keep quiet! Pipe down!" We decided to go out to the outhouse. That was a legitimate reason, or rather, an acceptable one, for leaving the house. As we went out the kitchen door, my Grandpa's steeple clock on the mantel shelf struck nine. We were dressed in our light cotton pyjamas, barefoot, with a flashlight for courage.

As on many farmsteads of those years, there was a separate building for almost every operation on the farm. My great-grandfather had settled on that land in 1863, and over the years the number of buildings had grown to include a hen house, pig house, sheep barn, forge, wellhouse, combination separator house and woodshed, carriage house/granary, and a calf house next to the main barn. The barn housed the horses and cows on either side of a big floor where the hay wagon could be driven in; beyond the cow stables was a shed for manure storage. All of these were enclosed by a fence, with a gate leading to the road that ran behind the main buildings. The outhouse was tucked between the carriage house and the calf house.

Brenda and I sat in the outhouse for a little while, talking, until we became chilly and decided it was time to get back to bed. We opened the door. To our surprise, a large dark muzzle poked through the opening. We quickly shut the door. We realized that our curious visitor was the new driving mare. My uncle had planned to hitch her first thing after chores in the morning, and, to save the time it would take to bring her from the pasture, he had left her loose in the yard, able to go in and out of the stable as she willed. We had been warned to stay away from this mare, as she wasn't used to us, and was said to be quite skittish.

We became skittish as well. We didn't dare venture out while she was nearby, so we sat down to wait for her to leave. Then we decided to sing, loudly; someone in the house might hear, and anyway it would keep our spirits up. So sing we did, mostly the songs we had been singing in the Gospel tent: "Life Is Like a Mountain Railroad," "Will Your Anchor Hold?" and "Pass Me Not O Gentle Saviour." The next line in that last piece is "Hear my humble cry," but there was nothing humble in the way we sang those hymns and many more. We opened the outhouse door. The mare was still there. The fun was gone. We were cold, and we had turned off the flashlight to save the batteries. We had to do something! We changed tactics. This time, we kept quiet for awhile. Finally, we heard the mare walk off. We ran like mad to the separator house, kitty-corner from us and halfway to the farmhouse. The mare heard us and reached the separator house door just as we shut it. Another period of waiting. Finally, she moved away again. Then we made a mad dash to the veranda, the mare just behind us as we raced into the house. Just as Grandpa's clock struck 11:00 P.M. We had been outside two hours.

Everyone else in the house was sound asleep, so we decided not to say a word about our adventure. But the truth will out. Not long after, my uncle was at the village on business. He met a neighbour who had been driving by while Brenda and I were singing loudly—so loudly we didn't hear his horse and wagon. He certainly heard us. "What," he asked my uncle, "was going on?" When my uncle got home, he asked us the same question, and the whole story came out.

Brenda eventually went back to England. I wonder if she is ever reminded of that night in the outhouse. I am. Especially when I hear "Life Is Like a Mountain Railroad."

The Day Dief Came to Town

DARLENE FOSTER

AS A YOUNG girl growing up on a prairie farm, I often felt that the world was passing me by and that nothing exciting would ever happen to me. Idle hours were spent daydreaming about visiting exotic places such as Paris, London, Rome, or even Toronto. Instead of doing homework, I would rehearse what I would say to the famous people I might encounter on these travels. I longed to meet people in the news, people like Bobby Darrin, Debbie Reynolds, Gordie Howe, or Prince Charles. It was clear that I would have to travel to meet interesting celebrities, as no one important knew that Irvine, the small town—well, actually hamlet—near our farm existed.

Things were about to change, however, when word came that John Diefenbaker, the prime minister of Canada, was to visit our placid little corner of the province. Mr. Diefenbaker, or Dief as he was fondly called, was popular in Alberta because he was a prairie boy himself, born and bred in Saskatchewan. 1962 was an election year, and Dief was seeking another term in office. As was the custom at the time, he travelled across Canada by train, making whistle stops along the way. He planned to stop at all the major centres as part of his campaign. The school was buzzing with the news that Dief would stop for a short visit on his way to Medicine Hat the following day. No one questioned why he had chosen to stop at Irvine, population 500, not counting gophers and coyotes.

Darlene on her dad's truck on their first farm near
Hilda, Alberta, 1955

At last my dream of meeting someone important was about to come true! I invited my girlfriend Sharlene to stay overnight at our house so we could ride the bus in to school together the next morning. We got up early that memorable day, took the sponge rollers out of our hair, fixed our faces, and put on our newest poodle skirts. It was a warm spring day, so we had no need to wear coats. The excitement in the school that morning caused so much distraction that the teachers gave up trying to teach us anything. Truth be told, they were excited, too. They closed the school, and we all walked down to the train station in plenty of time to meet our special visitor.

Word had spread. It looked as if everyone within a forty-mile radius had shown up for this historic event. The cheerleaders in the school colours of white, black, and gold shook their pompoms as they practised a cheer for the PM. The school band members tuned their instruments. Farmers parked their trucks and tractors by the side of the road, wiped their faces with polka-dot hankies, hitched up their jeans, and greeted their neighbours. Young mothers, pleased to have a reason to escape the house, were all smiles, pushing babies in buggies while toddlers trailed behind. The old people found good viewing spots, unfolded their woven lawn chairs, and waited for the train. Mayor Krauss, a kindly old man, was going over his welcome speech with the school principal, Mr. Gotfried, who took his wire-rimmed glasses on and off to get a better look at the handwriting. Sharlene and I made sure we were at the front of the railway platform, exactly where we thought our honoured guest would disembark. We planned to be the first to shake his famous hand.

According to our information, the Right Honourable Gentleman was due to arrive at 11:00 A.M. Roger Stickle, a grade ten student everyone called The Stick, kept track by ham radio. "He is running ten minutes late. He should be here by 11:10," Roger reported in his whiny voice.

It was 11:05. My heart was doing flip-flops. I turned to Sharlene. "Do I still have lipstick on? Is my hair in place?"

"You look great." She gave my hand a squeeze.

"Here it comes!" shouted The Stick.

In the distance, a speck of moving steel with a mane of black smoke was bringing our hero, the prime minister of the country, to our very doorstep. The iron horse grew larger and larger.

The cheerleaders were in position, the bandleader lifted his baton, the mayor shuffled his notes, the principal put on his glasses, and Sharlene and I smiled our very best Doris Day smiles. We stepped closer to the tracks.

"He's not slowing down!" shouted Roger.

The train whistle blew as the huge hunk of metal roared through the town. The noise was deafening. The platform vibrated under our feet, and hot dust flew through the air. Sharlene and I clung to each other as our poodle skirts flew over our heads.

The train slithered down the track and disappeared around the bend. I stared after it in disbelief. Then I looked around. Mr. Bauer was shaking his head as he pulled his handkerchief from his back pocket to wipe his face. Mary Schmidt was smoothing down her little boy's dishevelled hair. Old Mr. and Mrs. Weiss slowly rose from their lawn chairs. The band members began to put away their instruments. Roger, in a trance, packed up his radio.

Someone broke the awkward silence with a laugh. It was contagious. Soon everyone around me was laughing. I glanced over at Mr. Gotfried. He was laughing so hard he had taken off his glasses and was wiping his eyes with the back of his hand.

I looked at Sharlene who grinned. "At least we didn't get sucked under the train."

I shuddered.

Then I started to laugh, too. How funny we must have all looked! Did Mr. Diefenbaker even see us, standing there in foolish anticipation?

The farmers went back to their fields, mothers took their children home for lunch, the old folks went to the café for a cup of tea, and Sharlene and I, along with the rest of the students and the teachers, went back to our classes. At least we had had a morning off school and some much-needed excitement. For a long time afterwards, we had a good laugh every time we thought about the day Dief almost came to town.

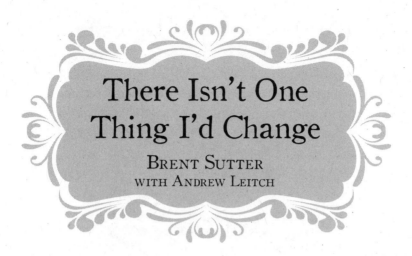

There Isn't One Thing I'd Change

BRENT SUTTER
WITH ANDREW LEITCH

FOR EIGHTEEN SEASONS I played NHL hockey. Five of my brothers played in the NHL, too, and eventually, the six of us became known to hockey fans as the Sutter Brothers. For seven seasons, my brother Duane was my teammate on the New York Islanders, and later, in Chicago, my brother Darryl was my coach. In 1988, our family set a hockey record for most members of one family playing in one game when Duane and I, playing for the Islanders, were matched against my twin brothers, Rich and Ron, and the Philadelphia Flyers. Sometimes I smile to myself when I think that big-city hockey fans from the suburbs of New York or Chicago would come to sit in the stands to watch a bunch of farm kids play the game we all loved.

I was born in Viking, Alberta, in 1962, the fifth of seven boys that would be born to the Sutter family. My parents farmed on a half section a few miles outside town, and we lived in a four-room house that didn't have running water. I remember cold trips to the outhouse in the winter, and I remember Mom melting snow for drinking water when the well was frozen. We didn't have much money. My clothes were hand-me-downs, and the only family vacation I remember was a camping trip to Red Deer. We grew grain, milked dairy cows, and raised pigs and chickens, but Dad said there were years that the farm would have been lost if it hadn't been for the income from beef cattle.

Brent (age 3, right) with older brother Duane (left)
geared up to play hockey on the farm, 1965

Looking back, I realize how difficult life must have been for my parents, but at the time, I was unaware of it. After all, our life was no different from the lives of our neighbours, so we didn't notice the things that were missing. Although we didn't have all the material possessions and options that kids have today, we had enough. We saved our quarters to buy candy at the general store. Although we had only two TV channels, we were satisfied with *Hockey Night in Canada, Walt Disney,* and *Bonanza.* We also grew up with a magical kind of freedom. We played with boys and girls who lived on farms for miles around, and we cared about each other and made our own fun in the wide open spaces, summer and winter.

All the boys were expected to work on the farm, and the type of work we were required to do changed as we grew older and stronger. We handled cattle, drove tractors, milked cows, and did all kinds of other chores that typical farm kids did. One of my earliest jobs was making sandwiches for lunches and doing the dishes for all nine of us. (What a blessing it was when

There Isn't One Thing I'd Change

my parents finally bought a dishwasher when I was ten!) Mom and Dad rotated our responsibilities so we'd all become competent at everything. One of my favourite jobs was working with the cattle; I always felt content surrounded by cows. I also loved to be out in the field on a tractor, where I could be happily on my own and have a lot of time to think. To this day, I love the sight of a combine swathing a path through a field of grain.

I loved farm work, and I couldn't wait to get up in the morning to get to work. I don't think I ever slept in in the morning, and I stayed outside, except for mealtimes, until nightfall. We all loved being outdoors. My brothers and I were always competitive, even with farm chores. We competed to do our work quickly and efficiently. We loved having something concrete to count to show for our efforts, like bales of hay. We would work hard to outdo the number of bales one of the other boys had baled the day before. One fall, the twins and I put up twenty thousand bales, and I was proud to look at that stack and see what we'd accomplished.

Maybe I'm lucky to have loved the work so much, because we didn't have a choice about doing it, anyway. On the farm, there was so much work to be done, and we simply pitched in. My parents let us know, from the time we were young, that we were expected to work hard and to contribute to the family. Discipline and structure were values that were instilled in us partly out of necessity. My parents had grown up on farms and married young, when my dad was twenty-one and my mom was seventeen. They learned their work ethic early, and they made sure we understood the importance of working hard. They also taught us that when we wanted something, we had to work to get it. Our parents stressed the fact that if we were going to do something, we had to do it well, no matter what it was.

The only chore I hated was weeding the garden. Mom's garden was so big it could have fed the whole county, and it was the boys' job to weed it. What slow and tedious work! Nearly as bad was picking roots. When we moved to our new farm in 1967, Dad cleared some land for crops. The roots from the trees kept coming up, and it was our job to clear them from the field so they wouldn't damage the machinery later. Every summer for eight years we were out on that field, pulling a sled back and forth and piling it high with roots.

Dad was detail-oriented. He kept the farm and the machines well maintained, and he kept things in order. He made sure we learned to do the same, to be organized, to pay attention to details, and to take care of things properly. Dad made sure we were self-sufficient. If I was out in the field and my machine broke down, I didn't dare walk back home and announce that it was broken, expecting Dad to bail me out. He would have said, "So why didn't you fix it?" He wanted us to be able to take care of ourselves.

My mother worked as hard as anyone I've ever known, and the older I get, the more I admire her. Her seven sons—though generally well behaved—could be a handful, and we liked to tease her. One of my brothers learned how to hypnotize chickens, and we found that if we worked fast enough, we could hypnotize the whole flock of them. Mom would come outside to the sight of a yard full of birds spread out on their backs, dazed and staring at the sky. Then she'd come after us with a broom, hollering. Luckily, we usually occupied our spare time with other activities, mostly hockey.

We all wanted to be hockey players. All of us played, summer and winter. In the spring, we played in the driveway, and as soon as the barn was cleared of hay—even if we had to clear it ourselves by chucking a few remaining bales out the doors—we were playing in the loft. We nailed chicken wire to the doors to keep the balls from flying out. We played every day, no matter how hot it got up there, and I'm sure we made a heck of a racket.

As soon as the sloughs froze, we were skating, and we all signed up with the local minor hockey club. When there wasn't league play on, we'd put on a big hockey event at our place on the weekends. All day Saturday, three of us would prepare the ice while the other boys did the farm chores. Then on Sunday, we'd all play hockey, often with kids from neighbouring farms. We played hard. We used pucks or tennis balls or, if we had to, horse turds. We strapped catalogues to our shins for pads. The nets were made from chicken wire and plywood until the year Brian brought back a set of proper nets from Red Deer. We'd have to move our game to a new location every time one slough became too scraped up from skate blades or the ice became weakened by the muskrats tunnelling underneath. On clear nights, we played by the light of the moon. More than once, Mom had to come out at one or two in the morning to tell us it was time to go to bed.

We all had our favourite professional hockey players. My favourite team was the Bruins, and my favourite player was Bobby Orr. As long as I can remember, I wanted to play in the NHL, and, like I had been taught, I worked hard to achieve that goal. My parents made sure we kept our priorities straight—school came first, and we had to keep up with our chores. But, to be honest, I didn't thrive in school. I had to scratch and claw my way through. And while I loved the farm work, hockey was—to say the least—my biggest passion. I never missed a day of hockey. Never. As long as there was ice, I was skating.

Everyone knew everyone in Viking, and the arena was the social centre of community life. Often on winter Saturdays, hockey games were played back-to-back from morning to midnight. Even when there wasn't hockey practice or a game, kids were skating. Often the girls would figure skate at one end of the ice while the boys played hockey at the other. I remember a hundred kids playing pom-pom pull-away.

We all took part in organized hockey, and my brothers and I got to our games no matter what. Sometimes it was a challenge. Often the country roads were snowed in by a good storm. Then we'd load ourselves into the neighbour's sled, and the snowmobiles would pull us two miles to the main road where someone would pick us up to drive us to town for the game. There was always a buzz in town when teams from Edmonton came for tournaments. They'd show up in their matching helmets, pants, socks, and gloves, while all we had that matched were our jerseys. We took pleasure in thrashing them and sending them home with their tails between their legs. We loved to win.

After a good hockey game, Dad would tell me I'd done well. After a bad game, he was silent all the way home from the rink. He wouldn't talk about it that night, but the next morning, over breakfast, he might look over at me and say, "That wasn't a very smart penalty, was it?" I'd agree. "Then you won't be doing that again, will you?" he'd say. I hated to disappoint him, so I made sure I learned from my mistakes. Dad taught us to apply the same values to hockey that he applied to farming: hard work, commitment, and focusing on details. He believed in skill, scoring, and winning—and working harder than the next guy to do it. We all grew up with that philosophy, which showed, I think, when we made it to the NHL.

I left home to play hockey not long after I turned fifteen. That was the youngest any of us had left—my brothers hadn't gone away until they were nearly sixteen. But I'd seen Mark Messier play in Edmonton the year before, and I knew I was ready to compete at that level. I remember the moment I announced my intentions. Dad and I were walking down to the barn together. I told him, "I'm ready to go." He told me it was too soon, but I said I'd already made up my mind. It wasn't easy for me to say that to my dad, but he knew I meant it, and he respected me for it. Although she wasn't happy about it, I think my mom knew it was coming. She had tears in her eyes, but she told me I had to go.

I remember coming back to Viking after my first year away in Red Deer, where I was continuing with high school and playing for the Red Deer Rustlers. I'd had a good year with the Rustlers even though I was one of the youngest players in the league. At home, I went out with my high school friends, who were celebrating their graduation. I was out until four A.M., which, by family rules, was unthinkably late. Mom woke me up at seven and didn't say a word about it. She prepared breakfast as usual, and then she and my nineteen-year-old brother Darryl went out of the room for a couple of minutes. When my brother came back, he sat down beside me, looked me in the eye, and said, "Who do you think you are? If you ever do that again, I'm going to beat the crap out of you." He pulled me back to earth, and I think I needed it. Although we were taught to be the difference on whatever team we played for, there was no place for ego.

From Red Deer, I went to Lethbridge, and then to Long Island, New York. In those first few years in New York, I didn't have a lot of options in the off season because my salary wasn't enough to keep me going all year. My brothers and I came back to the farm every summer. We'd pick up with the chores almost as though we'd never been away. We were farm kids, through and through.

Mom still lives on the property we grew up on, although she rents out the land now. Our old hockey sticks are still up in the barn loft, and my own kids often go up there to play. My kids are growing up in a world that is different than the one I grew up in, and they see the world in a different way. Farm kids today are much more connected to the wider world than I ever was, and they have so many more choices. Ironically, the one option that seems to be slipping away from them is the opportunity to own their own farms. It's difficult to make a go of it nowadays.

There isn't one thing I'd change about the way I grew up. My sense of the world and all the values I live by today were shaped by my parents, my brothers, and the way we, as a family, provided for ourselves on the farm. I'm extremely lucky, and I know it. In my last few seasons in the NHL, I earned enough to put away money to buy a farm of my own. Hockey has shown me the world and given me opportunities my brothers and I literally didn't even imagine—but to me, there's still no better sight than a combine cutting a perfect swath through a field of wheat, no better smell than the air at harvest time. There's nothing like the satisfaction I feel looking out over a herd of cattle that I can call my own. If hockey hadn't worked out, I would have found a way to make a life on the farm, and that would have been just fine with me.

Coming Home

GORDON TOOTOOSIS

WITH PAM CHAMBERLAIN

THE NIGHT I was born, in the late fall of 1941, my mother was home alone. My father was off working with a harvesting crew, and my older brothers were away at school. In the middle of the night my mother realized it was time, so she saddled up a horse and rode a mile or so to the midwife's house. I was born shortly after she arrived.

I grew up on the Poundmaker Indian Reserve, in the rolling hills of the Battle River Valley southwest of North Battleford, Saskatchewan. Although I was the seventh of thirteen children, it often seemed as if I were an only child. Like the rest of my siblings, my older brother Austin had already gone to residential school, and I was the only child at home. When I reached the age when children normally started residential school, the nearby school at Delmas burned down. Since the older students had to be sent elsewhere, all the schools filled up, so kids my age were kept behind at home longer than usual.

In the 1940s, my father was often away from home. He was busy campaigning to change the systems the church and the government had imposed upon the Cree people—leading the League of Indians of Western Canada, advocating for a national association of Indian people, campaigning for treaty rights, and working to improve education for Indian children by promoting the abolition of residential schools and the development of day schools on reserves. As a result, he was branded

Gordon (age 13) at home, leaving to work
for the summer on local farms

a communist—Communist John, they called him—and wherever he
travelled, he was under the surveillance of the RCMP. Of course, as a
child, I didn't fully understand all of his work, but I sensed its importance
because every time my father was home, there were people constantly
coming to see him. There were always people at our house, talking, and he
was busy all the time.

My father was self-educated, and he read a lot. It was rare for a person
of his generation on the reserve to be reading and writing that much. He
got all kinds of mail, and he handwrote hundreds of letters to leaders
across the country inviting them to meetings and calling them to action.
I also remember him translating for elders and others who didn't speak
English, at social functions, at conferences, with government officials, or
in the courts. Translating in the courts was especially important because
even if people did speak English, they often could not speak it at the
level used in the legal system. Legal language was, and still is, particularly
difficult because there are Cree concepts that don't exist in the framework
of Canadian law, and vice versa.

Coming Home

What I remember most about my father during my childhood is hearing him sing. Music has always been an important aspect of our life and our spirituality, because singing and drumming are a means of communing with the spirit world. Some of my father's songs had been passed down from one generation to another. Not only did he sing in community ceremonies, but he also sang at home a lot. We grew up with music. We heard it from the time we were babies, from even before we were born, and it was all around us and inside us.

———————◆———————

We didn't live in a small nuclear-family unit the way people do today. Rather, we lived as an extended family, and there were always people coming and going—my siblings, to residential school, and my father, for his political work. In addition, there were often Cree elders staying with us. These elders were returning from the States—they used the term "coming home." There had been an exodus in 1885 after the incident at Frog Lake.[1] People didn't want their families or themselves implicated, so they moved south of the border to places like the Rocky Boy Reservation in Montana. Many of these people were old by the 1940s. Although their kids had been born in the States and remained there, the elders still wanted to come home to Saskatchewan where they had many distant relatives. So people like my parents would take them in and care for them until they passed away, because there was no old age security or welfare for them.

These elders were our teachers. There was no television or radio then; I sat and listened to their stories. Sometimes a story was told as a series—the storytelling session might last an hour in the evening and end with a cliffhanger. All the next day, I would look forward to the next segment of the story until finally that night, the elder would start with a synopsis and carry on from there. When that particular person came to visit again, right

---

(1) On April 2, 1885, during the Northwest Rebellion and amid rising tensions resulting from hunger and mistreatment, a breakaway group of young Cree warriors led by Wandering Spirit attacked a settlement at Frog Lake, Alberta, killing nine people. The resistance was eventually crushed by the North West Mounted Police, and chiefs Poundmaker and Big Bear were imprisoned. Six Cree men, including Wandering Spirit, were hanged at North Battleford for their part in the attack on Frog Lake.

away I wanted him to pick up the story where he'd left off. These stories were so captivating that I wanted to hear them again and again.

The stories were about our history—who and what we were, as opposed to what society said about who we were. The stories were interwoven with our belief systems, with our world view, and they reinforced the Cree concept of *wahk-ku-to-win*, which, translated loosely into English, means "all my relations." It meant that in the living universe—the plants, the animals, the people, and the land—everything is spiritually interrelated and connected. According to these ancient stories, many of which had originated prior to European contact, the Cree had known that people of a great number of different colours would one day live here in North America, bringing with them their different ways of speaking and worshipping. The stories taught that we should accept these people, and their varied languages and religions, because they were meant to be here.

In the winter, we went to local halls to attend round dances—social dances in which we danced with departed spirits. Summer highlights were community functions such as sports days, sun dances, feasts, and other ceremonies. I particularly remember the sun dances—huge spiritual gatherings that involved, in part, round-the-clock prayer and then dancing and singing. The Poundmaker and Little Pine reserves share a border, and the sun dance lodge was right on the border. I remember asking my father why that was, and he said since 1885 it had been illegal for people from Little Pine to come to our sun dances, and vice versa. So the two communities built the lodge on the border. The Little Pine people camped on the Little Pine side, and the Poundmaker people camped on the Poundmaker side, but they still made one camp, and the police were always there to keep an eye on it all.

We had to be self-sufficient, and therefore my parents farmed, to the extent that it was possible on the restricted area of land available to them on the reserve. We sharecropped, growing wheat and oats, and usually kept a cow for milk. We kids were expected to help out. We hunted small game and helped with milking and gardening. My favourite job was working with the horses. We kids handled and rode horses a lot, from an early age. Since they were our only means of transportation, we knew how to handle a team and to ride horseback. Saddles were scarce, so we usually rode bareback, which meant that we learned to ride well because we needed to. In retrospect, bareback was the best way we could have learned to ride. I remember long evening rides, returning home from Thunderchild or Sweetgrass or from town on a Saturday night. By the time I was thirteen, I spent each summer working for local farmers and ranchers, herding cattle on horseback.

———————◆———————

My first language was Cree. Even when I went away to school, I understood very little English. My father always insisted that Cree was our first language, our god-given language; English was our second language.

The fall I was nearly nine, it was finally time for me to go to St. Anthony's Catholic school in Onion Lake, where I would spend two years. Believe it or not, I was actually excited when the grain truck that had been going from house to house in our community pulled into our yard. Even though my older brothers had warned me about residential school, it seemed at first like a big adventure, and a lot of fun, to pile into the open back of the truck with so many of the neighbours' kids and embark on this journey. However, as we drove northeast from Poundmaker toward Onion Lake, mile after mile, I realized we were travelling much farther from home than I had expected. I didn't fully understand that I wouldn't be coming home again until the following June. The second fall, when the truck arrived, I wasn't so naïve. I knew better what I was getting into, and it wasn't so easy to leave home. But it was the law—we had to go. Parents would sometimes try to hide their kids, but eventually they'd be found and turned over to the police.

My sister and two of my brothers were also at St. Anthony's, which made things somewhat easier. However, we were divided into different age groups and lived in different dormitories, so we didn't see each other very often. We weren't allowed to go home during the school year, and because my parents had no vehicle, they couldn't often make the seventy-mile trip to visit us. Although it was such a long way from home, occasionally my mother would travel by train to Fort Pitt to see us. We'd be permitted to visit in the parlour for a limited period of time at a certain time of the day, and that was all that was allowed. Afterwards our mother would watch us in the play area from a distance, but we weren't allowed to leave the yard to go to her. I imagine it was very, very difficult for her.

I suspect one of the reasons for the creation of residential schools is that government officials knew the Cree were very spiritual and accepting of different beliefs, so they thought we would be easy to convert. The government had an agenda, and our beliefs and language were a hindrance to their vision of progress. We already had our own language and spirituality. We had our own government. We had our own educational and judicial systems. We had our own astronomers and names for the constellations. We had our own history and heroes. Despite this, we studied Galileo and Christopher Columbus and John A. MacDonald instead.

At residential school, I was taught that my language, my songs, and those teaching stories of the elders were all the work of the Devil, and if I followed them, I would go to Hell. It hurt and confused me greatly to be told that my grandparents had gone to Hell because they were never baptized and had never gone to confession. It was very difficult to understand, and it made me very angry.

Like many other children in residential schools, I was abused—physically, mentally, spiritually, and emotionally. As a result, for forty years I was a very angry person, and that anger had a negative impact on my life. Through therapy, I regained the Cree perspective, which had always been there, underneath it all, and it helped me see my past more clearly. Through therapy, many years later, I was able to forgive the nuns. I found I could no longer really blame them as human beings. It was their job to teach us this new way of speaking and thinking, this new religion. They had never stopped to assess the fact that we already had our own language and beliefs. How could they have, since there was such a huge language barrier? We didn't speak their language, and they didn't speak ours. They believed—however mistakenly—that they were doing something good, something right, and they didn't know any better. They must have often been overwhelmed by the enormous job they had to do and the enormous responsibility they held. Yet, there was a lot of unnecessary abuse of power. Those teachers who sexually abused their students can't be forgotten or forgiven. They must have known what they were doing was wrong, by any standards.

The humiliation and abuse left their marks. Many of us were ashamed, afraid, and angry. We also felt betrayed. After all, we had welcomed the Europeans to our land and had accepted their presence. In return, they imposed their beliefs, systems, and culture upon us. We were so angry that many of us turned to alcohol—like I did for a time—and many of us never really recovered. There is still a lot of anger in Aboriginal communities, and forgiveness doesn't come easily, so I can understand why some people are still so angry. Much damage was done to us.

◆

When I was old enough to go to high school, Indian teenagers were still not allowed to attend the local high schools at Cut Knife or North Battleford, so I went to Lebret Indian School, a residential school 270 miles southeast of Poundmaker near Fort Qu'Appelle, which was, again, run by priests and Grey Nuns. Then after a few years in the States, I moved to Saskatoon to study art at the Technical Collegiate. A representative from Indian Affairs had seen my paintings and thought I could fit into and excel in the art program there, and I did. It was in Saskatoon that I first was exposed to TV and films. I fell in love with old movies and, watching the actors, I began to think, *I could do that.*

When I first arrived in Saskatoon in the early sixties, there were only three or four Indian families living in the city, unlike other Canadian cities that had larger Indian populations. Many Indian people in cities felt they just didn't fit in anywhere, except perhaps in a bar. As a student in Saskatoon, I sought other Indian students. We finally found each other, and the YWCA gave us a space to meet in, where we played games, got acquainted with each other, and started talking about who we were and why we were there. It was a way for us to counter the negative energy we were bombarded with every day. Similar gatherings had been springing up in cities across the country, and that's how the friendship centre movement started. The purpose of friendship centres was never to segregate ourselves—but to provide us with a place to belong and to help us understand why we were different from everyone else and how we could fit in. The centres were a necessary bridge between our culture and the society we were living in. They also provided a sense of belonging and family that was missing for many people. As we were growing up, many sibling relationships had been severed by the residential school system. Economics forced us to spend summers working out on farms or ranches away from our families. Many families were fragmented, and many of us felt alienated, so we sought kinship where we could find it.

◆

Growing up in a rural home helped reinforce my belief that I am profoundly connected to the world around me—the land, the plants, and the animals. Since childhood, I have retained my fondness for animals, particularly horses. I've always been fascinated with their power and intelligence. I still have a few horses boarded here and there. A favourite is a twenty-one-year-old sorrel gelding named Tex. Rodeo is among my many interests, and for many years I rode Tex in team-roping competitions. Even though he's an unpredictable, high-strung animal by nature, he's very competitive and level-headed in the arena. Tex has been a good partner. He's even been in the movies: his first film was *Ebenezer*, and his resumé includes *Unforgiven*, the *Lonesome Dove* series, *Legends of the Fall*, and *Big Bear*.

◆

For many years, I lived across Canada—in Whitehorse, Saskatoon, and Vancouver—and, for the most part, I have been able to feel comfortable wherever I was. After all, I see myself as being indigenous to North America, not merely to one small part of it. The idea that land can or should be divided up into parcels the size of Poundmaker, or Saskatchewan, or Canada, is a European idea—not a Cree one. Eventually, my wife and I reached the points in our careers where it didn't matter where we lived. As an actor, I fly to my jobs no matter where my home base is, and Irene is a social worker who has worked as a university instructor and director of social services agencies.

Things changed ten years ago when our daughter Glynis died of cancer. Irene and I took custody of her four children, and we decided to move back to Poundmaker and settle down here. Our decision to move home was primarily based on the importance of family and ceremony. We have a lot of family here at Poundmaker, and that's very important. Despite, or perhaps because of, the fact that our family felt so much pressure from outside forces while we were growing up, we remained very close over the years, and I am deeply connected to my extended family. We wanted our grandchildren to live among their mother's people and to remain attached to their Cree heritage. Also, I wanted them to grow up with ceremonies, especially the sweat lodge ceremony. The sweat lodge at Poundmaker is special because it's a family sweat lodge maintained by my brother, one where my siblings and I, and our kids and our grandkids, can gather as a family.

My grandchildren are also developing a love for animals and the outdoors. They ride and have attended rodeo clinics in steer riding and team roping. I tell my grandchildren some of the important teaching stories the elders told me long ago, but, because they aren't fluent in Cree, it can be difficult because I have to constantly interpret and translate from Cree to English. Some of the concepts and ideas in the stories cannot be fully conveyed in English.

Growing up here, amongst my family and surrounded by our culture, gave me a strong sense of who I am, which I have carried with me all these years. I want my grandchildren to have the same experience. I feel it's important for them to know who they are, first of all, and where they're from, and this is the place for them to find out—in fact, that's the whole purpose of the sweat lodge ceremonies. They'll develop self-respect and self-esteem so they can function in any society without feeling inferior to anyone. Once they are confident in themselves and their background, they can develop respect for other cultures and religions so they won't pass judgment on others. Fortunately, things have changed since I was a child, so my grandchildren can live at home and attend school. Their worlds are not as divided as mine was. They have friends in town and friends on the reserve. Like me, they can navigate in both cultures and accept people for who they are, while maintaining who they are. In this place, they have a strong base from which they can grow and then face the world. They are happy to be living here, and I am happy to be back because this is where my family is. We've finally come home.

Guardian Angels

CATHERINE R. FENWICK

*I learned that when people die they leave a space in the world,
and that long afterward the living can press their bodies against
that space, and listen.*

—Warren Cariou, *Lake of the Prairies*

I AM NEVER completely alone. While walking across a field on the prairie, hiking a forest trail in the mountains, sitting alone in a canoe in the middle of a lake, or cross-country skiing on the wide open plain, I am never alone. I tell them my dreams, joys, hopes, successes, failures, and frustrations. They listen to the small-minded thoughts I'd rather not share with the living. When I have decisions to make, I ask them, "What do I need to know?" They always answer. They are Gramma Katie and Gramma Irene.

In fearful times, one or both of them will be nearby, whether I'm driving my car in a blizzard, standing on a stage in front of a large audience, or sitting helplessly with a critically ill child. Fear rises from the pit of my stomach. That's when the grandmothers come and the choky anxiety melts away like early morning fog. The clearing starts in my belly and moves up to my lungs, heart, throat, and brain as I draw strength and peace from the memories of their lives. Katie was born in 1901 and died in 1940. Irene, born in 1900, died in 1988.

Catherine (age 19 months) with her pet cat,
Snowball, and the gentle farm dog, Shep, 1947

Our big old farm kitchen had cupboards that covered two long walls, a pump over the sink that belched water from the cistern in the basement, a big wood-burning cookstove, kerosene lamps, and a table that comfortably seated sixteen people. There was always activity in that kitchen, lots of good people and lots of good food.

Gramma Irene was a marvellous cook, one of the best pie makers and bread bakers in the municipality. I liked to watch her turn a musty-smelling, fusty-looking blob of dough into fragrant crusty bread. She punched that bread dough, lifted the huge pillowy blob and slapped it down on the kitchen table, white puffs of flour rising up. The dough looked like a big fat belly lying there. When sometimes she punched it hard, I wondered what she was thinking about. Other times, she kneaded the dough gently, singing or humming and talking with us kids. She beamed as she watched us tuck into the warm slices slathered in freshly churned butter. Even when I was very small, I got to crank the butter churn. I was always careful to do it just right.

Katie, after whom I was named, died before I was born, but she is alive in my memory. I saw her first when I was five years old and being chased by a large dog. I ran as fast as my little legs could carry me toward a shed, hoping to get inside and shut the door. Soon I realized that the shed was too far, the dog too fast. I screamed. The black-and-white border collie suddenly stopped, took a sharp turn to the left, and headed across the pasture after a rabbit.

I kept running until I reached the shed, where I sat panting on the door stoop. And there she was, not a person really, more like an image, a wispy shadow of a woman, a little older than my mother. Somehow I knew she was Dad's mother, the gramma who had died. She said, "Don't worry, my little Catherine. I'm always with you."

The next time I saw Gramma Irene, I told her what had happened. She said, "Well, I see you've met your guardian angel."

One Saturday morning when I was nine, my parents went to town to pick up groceries. I was left in charge of five little sisters—the youngest barely a month old. The end-of-January sun gave no heat. I threw coal into the furnace every couple of hours. The sun was about to go down when we started to get hungry.

Irma looked up from her paper doll collection. "Cathy, what's for supper?"

Four-year-old Susan came skipping into the kitchen. "Yeah, when are we going to eat?"

"I'll cook some potatoes and eggs. Go play with Maxine. Caroline, warm up a bottle for Sharon. I hear her fussing."

I loaded wood into the cookstove and started to peel potatoes. I cut them up, dumped them into the pan, and checked the burning wood. *Don't put too much wood in the stove. Too much wood will start a chimney fire.* Dad's warning was seared into my brain. *You're the oldest. You're in charge.*

I lifted the round stove lid to check the fire. The flaming logs were spitting sparks—sparks that were being sucked toward the back of the stove and into the pipe that was connected to the chimney. I heard a roar inside the chimney. I ran outside. Fireworks vaulted and landed on the roof. "Oh my God! Chimney fire!" I screamed. I ran back inside. "Caroline, grab the baby. Irma, help with coats."

I herded five little sisters into the animal-heated barn and made them kneel on the shitty floor and pray. We were just finishing the rosary when I heard Gramma Katie whisper in my ear, "It's okay now. It's over." I ran out to look. Our home was not burning down. There were no more sparks. We went back into the house, and I finished making supper.

We were eating when Mom and Dad came home. "Where were you?" Caroline asked, her eyes flashing. "Cathy made us kneel in the barn and pray."

I had to explain about the sparks.

A few years later, in high school, I was coming home from a country dance with friends in my boyfriend's car. My boyfriend hit the brakes, trying to make a tight curve at the bottom of a hill. The old car was going too fast. It rolled a couple of times. My door flew open. I was thrown clear and knocked unconscious—there were no seat belts in 1947 Fords. I awoke to see the frightened faces of my three friends staring down at me. I was shivering. Someone had covered me with a blanket. All of us had bits of glass, like sharp gravel, on our clothes and in our hair. I thought I might be dying and concluded there was nothing I could do about it. It was strangely peaceful. "It's going to be okay. No one is going to die." It was Katie and I knew we would be all right.

In my early twenties, pregnant with my first child, I was afraid. I worried about everything that could go wrong. I read medical books on obstetrics, frightening myself even more. *How will I deliver this baby? What if I can't tolerate the pain? What if I die? What if the baby dies?*

In my dreams I spoke to the gramma who had buried six children. She reassured me that I wasn't the first woman to give birth and that I would handle whatever happened. And I did.

One day, with my infant son I visited Gramma Katie's younger sister, Marian. She told me how Katie had grieved the deaths of her small children. One was stillborn, three lived for only a few hours, and two toddlers died from pneumonia. There were no antibiotics and the nearest doctor was twenty miles away.

"I remember when little Frances died. She was two years old," Auntie Marian said as she put the teakettle on the stove. "I was with Katie at the time. An RCMP officer and a doctor came from Indian Head to check the body and write out a death certificate. Stefan, your grandpa, made a small coffin out of boards and we lined it with white cotton from an old bed sheet. Katie bathed the baby and dressed her in a little pink and white flowered dress. Then laid her in that coffin. All day and all through the night she sat with her baby, eating only when somebody brought her food. She slept in a chair, her head resting on the little wooden box. The morning of the funeral, I helped her get dressed. Your dad helped her walk to the car while your grandpa carried the coffin."

"I can hardly imagine such suffering," I told her, cradling my own baby.

"Katie stood by the mound of earth until nearly everyone had gone from the cemetery. Your Uncle Joe wrapped his arms around her shoulders and helped her to the car. Back at home she went to bed and slept for thirty hours. I stayed to look after the other children. For days she wept, until it seemed there could be no more tears inside her. I remember when little Daniel asked, 'Where's Frances?' She said she didn't know what to say to him. How do you explain death to a toddler? Katie buried all those babies, and it never got any easier."

I said, "We live for such a short time as it is. It seems so unfair that a beautiful baby struggles for life, only to suffer and die before she has a chance to really live."

Auntie Marian got up to pour boiling water into the teapot. "Katie was only thirty-nine years old when she died. Again the RCMP and doctor came to the house. The doctor said she was worn out. Her heart just stopped. Your dad, the oldest, was eighteen. There were ten living children to care for. The youngest was only two weeks old." She sat down again and shook her head.

Gramma Katie's brother and sister-in-law took the baby. Grandpa and the older boys managed with the rest until he remarried, a few years later, and moved to Regina with the second youngest. Dad and Mom raised up the rest of the kids after they got married. Mom wasn't much more than a child herself, seventeen years old when she came to live on the farm. A year later I was born. Then came five more girls and four boys. I was eight when the last of Dad's siblings left the farm.

Irene, Mom's mother, gave birth to ten children and buried a baby boy. I remember her saying, "Life is hard. All you can do is keep going and know that things will get better. You have to do it. No one can do it for you."

Gramma Irene raised chickens from egg to table. One time I tried to help a chick laboriously pecking away inside its shell. "You poor little thing," I said, reaching for the wobbling egg, intending to break the shell.

Gramma gently took my hand. "This little chick needs to do the work so it can develop a strong neck. If you break the shell, its neck won't be strong enough for it to peck for food. It will die."

Once the chick had worked its way out of the shell, I watched as the feathers dried, then I picked up the trembling fuzzy yellow chick, and carried it to water and food. "Gramma, look how it grabs drops of water in its beak, throws its head back and swallows." I felt proud of my strong chick. It soon began to snap up small bits of grain, as though it had always known exactly what it needed to do.

These life lessons held me in good stead, when in 1990, at age forty-four, I was diagnosed with breast cancer.

"We caught it early, right?" I asked the surgeon.

"No, I'm so sorry," she answered, taking my hand. "We didn't catch it in the earliest stages. Let's wait for the pathology report, but I'm afraid the news will not be what we want to hear." She asked if I had any more questions. I shook my head. She smiled, slowly got to her feet, and moved on to the next patient.

I was numb, unable to cry. I thought about my children growing up without their mother. I felt like screaming, "Who will take care of my children? I want grandchildren. There's still so much I want to do. It's not fair. I'm too young to die." But there were other patients in the room, so instead of shouting, I wrapped myself in a blanket, curled up in the foetal position, stared out the window.

Suddenly there she was. She sat on the end of my hospital bed, her image clearer than ever. "Gramma Katie," I whispered. She wore a cotton housedress with a crisscross pattern in shades of brown and peach, low-heeled laced-up white shoes on her feet. Her worker's hands rested on her knees, fingernails trimmed, not painted. Shoulder-length brown hair framed her pretty face. I looked up into her gentle green eyes. I thought for sure she was coming to get me this time. She sat listening to my panicky thoughts. "No," she said. "This isn't your time. You have lots to do before you die."

I sat up. We gazed at one another. She smiled. I had never felt so at peace. I began to feel like I wanted to go with her. She said, "No, Catherine. Stay. Your family needs you. The world isn't done with you yet."

A flush of gratitude warmed my face. A few moments later, she nodded her head three times and was gone. I knew it would be okay, but I wondered what she meant when she said I still had lots to do before I die. I remembered the little chick and made a commitment to do everything I could to get healthy.

There were lots of things I still wanted. I hoped to see my children grow up and I wanted grandchildren. If her statement were true, it was possible that I would get my wishes.

Two weeks later I began an eight-month regimen of drug treatments. During that time I thought about ways to give meaning to this cancer nightmare. I realized I could help others by sharing my experiences of surviving surgery and chemotherapy. I became involved in the provincial and national breast cancer advocacy networks.

I had often dreamed of writing a book, and now I knew what I wanted to write about. *Healing With Humour* was published in 1995.

I began to speak about humour and healing. Speaking to a large audience was terrifying at first, but with Katie and Irene standing in the wings, holding on to my fears and insecurities, I walk onto centre stage. Through my many presentations to audiences across Canada and abroad, I am fulfilling Gramma Katie's prophecy.

My guardian angels continue to travel with me, to inspire and protect me. I'll never be alone.

Believe It or Not

PAMELA BANTING

Born on a mountain top in Tennessee,
Greenest state in the Land of the Free,
Raised in the woods so's he knew ev'ry tree,
Kilt him a b'ar when he was only three.
> —"Ballad of Davy Crockett"

FROM THE TIME I was born until about age thirty-five I led a charmed life. Or I thought I did. I felt fortunate almost all of the time.

In Sunday school, they tried, in their awkward way, to convince us pre-schoolers that our lives were charmed. They taught us, for instance, that *Jesus loves me this I know, for the Bible tells me so, little ones to him belong, they are weak but he is strong*, and while I was glad Jesus loved me, I didn't feel weak, nor did I see why in order for him to be strong, or to love me, it seemed I had to be. If Jesus liked us weak and meek, I thought, I could do without His kind of love or that kind of charm.

When I was in elementary school, my parents gave me a *Ripley's Believe It or Not* colouring book. Books of any kind were very scarce in our town, and I thought this one must be the best colouring book of all time. It had both entertainment and educational value, I thought, and I felt privileged to have it in my possession. I decided to take it to school

Pamela (age 3) in Birch River, Manitoba

to show my teacher and classmates. Even our school didn't have many books—only about three shelves per classroom. You could read the entire grade's worth in a couple of months or less. So I thought everyone at school would be as thrilled as I was to look at this book with its records of weird facts and strange happenings. One day, I placed my prized colouring book carefully in my bike carrier so that its cover wouldn't get dinted, and I headed to school.

As I approached the CNR stationmaster's long sandy driveway, the winds suddenly picked up. In front of the post office, a good-sized whirlwind was spinning sand and gravel skyward. As I watched, the vortex shifted, abruptly encircling my bike and I in its embrace. The deep, fine-grained sand of the Wellmans' driveway, which always bogged me down on my bike, was sucked up into the air and swirled around so violently that my arms and legs stung, and I had to dismount, straddle my bike, shut my eyes as tightly as possible, and cover them with my hands, just like what's-his-name in the Bible who feared to look upon the face of God. Then I heard a loud flutter as if an enormous bird were landing, wings pumping, right in front of my face. Terrified, I moved my hands away from my eyes expecting to see a hawk or an eagle, wings outspread, gripping my handlebars in its talons and about to peck out my eyes or carry me off into the wild blue yonder.

Instead, my colouring book had taken flight. The whirlwind had pulled the book right out of my carrier. Now fifty feet aloft, it was tearing the pages out one by one. Some of them ascended toward heaven and the rest scattered all over town.

I stood there amazed.

To have found myself at the centre of a whirlwind. To have had the same experience as Elijah—taken up into heaven by a whirlwind. Or Job, to whom God spake out of the whirlwind. Was God angry with me for having the hubris to take the book to school, to draw attention to myself as the possessor of such a wonderful object as *Ripley's Believe It or Not*? "Behold, the whirlwind of the LORD goeth forth with fury, a continuing whirlwind: it shall fall with pain upon the head of the wicked," it says in Jeremiah. Was that me? If I didn't want to be weak or meek, was I wicked? Was it wrong to want to possess books in a bookless community?

But the Biblical associations did not strike me very forcefully. Even though I was a little jaded about Jesus and his affections, I did continue going to Sunday school, but I was the heathen child of atheist parents and atheist forebears for at least three generations back. I didn't go for the religion: I went for the printed handouts they gave us from time to time and the little badges I could earn for attendance.

Rather than the wrath of God, it was the irony of that particular colouring book having been snatched away in a fantastic incident worthy of Ripley himself which seized my imagination. I was so awed by the irony of the situation that I didn't even try to gather the pages of my ruined treasure. Having *Believe It or Not* taken up in a whirlwind was almost better than having the book itself.

It was a sign that my life was charmed. I had been blessed by irony. By a cosmic joke. Since irony is, after all, a form of meaning or significance, I immediately grasped that I had a destiny after all. If nothing else, hereafter I would be the girl upon whom a whirlwind had descended, the one whose *Believe It or Not* book had been taken. I could be *in* Ripley. I could be *in* a book.

Of course, one's fortune is different from one's luck. I have never been lucky. When I was eight years old, one Thursday night at my request, my dad took my cousin Merle and me with him to the old Legion hall while he worked bingo. In the final game of the evening, Merle got a diagonal line of numbers, and she bingoed. She won five dollars, a large sum for a kid in those days.

To my surprise, at her "Bingo!" I felt a stab of jealousy in my belly. It was like a power surge in reverse. Power drained rapidly from me. I knew it was completely irrational. I understood that bingo was based on random numbers, but I felt *I* should have won the five dollars. It was, after all, *my* dad, not hers, who worked the Legion bingos, *my* dad who had taken the two of us to play that night. *Her* dad wasn't even a veteran, let alone a legionnaire. As we drove Merle home, I curled up in the front car seat, a silent little coil of jealousy, like a poisonous fiddlehead. Maybe my life wasn't charmed after all, I thought.

The only time I ever won anything was when I won five single-play records from radio station CKRC in Winnipeg. I successfully guessed which records would be in the top five that week. Unfortunately, the five prize records weren't as scintillating as the top five. Nevertheless, I was proud of myself. Proud that a young girl from the country had been able to compete successfully with all those city kids who always got good reception on their radios, not just on particularly clear winter nights; kids who had stores where they could buy popular records, not just whichever old-fashioned country-and-western odds and ends the warehouse at Marshall-Wells, Winnipeg, sent to our store when my dad filled out an order for "20 records"; kids who received the newspaper the same day it was published and who, therefore, had an extra day to contemplate the hit parade; kids whose letters didn't have to travel 350 miles to get to the radio station in time for the contest. A fortuitous aligning of the planets had obviously allowed me to win and to see my name printed as the winner at the top of the following week's contest. That was the first time I ever saw my name in print, and that turned out to be a better prize than the five free records.

There's something about coming from a small, remote or semi-remote community that lends an aura both of fortuitousness and unlikelihood to the events of one's life. For one to even compete on equal terms (let alone win) or to make one's mark on the culture at large, such as to see one's name in the paper, other than for some criminal offence, is regarded as so improbable that if it ever happens one leaps immediately right over notions of individual cleverness, intelligence, talent, insight, skill, effort, time, labour, practice, or sacrifice to notions of cosmic coincidence and planetary alignment.

The small town is based on the combined expertise of the handyman and the capable woman. The jack or jill of all trades is the heroic figure, not the master-of-one, not the musical virtuoso, the scientist, not even the teacher. It is not considered enough to excel at only one thing. Children and adults alike are expected to become pretty good at everything they do. In the small town, excellence denotes an imbalance in the use of one's time, a wilful foreclosure on one's other talents, and a cynicism about the range of a person's abilities. It makes more sense in a pioneer culture to be able to fix a stalled motor, to put up a building, to make a decent loaf of bread, to can, freeze, and preserve vegetables and wild fruit. It does not make sense to become a musician, writer, or professor. People who are unable to do anything with their hands or unwilling to get their hands dirty are derided in such a place. As a university student, more than once when I came home for a visit, my mom would take one of my hands in hers, and in that affectionate mother-daughter moment remark how soft and how obviously unused to hard work my hands were. There, soft hands translate as "useless individual."

Paradoxically, if someone does excel, win, or successfully compete, a sense of the miraculous descends upon not just that person but also the entire community. When someone excels, it seems as if being born there in that place is the criterion for success, something therefore that any local could duplicate. The charm in the charmed life extends outward to the place as a whole just as my colouring book ended up dispersed all over town.

When I was eight, and my mom's dad was dying of leukemia and of the excessive radiation he had been given to treat the disease, our parents took us with them to Winfield, British Columbia, for a last visit with him. Somewhere along the BC highway, we stopped at the Enchanted Forest, a roadside attraction where you follow a landscaped path through the verdant BC forest to encounter, at intervals, large, brightly painted fairy tale figures—Snow White and the Seven Dwarves, the Three Little Pigs, The Old Woman Who Lived in a Shoe, Little Bo Peep, The Fox and the Grapes, Goldilocks and the Three Bears, and Little Red Riding Hood.

This was my first trip out of the province of Manitoba. When I was four, my parents had taken me all the way to Winnipeg for the Shrine Circus, a distance of seven hundred miles round trip. For years afterward, they told the story of how, during the performance, they would say to me, "Did you see that acrobat?" or "Look at the tiger!" and I would reply in a curt and somewhat annoyed tone, "I *see* it." They were astonished that they could drive their little kid, who had never been out of the bush, all the way to Winnipeg for something as special as the Shrine Circus and that I would be unimpressed.

I don't remember being unimpressed or disappointed by the circus. More likely I was annoyed to think they thought I hadn't the ability to see for myself. If I can reconstruct that evening at the circus at all, I think I simply didn't see the point of having exotic animals like elephants, tigers, and bears perform tricks. I'd have been quite happy just to look at those animals live; I didn't see the necessity of having them stand on their heads or jump through hoops. It was unseemly, and it detracted from their power and presence. Here they were, taking elephants, tigers, and bears and treating them as if they were the dog next door.

Aside from being taken to the circus, this trip to British Columbia was the first time I had seen a truly different landscape. Long before we arrived at the Enchanted Forest, my brother and I saw for the first time the bluey-green water of the Bow River. Not content with the first few sightings of this turquoise water, we noted and exclaimed over each and every single glimpse of it that appeared between the trees as we drove along the mountain highway. The only rivers we had seen before were brown or red-brown like the Birch River, which ran by our land at home. We were charmed by this water. Water straight out of a jewellery box. Miraculous water. Jesus could have walked on this water, though the current might have been a bit swift for him.

When our dad agreed to pull over at the Enchanted Forest, I could hardly contain my glee. I thought I might burst with it. My brother and I played in the bush around home all the time. We had a very strong affinity for trees, and this forest was enchanted! We leapt out of the car, and Dad took Murray and me down the path while Mom stayed in the car with our baby sister.

Immediately we realized that this forest was different. But it was not the promised fairy tale characters that distinguished it from the bush at home. It was the smell of the conifer trees, and the moss growing not just at the base of trees but everywhere. For me, the springy, cushiony moss, the lush ground cover, and the enormous trees were the main attraction. At home, I not only knew each kind of tree, shrub, fern, wildflower, and weed, but it would not be an exaggeration to say that I knew most of the maple trees and clumps of red willow, each bluebell and columbine on our few acres of land individually.

I was delighted with the Enchanted Forest but perhaps not for the reasons our parents might have thought. I loved the vegetation; I thought the fairy tale characters were out of place. They were an intrusion. They weren't local, indigenous, or in any way meaningful. The fairy tale statues belonged in books, on TV, or in your imagination, not in the forest, which was enchanted enough in its own right. Anyone could see that the trees, the mosses, and the plants were the real enchantment, the path through the forest the magical thing.

Paths of any kind are marvellous. Paths are signs of the former or present inhabitants of a place—humans or animals—or more likely collaboration between the species. Paths are signs that others have passed that way and left little more than the cumulative evidence of their foot, paw, or hoof prints. In a bookless community, paths are your textbooks and your pleasure reading. Paths link you with the animals and assure you that you are not alone. Who needed Snow White and the Seven Dwarfs? Who needed Mickey Mouse? It was nothing but a letdown to round a curve in the path and be confronted with a giant red and yellow plastic fairy tale character.

Soon after I began writing this essay, I was going through a box of old diaries and journals when I chanced upon a thin black scribbler I had used for Composition in grade three. According to my carefully constructed table of contents at the front of the scribbler, the topic of the third assignment was "The View from a Hill." My response was to describe our family trip. The composition, here quoted in its entirety, is entitled "Mt. Sawtooth":

> *I was in BC. We climbed up Mt. Sawtooth. I looked down and saw green rivers, orchards, mountains, and streams down the mountainside. I saw a fawn too. It was so tame people could take its picture. I saw an enchanted forest. It was a beautiful sight.*

When I read this in the context of what I had just written about how the fairy tale figures offended my taste, I was embarrassed at what appeared to be a blatant contradiction of the way I had remembered the experience. Here I was, my adult self constructing a version of my child self as a little heathen, not quite raised by wolves but sufficiently bushed that Disney characters held little sway over my imagination, while the evidence in my very own scribbler—written the same year as the trip—seemed to contradict that version of myself with its testimony that the enchanted forest "was a beautiful sight." Had I succumbed to writing what I thought would please the teacher? Did the topic of a view from a hill immediately launch me into the tradition of the picturesque? I winced in shame at having caught myself romancing a reader with some version of myself as a half-feral child.

When I took another look at the composition, however, I began to read it a little differently. Although that final statement follows directly upon the previous sentence's reference to the enchanted forest, it does not unerringly refer only to the forest. It can refer, instead, to the matter of the whole paragraph. The view from Mt. Sawtooth was a beautiful sight, not just the enchanted forest; the sentence is a conclusion. Moreover, I have always been scrupulous about spelling and punctuation, even as a child, and *enchanted forest* is not capitalized, and so can be read as referring to the trees and other flora rather than the tourist trap. And surely it is significant that there is no mention whatsoever in the paragraph of the Disney figures. What is mentioned is the colour of the rivers in that country, and other elements of the environment. Seeing an almost-tame animal would have impressed me. I doubt I had ever seen a wild animal that had become habituated to people other than at the Shrine Circus.

Most of the animals and the people in our country shared a kind of mutually aloof regard. We both had such large territories in which to run that we could afford a respectful distance from one another. My dad thought nothing of picking saskatoons on one side of a berry patch while a black bear picked on the other. As kids, my brother and I were much more interested in wild animals than tame ones. One time when he was sixteen and out fishing somewhere north of town, Murray came across a wounded great blue heron. He caught it and was going to bring it home to try to heal its wing, but he couldn't figure out how to hold onto the bird while driving back to town. Despite its injury, the bird was just too strong to hold with one arm, and so he had to leave it to its fate. But the image of a good-looking, blond-haired, blue-eyed teenage boy driving through town in his blue Ford Fairlane with his right arm around a great blue heron is such a compelling one that I have added it to the collection of images associated with my charmed life, whether or not it ever happened.

It is something of a mystery to me that, born and raised in a place which lacked the amenities, comforts, conveniences, and culture that my urban contemporaries took and continue to take for granted, I came away from the Swan Valley not with a feeling of deprivation and lack but rather with a definite sense of having lived a charmed life. We were not raised in ignorance of the outside world. Though the paper arrived a day late, we always received the daily newspaper, as well as *Reader's Digest, National Geographic, Time, Chatelaine,* and *Ladies' Home Journal.* As kids we knew that cities had town water, sewers, libraries, museums, concert halls, and a million stores. We only had three grocery stores, one dry-goods store, one hardware (ours), a succession of pubs each of which burnt to the ground, three gas stations, a post office, a poolroom/bowling alley with three lanes where girls weren't supposed to go if they didn't want to get pregnant, and an electrical store which was actually a liquor store, long on Baby Duck and Gimli Goose. We knew that where we lived simply did not count. That the only way the outside world might hear of us up there in the bush was if a forest fire or flood raged through or a spectacular homicide was committed. However, we thought that being off the beaten track, despite the disadvantages, was an incredibly fortunate place to be.

In *Bone Deep in Landscape: Writing, Reading, and Place*, Montana-born writer Mary Clearman Blew posits that perhaps the frontier can be redefined as "the meeting point between conflicting narratives, and perhaps those narratives conflict within ourselves as often as with others." Certainly it would seem that knowing one lived in an economically and culturally disadvantaged place while thinking one is living a charmed life would qualify as two such conflicting narratives. Of course, the contradiction is not irresolvable: while it is not impossible, it is difficult to place the proper value upon something you have never had, and of course neither money nor season's tickets to the theatre is any firm guarantee of a well-lived life. Moreover, these two apparently conflicting narratives can easily co-exist if you view your place in the world through the lens of irony. If you believe that meaning is rooted in irony, then such a place can yield meaning galore.

Growing up with every individual tree as a companion, you have a natural scepticism toward cultural mythologies. You grow up without creating an opposition between culture and nature, significant and insignificant. For instance, learning the alphabet and learning to read were easy for me because I had already developed an eye for reading signs—tracks, details, and nuance—in the bush. Reading schoolbooks was essentially the same process. When I tell you that bluebells and columbines were my first friends before I went to school, I do not mean this metaphorically but literally. They were not imaginary friends; I did not personify them then, nor am I doing so now. There was always something interesting happening in or near the places where they lived: a bee visit, a few new-fallen leaves, a breeze swaying their tender but sturdy bodies. I could pick one blossom and sip its nectar—I could be a bee! And of course, despite the language gap, I could talk to them, though I imagine most of my days in the bush as passing without the necessity of talking when there was already so much sound and rhythm everywhere. Birdsong. Tree rustle. River flow.

Having a charmed life comes down to two things: living in relative proximity to wilder things and living within a contradictory narrative in which one is cast as humble and insignificant on the one hand and larger than life on the other. Believe it or not.

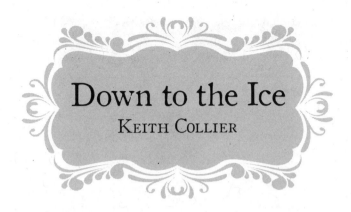

Down to the Ice
KEITH COLLIER

I GREW UP with no fence around my house and no asphalt in my
driveway. I took my backyard forest for granted, and early morning
visits of moose to my father's vegetable garden were common. I was
as comfortable in the woods as any Torontonian is on Queen Street,
and I have always felt an easy, respectful relationship with the natural
environment. That feeling has never left me, even after years of city living
and the realization that it may be a long time before I ever have a forest for
a backyard again.

———————◆———————

Ice defined the seasons in rural Newfoundland. Rural Newfoundland is
by default coastal Newfoundland, and when the first skim of ice appeared
on the bay on a frosty morning, the bicycles and baseball bats would be
put away for another season, and we would once again start tinkering with
snowmobiles, sharpening skates, and putting new tape on hockey sticks.

It was almost always after Christmas before the ice was thick enough
to venture out on. I would drive out onto the bay on a snowmobile to
check the ice, confident that the cold weather of the past weeks had made
the cove safe for us to play hockey. I'd chop away at the ice with a small
axe until I broke through. Any more than three or four inches of ice was
plenty to support a game of shinny in the evening.

Keith (age 11) up to his elbows in snow in the driveway,
with the bay in the background, 1994

I was four years old when my best friend cracked me in the head with a
ball-peen hammer, for no reason that I can remember. A few stitches and
an ice cream later, we were best friends again, and a decade later we were
still spending much of our time in his father's shed, puttering around with
hammers and nails and snowmobile engines.

It started when we found a couple of pairs of antique ice skates. The
leather was rotted and useless, but the steel blades were still in good shape.
It took us an hour or so to cut the rivets holding the blades to the skates,
polish off the rust, and sharpen them up.

My friend's father was a carpenter, and like all good carpenters, he had
scrap material all over the place. We found three pieces of lumber to make
the frame, nailed them together into a triangle shape, and braced it with
crossmembers. The skate blades were easy to attach to the corners, and the
front blade, at the point of the triangle, was even steerable, rotating freely
on a piece of old copper pipe controlled by ropes leading to the plank that
served as seating in the back.

A sturdy piece of spruce, limbed and fastened to the centre
crossmember, made an excellent mast. All we needed was a sail, and an old
tarpaulin was quickly liberated from a winter of obscurity.

Down to the Ice

Our icemobile was ready.

One Saturday morning in February, we carried our contraption down the hill to the ice-covered cove. We made our way out onto the bay, dragging the icemobile to the headlands. The wind was strong, onshore, and when we unfurled the sail, we had to struggle to keep the icemobile in place, using an axe to cut handholds in the ice until the sail was secured. When we were seated on the rough lumber plank, we let go.

We started to move immediately, the skate blades gliding smoothly over the ice. The tarpaulin sail billowed in the wind, and we picked up speed. We tried the controls, and the icemobile answered, steering to the right and left. The blades made soft swishing and scraping sounds over the ice, the sail fluttering. We laughed out loud. We had expected it to work, but we hadn't expected it to work this well.

We neared shore again in a matter of minutes, covering the half kilometre of ice in almost no time. The wind died down closer to land, and the icemobile slowed. Nearing the raftered ice at the snow-covered beach, we turned the icemobile sharply, side on to the wind, and she came to a gentle halt.

About four kilometres of water separated my tiny outport home from the slightly less tiny town where I went to school and to church. On Sunday, wearing skates and carrying small hand axes in addition to our sticks, my best friend and I set out to join a game of hockey taking place that afternoon. Other boys walked down to the bay, or arrived on ATVs or snowmobiles, but none arrived in as much style as we did. I don't remember who won the game, but the sail home in the failing light was beautiful.

The icemobile was an engineering success, but it had one major design flaw. From the seats on the back, our forward view was partially blocked by the huge tarpaulin sail.

On the east side of the cove, the ice was always soft, and a small patch of open water showed no matter how cold it was. One day, sailing home from another afternoon on the ice, we drifted too far east, and with our forward view blocked by the sail, we never saw the open water coming.

The icemobile made a splash as it tipped forward, the front skate plunging into the freezing water. The rest of it followed as the thin ice surrounding the open water gave way. The water swirled up to our heads.

I pushed off from the seat to get away from the icemobile. I was afraid of becoming tangled in the sail. I tried to swim, but my snowsuit was too heavy, full of seawater. It must have been freezing, but I don't remember feeling it. My feet sank and touched the bottom, and on my toes I found I could barely keep my chin above water. I knew then that I'd be fine, and I started to grab at the ice surrounding us, trying to pull myself up. The weak ice kept breaking away, and every time I hauled myself out of the water, the ice would fracture and I'd plunge back in, the sounds of splashing water and cracking ice too quiet to be heard across the cove.

When we were struggling free of the sinking icemobile, my friend's face was completely calm, as if this sort of thing happened all the time. I don't remember feeling scared, or even cold. I remember only reacting, thinking *this is what I must do*, and then doing it. I was trained from birth to deal with this. The ice was a natural thing, a part of my world, and I don't remember ever being afraid of it.

We finally got out of the water, away from the weak ice to where we could stand. The top of the icemobile's sail and one corner of the frame protruded from the water. By the time we'd walked the five minutes back to the warmth of the wood stove in the shed, the seawater had frozen our clothes almost solid. But it was nothing the roaring wood fire and a cup of tea wouldn't fix, and by the time we were warm again, our salvage plans were already in place.

◆

St. John's Harbour doesn't even freeze in the winter anymore, and in the city, snow and ice are inconveniences, dangers even, instead of a part of a natural cycle that was just as important to the life of the rural community as the summer fishing season. Sometimes when I open my front door after a snowstorm and see three feet of snow drifted against it, I see the shape of a snow cave or the tracks of a snowmobile.

I remember the cracking and groaning of the giant pans of ice heaving and separating in spring, breaking into smaller pieces, sometimes smashing wharves and boats before drifting away from the cove for another year. Walking along the shoreline in the dirtied snow, the yellowed ice would be shifting, cracking, melting away. Somebody braver than me would be farther out on the softened ice on his father's snowmobile, throttle wide open to keep the machine moving fast enough to stay on top of it, big rooster tails of melt water spraying into the air behind him.

I think back now and try to count the number of times I went through thin ice while I was growing up. Seven, I think—four times in salt water, and three times in fresh. Every time, the salt water was warm, almost welcoming, while the fresh water was brutally cold.

It's been years since I've felt the bite of cold water in winter, and it's a strange thing to miss, I know. But where, in the small backyards of the city, would I have ever found the space to build our icemobile? And where but in my small outport home would I have been so close to the sea to be able to use it?

The connection between the man-made and the natural still appeals to me. More than just a proximity to nature, it is a coexistence of civilization and wilderness. People shared a bond with nature in those rural coves and outports that isn't possible in a city. There, the sounds of animals and the ice were as familiar as police sirens and crowded sidewalks are here.

When the icebergs start gliding past St. John's Harbour, I know that the spring break-up has finished, and far away my cove is clear again. People are getting ready for summer, and the snowmobiles and skates are being stored away. I can still hear the scrape of blades on the ice, and I hope that when winter comes again, somebody will go down to the ice, and see the possibilities that we did.

Farm Kid

Rose-Marie Lohnes

A SMALL FARM in Nova Scotia dwells in my bones.

Our modest farmhouse was built by my grandfather when times were tough and money was scarce. The cellar walls were fashioned from hand-split granite stones. The floor resembled a patchwork quilt with its hand-placed slate stones my father and grandfather hauled from the pastureland on the hill. The south-facing door opened directly into the narrowest part of the L-shaped kitchen. One wall was peppered with nails on which overalls, coats, and other outdoor work clothes hung. The odour of working men clung to their seams. A wooden, metal-lined leaky sink and a drain board were attached to the opposite wall. On the drain board was a bucket of drinking water, and everyone drank from the same tin dipper. One well-worn toothbrush was stuck between the rough boards above the sink. It belonged to my grandmother. A toothbrush was a luxury, and neither my sister nor I had one. Instead, we each dipped a wet finger in baking soda and salt and rubbed it over our teeth and gums. One day I sneaked Grammie's toothbrush from the crevice and tested it out. I expected something that smelled minty like the toothpowder my father used to brush his dentures, but it had a strange musty taste and smell that assaulted my senses and lingered on my tongue.

A huge old Peacock wood stove dominated the kitchen. It was a demanding beast that chewed up wood hourly to provide heat in the

Rose-Marie (right, age 7) and her sister Sandra (left)
dressed up for Sunday school, 1948

winter and a surface on which to cook all year long. Pickles and jams simmered in pots on the surface; maple sap miraculously became syrup and sugar. Mom baked bread, pies, cakes, puddings, and other sweets daily. The kitchen, with the old drop-leaf table, was the hub of the house. In the winter, it was the centre of all activities for which heat and light were needed. An oil lamp sat in the middle of the table, and my father claimed the best circle of light as his own.

No one read in the evenings except my father and his eldest brother, Uncle Hallie. We children studied for school or worked to produce something for the house. My uncle retired to his room to smoke his corncob pipe and read Reader's Digest condensed books. He kept his door closed. Reading, except for reading the Bible, was regarded as a waste of time by my mother, who worked every waking minute of her life. This restriction made us want to read at every opportunity. I once sneaked a lamp under the wool puff to finish reading a story in my *Jack and Jill* magazine that had been interrupted by a strictly enforced bedtime. Luckily, the bedding snuffed out the lamp, but not before my mother smelled the distinctive odour of scorched cloth and doused the puff in the chamber pot. I had just added another task to my mother's workday that started at 6:00 A.M. and ended at 10:00 P.M. She swatted me with a kindling stick so hard that my bottom bore stripes—a deterrent against any similar future antics.

Someone had cut a round hole in the ceiling above the stove. This allowed some heat to fight with the cold in the "rough part," an unfinished space above the kitchen. The hole was covered once the kids went to bed in order to maintain some heat in the kitchen where my grandmother darned, spun, and knitted and my mother ironed, crocheted, hooked, and quilted. The rough part was our bedroom—a sanctuary for me and a sister not quite two years my senior. The ridge beam of our bedroom was a scant six feet at its peak, while the sides of the roof slanted steeply to the outer edges of the floor. It could have been cozy, but it had never been finished, and nails protruded through the roof. We often scraped our heads on them when we sat up in the dark without thinking. The rough part also doubled as a storage area for old trunks. Nails driven into the wood served as hangers for one Sunday dress and an old plaid housecoat each. After we butchered in the fall, the room was redolent with the aroma of home-cured bacon, smoked hams, home-made puddings, and sausages that were hung from the beams to dry, their skins puckering like old people's skin.

I did a lot of dreaming under that rough shelter. On bitterly cold winter nights when the nails became encrusted with frost, they gleamed in the moonlight and became a thousand stars. On those nights, I was a dreamer. When the snow thawed, or when it rained, the stars dripped rusty water onto our bed. My dream world collapsed.

My sister and I slept on a straw tick that we stuffed to capacity after the wheat was harvested. The first few nights on a newly filled straw tick that was higher than my head proved a challenge. Once I had scaled its cliff-like sides, I sank into its welcoming warmth. I spread my arms and imagined myself an angel floating on a cloud. The straw felt that soft. Later, bits of straw worked their way though the ticking and pricked our skin. We stayed cozy under a homemade bedcover fashioned from sheep's wool enclosed in flannelette, tied with bits of yarn, and encased in bleached flour bags. As winter progressed and the tick moulded to the shapes of our bodies, we fought over who was on whose side of the bed. The webbing on the bed frame sagged, so we had no choice but to roll into a heap and stay warm through bodily contact. By the time morning arrived, the temperature in our room equalled that of the outdoors. The water in the washbasin froze; frost formed on our iron bedstead. I once tried to remove a piece of spruce gum from the metal headboard by licking it free. My mother rescued my tongue by pouring hot water over it—a lesson I did not need to have repeated. I remember the spanking that followed—for lying. I had pretended to spit the offending gum in the stove before going to bed.

Each of the bedrooms had a chamber pot. My mother used a chamber pail with a cover—a luxury! Every morning we emptied the chamber pots into the bucket and dumped the contents into the outside toilet. Our outhouse was a two-holer and, yes, we went there together, especially at night. It was located a considerable distance from the house for very good reasons, but it was a scary place for a child to go alone. It was very dark in the country at night, and bone chillingly cold in winter. The boards that formed the toilet seat attracted dampness created by the decomposition of the matter below. The holes became rimmed with frost. I used to sit on my mittens until the frost melted. In summer, there were snakes along the path to the outhouse, and the interior attracted rodents, spiders, flies, maggots, and other vermin.

Our outhouse had no toilet tissue. We used an old Eaton's catalogue (newspaper ink comes off on your skin). We tore off a page and rubbed it between our hands in an attempt to soften it. My mother called it "wraddling it up." Tacked to the wall was an old calendar picture of a black bear with a fish in its paws standing on a rock in the middle of a bubbling stream. A five-gallon bucket full of lime and an empty orange-and-blue tobacco can stood in the corner. After each visit, we sprinkled lime over the latest deposit. This was especially vital in the summertime.

Some of our neighbours dug deep holes, put their toilets on runners, and moved them to a new hand-dug pit when each hole filled up. My father, however, built a coffin-shaped drawer on skids and put it under the toilet seat. Once the box was full, he hitched our old mare to the end of the box and hauled the load up over the hill to the pasture where he dug a trench and buried the malodorous sludge—an onerous task.

My father rose at 5:00 A.M. all year round. In the winter, he made a fire in the kitchen stove and another in the box stove where flames flickered through the isinglass window in its front door. The box stove was in the parlour—a room, together with a spare bedroom next to it, that was reserved for our rich relatives who visited once a year. The hand-crocheted lace doilies in these rooms remained spotlessly white.

My mother served breakfast promptly at seven o'clock each morning when my father returned from his barn chores. He was a stickler for being on time. My morning meal usually consisted of oatmeal porridge with brown sugar and full cream. My father and the occasional hired man ate plates stacked with baked beans, fried potatoes, fried smoked ham or bacon, and toast slathered in home-made butter. When Mom fried bacon, she reheated the bacon fat and added molasses to create syrup she called Yankee butter. The men dipped their bread in this fat-laden sugary mixture and washed it down with mugs of boiled black tea. Dessert followed, usually a large slice of homemade pie or doughnuts washed down with whole, raw milk.

My father eschewed anything not produced by the farm or the sea. He often compared farming with the factory work he had done in Halifax and in the States. His list of good reasons to be a farmer was endless: "Farming is not a nine-to-five job." "The farmer is his own boss." "There is something inexplicable about the feeling of working the earth with bare hands." "Fresh air. Ah, fresh air," he would say, standing up from his weeding to take a deep appreciative breath that made the bib on his overalls expand so he looked like a proud rooster crowing at dawn.

As a child, I did not share my father's love of all things rural. Fine for my father, he was my boss. What I saw was that we had to be home to tend the animals. While other children played, I worked: shovelling manure; milking cows; killing, plucking, and eviscerating chickens; spreading DDT on crops with my bare hands; raking whole fields of hay in the hot sun; planting and weeding long rows of vegetables; and spending hours picking tiny wild berries.

We didn't have any money, unless you count the nickel a week that my mother gave me to buy an orange at the local store. We drooled over the penny candies, the chocolate bars, the soda pop—the largesse we could not afford. I did not see the glory in country living although I had nothing with which to compare it, and everyone in the community lived in much the same way. We were probably poor, but no one except our rich American cousins ever told us we were.

Whatever the season, I worked mainly with my father. We owned a small mixed farm, so there were various animals that needed attention. My father, of necessity, ensured that work got done. Our main source of income was derived from farm produce. We delivered eggs and milk to a few neighbours; sold turnips, cabbages, and potatoes; sent cream to the dairy; cut firewood and logs in winter; and raised animals for slaughter.

Spring chores involved the birthing, shearing, and dipping of sheep. In the spring, when a lamb was born too early or too weak to suckle, it was wrapped in a potato sack and warmed on the oven door until it was able to drink from a bottle and nipple. This is one of my fondest memories: the oven, the warmth and softness of the baby lambs as we held them to drink, their appreciative nudges when they were sated with warm milk.

Adult sheep were penned and then caught individually so their thick, winter-dirty fleeces could be shorn and washed in preparation for carding and spinning. The sheared wool formed a soft, cloud-like mountain, and the exposed sheep reminded me of the ruler in *The Emperor's New Clothes*. The sheep were dipped into a vat of purple liquid to kill vermin. Purple sheep! You can imagine how exciting this was to a small child. Later, I helped my mother and my grandmother pick the dried manure and dirt from the wool, hand wash it, and then spread it to dry on an old canvas army tent. After the wool was dry, my sister and I lay on it in the sun, revelling in the distinctive odour of sheep's wool and hot canvas.

We obtained water from the well just up the hill from the barn. We lowered a twelve-quart bucket on a pole with a spike in the end to prevent the pail from slipping into the well. We drew and carried water to satisfy the needs of two draft horses, a dozen cows, six calves, five pigs, two dozen hens, and a small flock of sheep. The pigs were housed in the manure shed, while the sheep pen and hen house were separate. There was no way to avoid entering the hen house in the morning, and I couldn't hold my breath long enough to feed and water hens and collect eggs without inhaling the acrid smell of ammonia.

My chores included milking the cows by hand, cleaning the manure gutters, and feeding and bedding down the animals. I was eight years old when I milked my first cow. I learned to wash the teats with warm water and massage the cow's udder so she would release the milk. My father insisted that laying my head against the cow's flank made her more content and thus easier to milk. The barn odour clung to my clothes, a noxious miasma that followed me about, unbeknownst to me, until my clothes were washed each Monday. My father made milking into a game by teaching me how to milk fast enough to create foam in the bucket, after which I was allowed to squirt streams of milk into the mouths of expectant barn cats. This made doing chores before breakfast a bit more enticing.

I anticipated the return of spring with some reservations. All field work was labour intensive. Everything was done bare-handed, which inevitably produced painful blisters that had no chance to heal in the heat of the season. My father never planted in moderation. We helped him plant acres of potatoes and turnips, dozens of tomato seedlings, row after interminable long row of peas, beans, and corn. Once the young plants emerged, there was thinning, hoeing, and hilling to do.

My sister and I were sent to the turnip patch with a lunch bucket and a glass jug of vinegar drink. My mother put a cup of sugar and a cup of cider vinegar in this gallon jug of water; we suspended it in the river to keep it cool until lunchtime. At noon Mom rang the bell. We cooled our feet in the river and consumed our lunch, then continued thinning turnips using a stick my father had given us as a spacer. The rows seemed endless—the end of a row not even visible when we stood on tiptoe. Each plant had to be watered from the nearby river. Daddy promised us each a nickel a row if the end product met with his expectations. I don't recall getting any nickels.

We cut hay early in the morning, often with a hand scythe. The swaths lay drying until after lunch when they were turned and dried. The next morning the hay was turned again, then stooked in the early afternoon in readiness for loading it on the wagon later. Many nights, we hauled loads of hay off the intervals by the light of the moon and worked in the hayloft in the diffused glow cast by an oil lantern.

One of the most enjoyable midwinter jobs was the stocking of the ice house. Our ability to keep fresh food from spoiling in the warmer weather depended on our success in getting good ice. When the ice in the lake was at least a foot thick, we sawed out manageable-sized chunks. These were placed on the stone drag or sleigh and hauled home by our team of horses to the lean-to where blocks were laid in rows with military precision. We packed the spaces between them with sawdust. On a sunny day, the blocks shone like crystal, creating silvery worlds—ice palaces housing princesses, unicorns, and fairies.

In many ways, my father regarded me as a son. At about age seven, under the tutelage of Uncle Hallie, I was allowed to split kindling on the chopping block in the yard to start the morning fire. From the time I was eight, I stood on a stool to harness the horses, teamed them in the cultivator, the plough, and in all the equipment that had to do with haymaking. Traditionally, these tasks were done by males. I worked like a man, but I was still expected to behave like a girl.

I delivered a litter of pigs when I was ten years old and happened upon a farrowing sow during my daily barn chores. My father arrived as I was placing the last of the dozen slippery piglets safely away from the labouring sow. I received no thanks, but was banished to the house as though I had done something wrong. Girls were not allowed near anything that had to do with breeding or birthing, while boys were encouraged to be present. Boys, even those who had no sisters, did absolutely no housework.

Indoors, we pulped turnips, kept the woodboxes filled and the copper boiler heated on the stove for our weekly baths. All inner garments were changed on Saturday night after our weekly baths so we had clean clothing for Sunday school and church. My sister and I were scrubbed first, in a washtub in front of the kitchen stove while my father was in the barn. Then my mother used the same water and my father bathed last. (We know because we sneaked a peek down the hole above the kitchen stove!)

Mom scrubbed all the dirty wash on a scrubbing board every Monday morning using Sunlight or homemade lye soap. She hung the wash on an outside line regardless of the weather, and we brought it in to finish drying on a rack beside the stove. My thumbs became numb with cold when I freed the clothing from the metal line. I was amused as I watched my father's long underwear morph from a huge snowman into a pile of fabric at my feet in the heat of the kitchen.

In the winter, we wore undershirts and buttoned waists with long garters attached to lisle or wool stockings (no slacks for girls!). Everything itched. Ubiquitous navy fleece-lined bloomers with knee-hugging elasticized bottoms kept our thighs warm. Knitted socks were inserted in rubber boots with a layer of newspaper wrapped around the socks on really frigid days for extra insulation. I remember always being cold and wet when working or playing outside in the winter. Wool is warm, but it is neither windproof nor waterproof. When we came home from a day outside in the snow we stuck our feet, wet wool socks still on, into the oven. The smell of scorched wool often resulted in a reprimand from our grandmother, who knitted and darned the socks. The smell of drying wool was synonymous with winter.

We dug tunnels in the snow, built forts to protect us during snowball fights, and coasted downhill on pieces of old linoleum or on bobsleds. On cold wintry evenings we played cards, checkers, reassembled our one jigsaw puzzle, and played crokinole on a homemade board with Uncle Hallie and Grammie. My sister and I shared a colouring book and one package of eight crayons. We amused ourselves by cutting paper strips from an old Eaton's catalogue. We created the outline of a house and filled the rooms with furniture and people from the catalogue. One year an aunt sent us a book of paper dolls that actually stood up.

In summer we swam in the river, played ball, played house in the stone walls that separated the properties, hid in lumber piles, and rode our rickety bikes. Sometimes we played hide-and-go-seek in the cellar among the barrels of apples, salt pork, sauerkraut, pickled beans and cucumbers, meat and herring preserved in salt brine, bins of vegetables, and cupboards filled with preserved fruit and pickles, all the preserves put up by my overworked mother.

Our community of less than two hundred souls was close knit. We often met at the school for old-fashioned eight-square dances, pie sales, and community suppers. We also congregated in neighbours' kitchens to make fudge, decorate Easter baskets, or pull taffy. We celebrated births at community baby showers, and we mourned deaths at community funerals. Our church tolled the bell when a community member died, once for each year the person had lived. My grandmother died in her eighties. As a small child, I thought the mournful tolling would never end.

School was both a respite from work and a place to meet our friends. In our one-room school, the benches and desks were bolted to the floor, we wrote on slate boards, and the strap was displayed prominently on the teacher's desk. In a woodshed attached to the school, strappings were administered to those who broke the rigid rules. (Mine were for talking, passing notes, tying shoelaces to desks, dropping my pencil three times, turning around in my seat during a lesson, and putting someone's braid in an inkwell). We recited lessons by rote, competed in a weekly spelling bee, were promoted once the work for a grade was successfully completed twice, performed in the yearly Christmas concert, and took daily halibut-liver capsules. In the winter we were allowed to stay at school for lunch. This often consisted of salt fatback between slabs of homemade bread spread with blackstrap molasses. On Arbor Day we scrubbed the entire school, planted a tree, and were treated to a picnic and games in the afternoon. The work ethic instilled at home was strictly reinforced, but we had our share of fun, too.

As farm kids, we were different in many ways from kids who grew up in urban areas. Our distinctive accents and worn hand-me-down clothing made us open to ridicule. We worked hard just to survive.

I was resourceful. I bought a piglet, named her Betsy, fed her, and cared for her from birth. My father slaughtered her so I could earn enough money to buy a bicycle. I cried while helping scrape the carcass, and I cried for days while my mother tried to explain the reality of raising animals for slaughter. Experiences like this one, however distasteful and difficult at the time, taught me to be adaptable, to have a deep respect for manual labour, to respect the forces of nature, and to always do whatever job I attempted to the best of my ability. In retrospect, I must admit that I learned some valuable skills under the tutelage of a hard taskmaster.

Our family was a paternalistic one. My father dictated what, when, and how things were done. I would have done anything to win his approval. I once scrubbed the stable floor so he would praise me for a job done well enough to suit him. He did, so I scrubbed it weekly from then on. This need to please meant I did not develop into a person who made good, informed choices about relationships or finances.

Somehow, from my father, a gregarious man away from home, I did learn an enjoyment of simple pleasures and an ability to get along with people of all ages and from all walks of life. I am grateful that I had the opportunity to live in a community where there were no locked doors, where everyone knew my name, and where bare feet were the norm. At heart, I will always be a farm kid. But inside that kid there was always a dreamer. I craved romance that contradicted my father's strictness. I wanted time to play. I wanted to explore the world I read about in the books at school, wear clothes like the ones in the Eaton's catalogue, meet people outside the community, cook what I liked, have money of my own. I wanted to be free to make my own choices. I wanted a different life.

I developed a love-hate relationship with farming. I grew to hate the restrictions placed on me by a moody father who demanded perfection without praise, dependent animals, the vagaries of the weather, and the uncertainty of what might be cancelled to accommodate the needs of the farm. I accepted my role as a farmhand until I was sixteen. Then I left home.

That dreamer became an optimistic realist, an overachiever with the need to have a challenged mind and busy hands, a writer of poems and a lover of drama, art, dancing, and music.

I know why I embraced modern conveniences, why I have a closet full of clothes, why I love homemade food, why I am known as a diligent worker with myriad practical ideas who can be relied on when the going gets tough. I also know why I did not become a farmer or, worse still, a farmer's wife.

I Am...a Farmer

Marianne Stamm

OCCUPATION: _____. THE line from the hotel guest registration stares at me, accusingly. I falter. Every other time I have proudly penned *Farmer*. What do I write now? I've always been a farmer. I've been farming since I was a little girl helping pick up apples for cider in Switzerland. I've been farming since I was a six-year-old steering a tractor on a pioneer farm in northern British Columbia, too small to reach the clutch. My father had to jump up and stop the tractor for me.

Some might say I wasn't really a farmer—I was just a farmer's daughter. They don't understand. A teacher's daughter doesn't go to school with her mother and help teach. She isn't responsible to help make sure the school runs smoothly. A farmer's daughter is. We knew from the time we were small that our help was essential to the success of the farm. Our parents needed us to pick roots, feed calves, and help with haying. If I didn't take care of my younger siblings at the edge of the field, playing with them in the bush while my parents worked, they wouldn't have been able to get the work done. We children were part of the farm. We were farmers.

The eldest of seven children, I was born in Switzerland in 1958, on a typical mixed farm of twenty-five acres near Lake Constance. Like most Swiss farms then and now, ours was home to several generations. We (my parents and, eventually, four girls) shared the kitchen and meals with my

Marianne (far left) with her father and sisters Barbara, Maya,
and Rosette (left to right) on their pioneer farm, 1964

aunt and uncle. Mom's sister was married to Dad's brother, and they had
two daughters. The big farmhouse also included a small apartment for
my grandparents and my father's youngest brother, Sami, who was only
eight years older than I was. Sami was like an older brother to me. It was
Sami who showed me how to escape the narrow confines of my playpen.
My mother was not impressed. Much of the work in field and orchard was
done manually then, and the women were glad to know their children
were safe in the playpen at the edge of the field.

Twenty dairy cows supplied most of the income, supplemented by
some seed wheat and potatoes. What I remember most about the farm
was the big orchard. The Thurgau area of Switzerland is well known for
its orchards, supplying much of Switzerland's grocery stores with apples,
pears, and fruit juice. Apple harvest was always a joyous time, when
relatives would come to help, voices calling back and forth between the
trees. They shared stories and news while sipping steaming cups of coffee,
sitting on empty crates during breaks. There was one job even the very
littlest of children could help with. Some apple trees, special varieties, were

I Am…a Farmer

shaken until all the apples lay on the ground. These were picked up, crated, and sold for cider and juice. The whole family gathered under the trees, filling the baskets with the aromatic fruit, chatting and joking together. It was my first real job on the farm.

It was always clear to my father and his brother that one of them would eventually have to leave—the farm could not support both of them with their growing families. Tradition had it that the younger brother would inherit the farm. My father was the oldest. He had always dreamed of big things—vast fields and a large dairy herd. His brother had been in northern British Columbia, Canada, for a year, working for a Swiss farmer there. He'd come back telling of the wide expanse of land in the Peace Country. So it was that in the spring of 1963, with three girls, an eight-month-old baby, and the equivalent of seven thousand Canadian dollars, our family set sail across the ocean for Canada. I always marvel at the courage of my parents. They spoke no English and had never been to Canada. They were breaking all ties for good as everything they had was put into the new venture. Certain we had seen grandparents, family, and friends for the last time, we gathered them together at the train station in Weinfelden to say goodbye. In the bustle and emotion of leaving, my parents almost forgot my little sister, Rose, in her bassinet beside the train. Someone passed her through the train window at the last moment!

My father would have loved to buy a dairy farm in the Fraser Valley, the dairy centre of British Columbia. The little money he had brought with him was not enough to buy land there, though. So he went to the Peace Country, where his brother had worked, and eventually bought a farm in Cecil Lake, about thirty kilometres east of Fort St. John. This was still pioneer country and homestead land. Most of the country was bush. We arrived there late in the fall of 1963. There was a tiny house, no running water, and an outdoor biffy. It was not an easy transition, especially for my mother. But she appreciated one thing—it was her own house. She didn't have to answer to her mother-in-law or share the kitchen with her sister.

Those were hard years, in many ways—not just for our family, but for most of the families who had come to wrestle a farm out of the wilderness. I was six years old when we came to Cecil Lake. My sister Helen, the fifth girl, was born during the bitter cold of February during that first winter in

Canada. Not even in grade one yet, I cooked the *Rösti* (Swiss hash browns, a traditional farm breakfast in Switzerland) on the wood stove while Mom was in the hospital and Dad was milking our two cows by hand. This was a family farm, meaning that each family member was necessary in making it work.

Land was cleared, little by little. We spent summers picking roots. It was hot, dusty, tedious work, especially for little girls who wanted to play. The community store sold a special sort of hard red raspberry candies that dissolved on our tongues in delicious flavour. They were an effective bribe. We played, too—our parents were not tyrants. We spent many hours in the bush at the side of the field building moss forts under the spreading branches of the spruce trees. My mother appreciated my babysitting the younger girls so she could continue working.

Once land was seeded into grass, it meant that summers were spent haying. At nine years old, I became the chief tractor driver. I watched longingly as the neighbour children biked by on their way to baseball practice. There was no question of my going. I was needed for the baling. Daydreaming was my substitute for baseball, and I learned to see the beauty around me. Driving the old Fordson tractor, I had plenty of time to marvel in awe at evening skies flaming with fire. More than once I watched a spectacular sunset and missed the turn at the edge of the field until I heard a shout from my father or a hired hand, piling the bales onto the wagon behind the baler.

Once, when my parents and I were baling, my mother called out to me to stop the tractor. The ground was covered in red—wild strawberries— and Mom couldn't bear to drive by them. She figured if God had let them grow that profusely, it was the least we could do to stop and pick them. So there we were, the three of us on our hands and knees feasting on the distinctive warm sweet flavour of wild berries.

My mother was an avid berry picker, and we spent many hot summer afternoons in some wild berry patch. In the spring, on the way to town (Fort St. John), we would watch for the white blooms of the saskatoons in the Beatton River hills, wondering if the berries would be good that year. I loved to roam the hills, searching for bushes hanging heavy with bunches of dark sweet berries. Our pails full, our mouths stained a delicious purple, we would return home to the job of canning. We all took pride in seeing

I Am…a Farmer

the shelves in the cellar fill up with the jars of our labour—golden peaches beside dark blue saskatoons, green beans, and cherries. On July days we scrambled along the steep banks of the Kiskatinaw River for raspberries, getting scratched by the brambles, stumbling over protruding roots and old logs hunting for the crimson bounty.

On Labour Day, we often piled into the family truck and drove two hours to Milligan Creek to pick wild blueberries. Even my father came along! He joked about his big hands mashing the berries, grinning merrily at his girls. Mom packed a big picnic lunch of homemade bread and cheese, making sure she didn't forget the pot of coffee with lots of cream and sugar. I scavenged for the best spots, where the dusky berries covered the ground, often offset by the brilliant dark red of spicy cranberries, the slight risk of bears nearby heightening the keen sense of adventure. Each of us had a tin juice can to pick into and by evening we would fill two or three of those old eight-gallon metal cream cans.

Our mother often walked with us, on Sunday afternoons, through the bush close to our home. In spring, we would delight in the delicate green of new leaves of aspen poplar and birch. Later the spruce trees would sprout new shoots at the end of their prickly branches. When Mom saw that, she would call her crew together, and we would all head out to the bush to pick the new shoots for her spruce juice. The shoots had to be picked while still in bud, before they were fully opened. Mom would then put them in a big pot, cover them with water, and cook them for about twenty minutes. Then she filtered the liquid. For every two cups of liquid, she added one cup of sugar, cooked the mixture up again, and poured it into hot sterilized jars to seal. Diluted with water, it made for a refreshing summer drink.

On our walks, Mom would point out the wildflowers—nodding bluebells, bright yellow arnica, which could be used for a tincture for bruises and swellings, the heady scent of wild roses, Solomon's seal, tiny delicate twin flowers. How excited she was when she found a true orchid in the wild—the dainty fairy slipper. Sometimes we would have contests to see who could notice something extra special—a delicate plant, a unique cone, or a distinctive combination of colours and textures. We carried home bags of mosses, pine cones, lichens, and dried rose hips to craft into pieces of art. Mom could always make something beautiful out of what was growing around us.

The farm expanded, and our responsibilities with it. As we children grew older, we worked where our natural interests took us. My sisters Barb and Rose enjoyed working with animals and spent much of their time in the barn, milking the growing herd of cows or feeding the calves. Maya was happy to stay in the house and help Mom with the cooking and housework. I was the machinery operator, often in the fields or helping with repairs. I took pride in my greasy jeans, as they were proof of my proficiency as a mechanic and operator.

In the fall semester of my last year of high school in Fort St. John, I missed enough days of school helping with the grain harvest that it merited a remark on my report card: "Marianne could have done better if she had been in school more." I was upset with the teacher. Didn't he know that a crop was more important than a mark on a report card? I remember that fall—the long hours, the scratch of barley on my skin on hot days, and the pride that filled my heart at being able to help take the harvest in. I remember daydreaming—how I would run the place if something happened to my parents and I had to take over. I was a farmer.

My accounting teacher encouraged me to go to university to study as an accountant. I had the highest marks in the class and won the secretarial award in my final year. But whenever I thought about a career, I couldn't decide what it was I really wanted. There were so many exciting things to do! I felt that if I was a farmer, I could do most of them. University or college didn't entice me then. I didn't really know what direction my life should take.

After finishing high school in Canada, I spent a year in Switzerland. I worked in an office there, set amid beautiful foothills outside of the village of Langenbruck, south of Basel. I was secretary to the European director of a large mission. It was a fulfilling job—until the farming neighbours started making hay. The scent of the drying grass wafted through my open office window. Hoping they might need me, I went over to ask if I could help, but they assured me they were all right. From the edge of the hilly field, I watched the family working together on the steep slopes, hearing their easy banter as they worked. Tears filled my eyes.

I Am…a Farmer

Switzerland was wonderful, but my round trip ticket was expiring, so I went back home. I found an office job in a large lumber mill in Taylor. It, too, was set among beautiful rolling hills along the Peace River. I lived at home and again spent evenings and weekends in the summer helping with the haying or the garden or, later, the harvest.

One day in May I came home from the office to find a handsome young Swiss farmer at the table. He and his brother were travelling through Canada and the USA for two months and had received our address from mutual friends in Switzerland. A week was enough to light the fire of romance. When Robert asked me if I could see myself at his side on a farm in Switzerland, I was happy to say "Yes." Those were the days before cheap telephone rates and email, but he was a faithful letter writer, averaging three a week—enough to win this woman's heart. I couldn't always read his writing, but the "I love you" was clear enough! I followed him to Switzerland that fall, and we were married within the year.

It was quite a transition from the pioneer farm in the Peace Country to an established traditional family farm in the Old Country. The Emmerhof, eighty acres including rented land, was a larger farm by Swiss standards. It was situated on a level rise in the Jura Hills—a low mountain range that runs parallel to the north side of the Alps—along the German border. From my kitchen window I could look out over the Black Forest, and from the deck on a clear evening I could see the famous three peaks of the Swiss mountains Eiger, Moench, and Jungfrau. I never ceased to thrill at the views. It was a mixed farm, growing wheat, barley, canola, corn, and sugar beets, a labour-intensive crop. The barn held around a hundred head of feeder beef, which were bought in twenty-calf lots at three weeks of age and fed to maturity with grain and corn silage.

We lived a mile outside the large village of Schleitheim (only twenty minutes away from the famous Rheinfall). Our nearest neighbour was not even a quarter mile away. I would often chuckle when people asked if I didn't find it lonely so far away from other people. They had no idea where I'd come from!

There were many adjustments to make. The hardest one for me was finding my role on Robert's family farm. I had been an integral part of our family farm, growing into my responsibilities and knowing my worth there. On the Emmerhof it was the same—each individual knew his or her place, found over a lifetime of living together. They had to learn to make room for me, and I to gracefully allow them time to do so. There were cultural adjustments. The Swiss farming community placed great worth on tidiness, both on the farm and in the house. Presentation was important. These are not valued attributes for a pioneer, whose energy goes into building up, battling the elements, and carving out a place.

Gender roles were still firmly entrenched. Women helped on the farm, in the fields, in the barn. But they did not manage, at least not visibly. Farm seminars and conferences were attended by men. It never occurred to me to accompany Robert to them. Women went to workshops on sewing, mending, cooking. I had attended a five-month "domestic sciences" school for farm women before getting married. One of the courses was on Swiss politics, and I was appalled at how little interest most of the young women showed. Their men would tell them how to vote. My social studies courses in Canada had taught me otherwise! Even as I rebelled inwardly at some of these roles, I did not fight them outwardly. It was not done. The rule *"me hets scho immer so gmacht"*—we've always done it this way—was still practised in the rural Switzerland of that day.

In Canada I had mowed hay on a quarter section with a big swather. When I left, the round baler had replaced the old square baler. Now I walked behind a square baler again, on a few acres, pulling a hand rake to scoop up the stray wisps of missed hay into the baler so nothing was wasted. While machinery had replaced much of the manual labour, there were still many jobs to be done by hand. The farms were small, and everything was utilized. The strips of grass around the grain fields were mowed and made into grass silage or hay. Even the grass under the fruit trees in our small orchard was mowed and raked, partly by hand, for silage or hay. Faithfully, most Saturdays, my mother-in-law would sweep the whole paved yard. (That's when the small yard began to feel huge!)

A major challenge was learning to live and work together in close quarters with Robert's family. It was a small, tight farmyard compared to our expansive western Canadian acreages. As an independent Canadian girl, I was lucky enough to have my own house on the farm, newly built for us. Most Swiss farms would have a separate apartment for the young

I Am...a Farmer

couple, but often it was in the same house as the parents. My parents-in-law lived in the old farmhouse, attached to the barn—typical for that area. Robert's youngest sister, Barbara, was still at home then, in high school. On weekends, many of his six siblings came back home from various jobs and schools. They were a close, boisterous family, and my business was their business. The lessons I had learnt at home in Canada about working together as a family became invaluable.

I came to appreciate Robert's family as a treasure for our two boys, Mike and Dan. Having grown up without any extended family, I recognized the powerful influence of loving grandparents, aunts, and uncles in the lives of my children. I was happy with my young husband, Robert, and our growing boys. I was becoming a more equal partner, to be consulted for important decisions. In the labour-intensive times of haying and harvest, and thinning sugar beets by hand, all of us were there together. I was still a farmer.

Fifteen years ago we moved back to Canada. Robert had been on the regional agricultural board in Switzerland. He sensed big changes coming to agriculture in Europe, especially Switzerland, that he recognized would change the face of farming there. (Although many wouldn't believe him, saying those changes would take years to come, the changes came even faster than we had anticipated.)

We decided to immigrate back to my home country. We bought a grain farm 150 kilometres north of Edmonton, Alberta, near the community of Westlock. Those years in Westlock were the height of my farming career. Now it was just Robert and I and our two boys. As a young wife I had left the bigger farms of Canada for the small plots in Switzerland. Now we were back in Canada, in the midst of wide open grain fields waving golden in the evening sun of harvest. I traded the Black Forest and mountains for flat prairie, under a magnificent circle of ever changing skies. We went from eighty acres to eleven hundred. The tractor we used to seed the fields in Switzerland now tilled the garden. We were farming again, but this was different. I had grown up in this country, but I had not been one of the responsible partners. Now I was part of the management team. So much was new to us. We asked so many questions of everyone we met that I wondered they didn't tire of us. That first fall I stopped more than once at the edge of a neighbour's field and rode on the combine with him, pestering him about all those things we weren't sure about—when and how to swath canola, for example. The farming community seemed eager to help us in any way they could, readily supplying information, or a piece of equipment, or a helping hand. Both the community and the local church we began to attend made it easy for us to fit in and find new friends. Our boys came home after the first day of school declaring, "It's awesome, Mom!" We agreed.

That is, *I* agreed. Robert was having second thoughts. Starting on a new farm meant we had to make a host of decisions concerning land, buildings, and machinery. Most of these decisions carried substantial financial consequences, had to be made with a lack of adequate knowledge, and carried considerable risk. The responsibility of it all weighed heavily on Robert. He began to think he had made an awful mistake. We'd bought the farm almost at the end of a downward trend in the Canadian farm economy, but at the time we didn't know that any more than anyone else did. Robert often came home telling me about another farmer who had told him again: "You'll never make money in grain farming." My usually strong confident husband became anxious and depressed. But I had grown up on a pioneer dairy farm, and my father had heard similar words: "You'll never get the quota to be a dairy farmer." I had watched him fight the odds to become successful. Robert and I would do so, too. We did, ending our first year on a positive financial note. Robert's spirits lifted as the grain began to pour into the bins. After that first year, he never looked back.

Robert was responsible for the production end of things, and I took over much of the business management. My school and job training were an advantage now. In Switzerland all grain was brought to strategically placed elevators and sold to the government. There was no marketing involved. In Canada I learned how to sell grain and what puts and calls were. I learned that the weather in Brazil affected us in Westlock, driving canola prices up or down. I taught the grain buyers who phoned that I was the one they wanted to talk to, not my husband. I thrived in my new job. Robert and I made a good team, building up a successful and growing farm. We bought more land and upgraded machinery. During our first summer here, Robert, the boys, and I spent many hot days building bins

I Am…a Farmer

for grain storage. The second summer Mike and Dan groaned when we mentioned bins again, but they were as proud as we were to see the shiny row of new steel.

Some people might say I was a farmer's wife. I was that—I was married to a farmer. Being married to a farmer didn't automatically make me a farmer, though, anymore than being married to a teacher or doctor would make me one myself. Not just the farmer's wife, I was a farmer too. I was one of the only women in the local Grain Marketing Club. Sitting at a table with mostly male farmers, I attended agricultural conferences such as the annual Farm Tech Conference in Edmonton. Other farmers sometimes asked me for my advice about selling their grain, and I was invited to take part on several agricultural boards. I was proud to be a farmer in my own right, proud to write *farmer* as my occupation.

And now it's over. This spring I watched someone else seed our fields. I asked Robert how he felt about that. "I'm glad I don't have to do it," he answered. The stab of pain I felt was more intense. With the onset of spring, the first robins, the tentative ribbons of green quack grass along the country roads, came an ache of not belonging anymore.

But we had agreed together that it was time to move on with our lives. Together we decided that this was a good time to quit active farming and rent out the land. Robert, who is closer to sixty than fifty, feels he would like to do other things while he has the energy. The boys have chosen other careers—Mike is an electronic engineer working in Switzerland, and Dan is studying for a child and youth worker diploma. Neither will be taking over the farm. I, too, had lost some of my passion for the farming game and was excited about new prospects we saw ahead. We have twice spent a month in Zambia, Africa, helping with an irrigation project and would like to return there. I sometimes think of going to university, after all. So many open doors and opportunities lie ahead!

Why, then, do I find it hard sometimes? That early training does not easily leave me. The value of hard work was deeply instilled, at an impressionable age. Now that I spend much of my time writing or travelling, the very roots of my sense of worth are attacked. I was raised to believe that farming the land was a sacred profession. Do I feel deep down that I have betrayed that? Am I less of a worthy person if I am not attached to a piece of land?

I did not stop being a mother, though, when my children left home. And so, I am beginning to see, a farmer does not stop being a farmer when she leaves the land. I am still asked for my thoughts on marketing and management strategies. More than one farmer has asked me to help him with some aspect of business management. We plan to work more intensively with Zambian farmers on agriculture projects. My farming career does not seem to be over yet.

But it is changing, as it has changed so many times. Even when I have had the privilege of choosing it, change is not always easy. It is an opportunity to rethink my values, re-evaluate my sense of worth, and reconsider where I want to go. Maybe one day I will say *Writer* when asked for my occupation. But for now, I defiantly stare back at the line on the hotel registration card and proudly pen *Farmer*.

Going Malting

JANICE ACTON

I T HAD TO be important for my father to listen in on someone else's phone call. There was an unspoken code among the people on our party line that we wouldn't listen in on each other. But people were human and, once in a blue moon, they just couldn't help themselves, like my father during harvest time when the barley test results were coming in.

We were number 5 on party line 82. We knew it was our call when Mrs. Koslowski, the telephone operator, rang us with five long, steady rings. I remember thinking that something unusual must be happening the morning my father got up from the breakfast table and tenderly lifted the telephone receiver after three short rings. He put a finger to his mouth and frowned at us to all keep quiet. My mother, who was cracking egg yolks into a pot, turned into a pillar in front of the stove. My sister and I stared at one another, spoons frozen midway to our mouths. I could hear the clock ticking on the wall and the wind blowing through the lilac bushes outside the kitchen window.

A few seconds later, my father delicately set the receiver back into its cradle. He looked at my mother and announced, "Robertsons have gone malting."

My mother resumed stirring the eggs for her mayonnaise so they wouldn't curdle. "Well, you know they always have good success with their barley. They've got the soil for it."

Janice (age 8) with Scottie in the wheat field, 1956

My mother was a pragmatist. She faced adversity by anchoring herself to the practical, planning tomorrow's meals out of today's leftovers and buying our clothes a size too large so we could grow into them. "Just get on with doing what you can and leave the rest." Years after we had moved to the city, she confessed that she was not as calm as she appeared at the time; she admitted that the uncertainty of farming kept her, as well as my father, tossing with worry long into the night.

She emptied hot water out of waiting masonry jars, then filled them with steaming lemony mayonnaise from the double boiler. To nobody in particular she said, "Going malting happens once in a blue moon—when you've got the right soil."

My father was unable to accept the news with the same equanimity. First he walked over to the kitchen window and stared out for a few minutes. Then, in one motion, he turned around, grabbed his cap off the hook, and strode out the door. By the time we heard him call out, "I'm going down to Jordie's," the screen door had snapped shut and he was already around the corner of the house.

I ran out after him and managed to jump into the back of our old half-ton truck just as he was grinding it into gear.

Going malting was the biggest bonanza known to the small prairie farmer. No lottery ticket was more jubilantly celebrated than was the pronouncement that one's barley had gone malting. Receiving the premium price from the country's top whiskey malters was like finding the pot of gold at the end of the rainbow. Going malting made all the difference between really making it and barely getting by. It was no coincidence that Johnny Walker, the king of whiskies, was the liquor of choice down at the Men's Parlour in the hotel or at Gage's Garage & Farm Implements when the men pulled out a bottle for a nip on a rainy day.

A few farmers were not as reliant as we were on barley. My uncle, for example, made a handsome profit growing the novelty crops such as soybeans, canola, peas, and mustard seed that were being promoted by the agribusiness titans and the Eastern Commodity Markets. However, my father preferred to take his chances with Mother Nature and the holy trinity of traditional small-farm grain crops: wheat, oats, and barley. He figured, according to the law of averages, if he tried hard and long enough, our barley would eventually go malting.

Part of the farmer's ritual at harvest time was scrambling to send off a sample of his barley to be tested for malting quality. It took a keen eye and a lifetime of experience to recognize the precise moment when barley was its best. The moisture content had to be less than thirty percent, when a fingernail could barely dent the kernel. At the same time, the kernels had to be plump, mature, and uniform in shape and colour, free of smut and stains and blotches. When the barley reached this stage, the farmer rushed his sample into town and sent it by train to Winnipeg. Then he waited. And waited. Fingers crossed. Hoping the tests would come back positive. Hoping there would be no early frost or rain to loosen the hulls from the kernels in the field if the results did come back positive. The lab results were telegraphed back to the railway agent in town, who then phoned the lucky farmers whose barley had gone malting.

Waiting for that hoped-for call made everyone antsy. The men went through the motions of harvesting their other crops, but their minds were always on the call. Farm wives shelled buckets of peas and canned dozens of jars of pickles and jams, but never strayed out of range of the phone.

Once one farmer received the news, it wasn't long before others also learned if they had gone malting. So, when my father learned that morning that our neighbours, the Robertsons, several miles to the west of us, had gone malting, he became restless and was eager to know if others had received the call. Besides, the morning dew made the swath too wet to combine. If he started harvesting when it was this damp, the straw would bung up the rotors, and he'd spend the rest of the day untangling the mess and running back and forth to town to buy repair parts for the combine. So he figured he might as well go to Jordie's. And I never missed an opportunity to go to the Cotters because David, the youngest of their four boys, was my best friend.

Once we got to Jordie's, my father didn't bring up the topic of barley right away. For what seemed forever, he and Jordie leaned against the truck, crushed handfuls of wheat heads in their calloused palms, popped a few kernels in their mouths, and talked about crop yields and which fields in the district looked best. After that, they each put a foot up on the bumper and got into the weather. They speculated that we might get another bearcat of a winter like the one in '47 when the trains didn't run for ten days. They talked about unpredictable blustery days, cold grips, smeary frost, squalls, lulls, warming trends, foul stuff, and barometer readings gone haywire. Jordie shook his head and laughed about the weather being a crapshoot with no halfway in between: "It either comes in piles, or else it's nothin."

When that topic was exhausted, my father finally got around to asking the burning question. He raised it casually, almost as an afterthought.

"Did you go malting?" He looked down at the dust and kicked a loose stone.

Jordie's answer was as predictable as the return of the red-winged blackbird each spring. He inhaled. "Yup." Then, as if this were the least important thing in the world, he picked a fleck of tobacco off his tongue with his nicotine-stained fingers and spit on the ground. For Jordie, going malting was no big deal. Going malting would no doubt translate, once again, into the purchase of yet another state-of-the-art piece of equipment.

Jordie was known for having the newest and the biggest of everything. One year it was a Massey-Ferguson tractor with a heated cab. Another year it was a two-ton truck. Another year it was a twelve-passenger Bombardier that rode over snowbanks smooth as a limousine. Another time it was a robin's egg-blue Dodge that sported fins like those on the Batmobile. Because David was my best friend, I could ride in the front seat of whatever Jordie bought. But just once, I wished my father could be the one to buy something that nobody else had.

I resented the unfairness of a world in which Jordie's barley consistently went malting, but ours—just across the barbed-wire fence—never did. Through some act of God or fluke of land surveying, the soil consistency changed at the top of the hill just south of the fence, about a hundred yards into Jordie's field. Some years we could actually see a demarcation line running through the barley where the quality abruptly shifted from the average growth on our side of the fence to the luxurious four-foot stands with graceful whiskered heads hanging heavy and swaying in the wind on Jordie's side.

I wondered what kind of fickle and mean-spirited God would, year after year, render this kind of unfair judgment? I resented putting on a dress every Sunday and trudging off to sit in a cold varnished pew. Going to church seemed to be a futile exercise since God still thumbed His nose at us at malting time.

———◆———

My father was a dreamer. He felt the land in his heart and lived its vagaries in his soul. He knew that farming was one part science and three parts fate. He said you had to be either crazy or a poet to contend with the gods of farming, with all their irrationality, unpredictability, and quirky contradictions.

When he confronted something that didn't turn out the way he'd hoped, my father would mutter, "We look before and after and pine for what is not." My father came by this philosophical penchant legitimately. His ancestors came from the same stock as Robbie Burns. His grandparents held the dubious distinction of going bankrupt on the same tenant farm in Scotland as the great bard himself. From this inherited wisdom, my father divined his understanding of farming's inevitable frustrations, discouragement, and hope. He always had that hope—eternal hope—although there were days when I looked into my father's eyes and saw its pilot light flickering against the mighty odds.

My father's dreams were never grandiose or unrealistic, aside perhaps from his dream of going to Hawaii or his notion of renovating the barn for us to live in because it was better built than our small stucco house. His dreams, along with his grease-stained overalls, were the garments he donned every morning. They were woven into the simple pleasures he enjoyed every day: walking to the barn through the fox grass, spending a rainy day in the shop building a birdhouse, bringing home a handful of cowslips found among the tangled grasses, searching for Indian arrowheads in the freshly ploughed fields, and carving whistles from a willow branch in the springtime. My father's dreams shielded his hopes against the cold irrefutable limitations of our stony soil. They motivated him to keep struggling and fuelled his ongoing attempts to convince my mother that, despite everything, we really did live the good life.

For my father, farming was more than the physical act of cultivating land and harvesting crops. It represented an ideal way of life and nourished his love of freedom. When the first echoes of war reached the prairies, it was as if the German bayonets were pointed directly at his breast, and an anti-fascist sentiment rose up from deep within him. When he enlisted, it was not for loyalty to Britain but to preserve the kind of freedom and independence he saw embodied in the farming life that he so loved. In the big scheme of things, freedom meant that someday the CCF might be given a crack at forming the government. Locally, it meant having the choice of shopping at the Co-op store and lumberyard or at the privately run Red and White grocery. It meant being able to sell our grain to the Wheat Pool instead of the Cargill monopoly.

Admittedly, his signing up for the Air Force was not entirely driven by idealism. Like thousands of other farm boys, he knew that putting on a uniform would earn him a regular, albeit small, income. This, plus the modest salary my mother hoped to receive as a newly graduated nurse, made it possible for my mother and father to marry in the early years of the war.

Following the war, my father yearned to return to the farm, and his hopes were high. He believed the Canadian prairies, which had fed the

Allies throughout the war, would continue to be the breadbasket of the world. He envisioned eggs and butter and bread flowing from small farms, ensuring a new era of prosperity for the whole nation. My father reckoned that since his parents had managed to make a modest living on the farm, our chances would be even better, given the new rust-resistant varieties of wheat and modern farming techniques.

However, it took time for the engines of industry to retool and the conveniences of modern life to trickle down to our part of rural Saskatchewan. By the early fifties, our town and city relatives who enjoyed dial telephones, flush toilets, electric appliances, and plastic wrap found us still driving to a one-room schoolhouse by horse cart, hauling our drinking water from town in large creamery cans, canning acres of vegetables, and melting snow to wash clothes. In fact, there was little to distinguish the early post-war years on our farm from the thirty-five previous years when my grandparents lived on it.

In his quest to grow more robust crops, my father followed the agricultural husbandry practices promoted by the Department of Agriculture's brochures. He read the *Western Producer* and listened to the CBC's noontime *Farm Radio* broadcasts. He drained sloughs and bulldozed stands of poplar and willow to expand acreage. In the spring, he sprayed the crops with DDT, and in the fall, he burned the stubble, leaving black scars in the fields.

By the mid-fifties, he was discouraged to find that the yield of wheat was little better than it had been during his father's harvests. Every spring my father found himself, with other scuff-booted farmers, sitting in the bank manager's marble-and-brass waiting room, cap in his fidgeting hands, waiting to negotiate a loan for the next season's seed and fertilizer. Each year the loan was successfully arranged, but his dreams proved to be short-lived and elusive. At the end of each year, there was inevitably just enough to get by. Just enough to pay down a bit of the debt. Just enough to buy a second-hand cultivator. Just enough to purchase a new set of clothes and shoes before we started school. Occasionally there was enough for a few days of camping at Katepwa Lake.

And so, year after year, we sank a little deeper into a pattern of economically diminishing returns and slid imperceptibly into a state of poverty made palatable only because it was a condition shared by so many. So many factors were beyond our control. Escalating fuel costs. Ever-increasing taxes. Higher interest rates. An unpredictable Crow Rate. A back-and-forth curse of first, too-dry, and then, too-wet, years. Despite my father's heroic efforts our land gradually joined league with market forces; crop yields were insufficient to keep up with rising costs.

My father, like Faust, was prepared to give his very soul for the beauty and perfection he believed was possible on the farm. But in the end, he never had more than a fleeting glimpse of the harvest he longed for, the bumper crop he believed would unchain us from debt.

◆

While we were at Jordie's that morning, my father kept up his end of the friendly bantering. He never let on that anything was bothering him. When Jordie's wife, Marlene, called us into the house for coffee and buns, my father continued the small talk as if everything were normal. However, I knew something was wrong the moment we got into the truck because he didn't say a word the whole way home. When we got back to our farm, he lingered under the honeysuckle tree, leaning over the fence railing and staring off into the field of swathed barley waiting to be combined. I now understand that he needed time to calculate the repercussions of going another year without a malting crop.

I ran into the house where I found my mother bent over the kitchen table pressing graham cracker crumbs into the bottom of a pie plate. It was one of those wonderful double-header Tuesdays when she made mayonnaise and lemon pie the same day.

"Cotters have gone malting, too, Mom," I breathlessly announced.

My mother accepted this capricious act of fate with her usual combination of practicality and acceptance. "They usually do," she said, wiping her hands with a tea towel. "They've got the right soil for it."

"How come our barley never goes malting?" I asked.

As she had many times before, she patiently explained, "Our land just isn't as good as it is farther south. It's not as heavy. It's not the kind that's good for barley."

"Won't ours ever go malting?" I wailed.

"Maybe," she replied, without commitment. "It does happen once in a blue moon."

———————◆———————

Before bed that night, I sat on the porch waiting for the harvest moon to rise. The wind smelled of clover, and crickets chirruped in the tall brome grass surrounding the two old cotton poplars. Eventually, I saw an iridescent sphere rising behind the poplar bluff at the bottom of the yard. My heart did an excited somersault. Then I watched as the moon crawled above the silhouette of the trees—round, magnificent, and orange.

Part III
Departures

Our Family's Homesteading Days

HABEEB SALLOUM

MY FATHER'S WISH to be a farmer was fulfilled. He was granted by the federal government a quarter section of land as a homestead eighteen miles north of the town of Val Marie. In the meantime, he had not been idle. He had saved a few hundred dollars from peddling, and with this he bought another quarter section of land, a team of horses, a wagon, and a plough. Unlike many other Arab immigrants of the time, my father did not intend to save money, then return to the old country to buy a house or a piece of land. He had decided that Canada was to be his permanent home.

I have often wondered how my parents felt when they reached their empty land. In the old country, they had been used to seeing relatives and friends; now they were alone with not even a neighbour's house in sight. As they looked across the barren land, how they must have longed for their home in the Karoun or even their little shack in Gouvernor, which at that moment must have seemed like a palace. Surely they must have known that homesteading on the unbroken prairie was no easy task.

Nevertheless, in that summer of 1927, my parents were young and ambitious. To begin from nothing must have been an unnerving experience, but there was no turning back. They were pioneers in a land they had chosen and were determined to settle, ready to conquer whatever came their way.

Habeeb with his mother and siblings (left to right): Rose,
Habeeb, Helen, Mother, baby sister Mary, Fred, and Eddie,
outside their home on the homestead in 1930

Their first task was to build a habitable structure before the cold winter winds blew across the land. The previous owner of their quarter section had partially constructed a small framed building. However, he had left before even the outer walls had been completed. This unfinished shell served as a shelter for our family during the hot July and August days, but my father knew he had to do something before the icy winter blasts compelled both man and animal to seek a warm refuge.

Without money, he could not buy the materials he needed, but his background came to his aid. In Syria, people had built their homes from the soil and rock of the countryside, and my father was well-acquainted with their building methods. He had helped many of his relatives and friends erect their homes, and now he put this knowledge to work.

Near the frail structure where we lived, a part of the land was pure clay. With my mother's help, my father mixed clay with straw and water, creating a building mixture known as adobe—a word derived from the Arabic *al-tub*. They filled it into the inner walls and ceiling of the frame

Our Family's Homesteading Days

structure, and when the adobe hardened, the building became a habitable home, comfortable in the extremes of both summer and winter. In later years, the adobe was painted and proved both pleasant to see and highly durable.

At the same time as the house was being finished, my father started to plough the land to ready the soil for the next year's crop—our first harvest, which my father thought would set us on the road to prosperity. However, preparing the soil was no easy task. Not only did it need to be ploughed, but thousands of rocks had to be hand picked from the fields.

Every morning my father would wake my brother and me at 4:00 A.M. and take us to the fields to help remove the many rocks. As tiny tots, we could pick only the very small stones, while my father laboured with the large boulders. We picked stones morning after morning. The task was unending, so that, even as a child, I came to loathe the sight of piled rocks. Around 7:00 A.M., we would return to enjoy a hearty breakfast which my mother always prepared. After the meal my father ploughed the fields while my brother and I helped with the chores around the house. These were pleasant tasks, however, compared to the picking of the stones.

The virgin land being ploughed by my father hosted many wild animals and birds that were to be found on the south Saskatchewan plains. Almost every day when my father returned from the fields, he brought a few prairie chickens or rabbits for our daily meals. There was no problem keeping the extra meat. In summer we put the meat in a pail, then lowered it into the well to just above the water line; in the winter, an outside shed made an excellent refrigerator. Besides the wild partridges and rabbits, we raised chickens and a few sheep and cows that lived off the little grass and bushes that grew in the valleys.

Even though meat was important, it was only one item in our diet. During the spring and summer months, my mother scoured the nearby fields for the roots and edible wild greens—*silq*—known to her during her youth in the old country. In spring and early summer, the tender wild shoots of lamb's quarter or pig weed, sorrel, dandelion, and a host of other prairie greens were part of our daily meals. In the Middle East, many of these weeds were well known, so my parents continued the tradition of using them in their daily cuisine. Our kitchen overflowed with endless dishes made from these tasty and nutritious wild greens. Without question, these greens were responsible, to a great extent, for not one of us children ever needing to see a doctor during our growing years.

In addition to the wild greens, every year my mother had a thriving vegetable garden, which, with my brother's and my help, was watered by hand. From this excellent garden she kept us fed for the whole year. What we did not eat during the summer, she dried or cooked in jars for winter use. Hence, even though money was very scarce, we always ate well.

The excellent crop in 1928 made my parents forget the hardships of their first homesteading year. They planned for a rosy future, but fate did not look kindly on their many dreams. Thereafter, the bountiful years were few and far between.

In 1929 there was a small crop, but nothing to compare with the previous year. The stock market crashed, bringing on the Depression, and, as if to magnify the catastrophe, Mother Nature refused to send the life-giving rains. It would be some years before the grain would grow again.

In no time, the land in that part of southern Saskatchewan became a desert waste. For the next three years, nothing grew, and the soil blew back and forth like the deserts of Arabia. How many times my father and mother must have cursed the day they came to this land where they had thought the streets were paved with gold.

During those years our neighbours, the nearest being three miles away, began to abandon their parched farms, but my father, with an expanding family, could not afford to move away. Besides, the harsh life that was forcing many of the people to leave did not affect us in the same way as it did our neighbours.

Like many Arab immigrants, we were able to survive better than many members of various ethnic groups due to the experience of agrarian, subsistence-level living that had been practised by my parents in their homeland. In the Biqaᶜ Valley, my parents had grown chickpeas and lentils—vegetables that had, through the centuries, adapted to the desert climate. These we now seeded, and every year our garden of chickpeas and lentils thrived, aided by hand-drawn water from our well.

My parents' ancestors in Syria had cultivated tasty chickpeas and lentils for untold centuries. When our family immigrated to Canada, they brought their love for these ancient legumes with them. In the all-encompassing drought of the Depression years when hardly any grains or vegetables grew and people went hungry, we thrived on our dishes of chickpeas and lentils. None of our fellow farmers were familiar with them and we, like other Arab immigrants, kept the knowledge of cultivating the legumes well hidden. Now, when I look back to those years, I think how foolish we were. Instead of acquainting others with these ancient, healthful foods, we were ashamed to mention their very names. In fact, as children, my siblings and I thought our parents were forcing us to eat inferior food.

Although we had enough to eat, clothing was another matter. My mother made our shirts, overalls, and other garments from canvas or flour bags and any used, discarded clothing she could find. Like most Arab immigrants, my parents' desire to survive and try to prosper in a foreign land gave them the impetus to improvise.

For us children there was not much excitement growing up during these years. Going into town (Val Marie) was an event my older brother and I looked forward to with great anticipation. In the period we lived on the homestead, I remember journeying only twice with my father to Val Marie, which appeared to me to be a huge metropolis—a fairyland centre which filled my dreams. The eighteen-mile trip to Val Marie by horse and buggy or sleigh was usually, especially in winter, a two-day journey. With no money for a hotel, we slept overnight with our horses in the livery barn, spreading out bales of hay for our beds.

During the homesteading years our prolific family increased by four, a brother Fuad (Fred), and three sisters, Hilla (Helen), Mariyam (Mary), and Furzliya (Phyllis). With the closest doctor twenty-two miles away in Ponteix, the children were delivered by a neighbour's wife, who had some training as a nurse, assisted by my father.

Births were not the only occasions when a doctor was needed but could not be reached. I remember vividly many a cold winter night with my mother crying in pain, having no medical help to relieve her torment. There is no doubt that these undiagnosed pains—caused, as she found out later, from gallstones—affected her in the coming years. But the pains of childbirth and gallstones were only the visible, physical suffering.

Deep inside she had other torments. During the long winter evenings she would relate to us nostalgic stories about life in Syria. Her eyes would shine as she talked about the orchards and vineyards heavy with grapes that, at that time, I had neither tasted nor seen. She talked of sunny climates and a land full of people. She would reminisce about the village of Karoun, where she had many relatives and friends, comparing it to the homestead, where we had a visitor perhaps once or twice a year. Even as a child, I deeply felt that her life was lonely.

I was nearly eight years old and my brother ten when the first school was built three miles away from our home. We attended it for a year, but by the next summer the majority of the farmers had moved away, and the school was closed.

———◆———

My older brother and I often found circles of stones where, we were told, the Plains Indians pitched their tents. Scattered around them we found a few vestiges of the people who once owned the land—a number of arrowheads and some stone hammers. Growing up in the same manner as all our neighbours' children, we never dreamed that the land we lived on had been taken away from its millennia-old inhabitants, then given free to others brought from the four corners of the Earth. Our digging of what we thought was an Indian grave and our endless search for arrowheads were to us games in the world of fantasy. In our minds, the people who left these remains were not humans like us. They were like the fictitious characters in the tales from the Arabian Nights stories that our mother often related during cold winter evenings.

We must have picked up this outlook from our few playmates at school—no doubt influenced by their parents' thinking. As poor Syrian immigrants with deep feelings of inferiority, we mimicked those we thought were real Canadians. The history of the conquest of the West with its broken treaties and betrayals was never known or discussed in our family circle. Yet, we had inherited the bounty of these unfulfilled promises. No one acknowledged the fact that, like almost all the western pioneers, we were living on stolen land. By the time my parents and other newcomers inherited their lands, it was as if the Plains Indians had never existed.

The improvisations of my parents helped us survive during those barren homesteading years, but my father knew he had to find another place if his family was to have a decent future. The turning point came when he met a fellow Arab émigré in Gouvernor. Albert Hattum, who hailed from a neighbouring village in the Biqa^c Valley, was a farmer who had settled north of Gouvernor. They discussed their lives in the New World, and when my father informed him that he was looking for new land, Hattum told him there was a farm for rent a few miles away. Some weeks later my father rented this farm, and in early March of 1933, our friend came with a team of horses and a wagon to help us move.

A blizzard was blowing as we loaded our possessions in four wagons, getting them ready for the next morning when we planned to make the thirty-mile trip to the new land. My father, our friend, my elder brother, and I each drove a wagon on that cold, blustery day. I still remember the biting winds cutting through the blanket wrapped around me as our friend, Hattum, from the wagon behind spurred me on with encouraging words: "Son, you are a man now. Take courage! The trip will end soon." I can still hear his voice as he shouted to my father across two wagon lengths: "That son of yours will be a great man one day. Look at him now driving the horses in this cold without complaint."

It was dark that March evening when we reached our new farm situated between the towns of Gouvernor and Neville. I felt elated, for we had driven through a countryside that was inhabited, unlike the deserted lands around the homestead we had left. On our new farm, there was a house with a barn and ploughed fields. In the coming days, like a general, my father organized us so that each was responsible for his or her own task. His instructions were carried out without hesitation. The house was in rundown condition, but habitable. That spring and summer we cleaned, repaired, painted, and reconstructed many parts of our new home.

To me, this new farm was heaven compared to the old homestead. Now we had neighbours who lived close by, and hardly a day passed when we did not see someone who would come over for a visit or just to chat. For me, even more satisfying, there was a school only three miles away. I was happy. School was to me then as the cinema and television are to the children of today. My mother also appeared happier as she went about her many tasks. Now she had friends among the neighbours, and on rare occasions some of our relatives would come to visit our modest home.

However, all was not bliss. Like the days on the homestead, the winds blew the soil from the parched land. Only in 1935 did we get a fair crop, the first since 1928. Until I left home in 1940, this was the only bountiful crop I can remember. In 1937 the land was so dry that even thistles failed to grow.

During sunny days the wind blew the soil so thick that midday became midnight. In those years, the town of Gouvernor gradually disappeared as the surrounding land became desert and the farmers moved away. In my mind, it was a strange irony. The desert seemed to have followed us from Syria. We were fated not to escape the blowing sands.

Tombstone Community

RUDY WIEBE

SCATTERED HERE AND there across Western Canada are
communities which stand as tombstones to the "homestead method"
of rural settlement. A number of them were established during the
depression years of the 1930s when, desperate for an honest livelihood,
thousands of impoverished families felt that if only they had land to live
on, they could avoid both hunger and the dole. And there lay such an
immensity of Canada beyond the strip of southern settlement and below
the rock of the Canadian Shield; surely it could be settled in the tried
and proven way: 160 acres and five years with minimum improvements
and the land was theirs. Get enough families to settle in one area and
presto!—a stable community had begun.

Prairie governments were nothing loath to encourage such thinking.
Settlers, often enough innocents from Europe, moved in, registered on
their land, and began to pioneer. In the years that followed they proved
again what had already been discovered with great hardship in the Cypress
Hills area twenty years before: that homesteading, which succeeded quite
well in founding stable communities in the more fertile black-soil parts of
the prairies, broke down completely when a quarter section of thin rocky
soil in the short growing season of northern latitudes was counted on to
support a family.

The Speedwell-Jackpine community of Saskatchewan where I was born stands as one such tombstone to the 160-acre homestead idea. As a place on the map, Speedwell no longer exists. The vital services of a well-populated, working community—school, post office, store, church—now can be found only twenty miles away—in Glaslyn, a small town some forty miles north of North Battleford. Yet during the early 1940s when I was growing up, Speedwell district had a post office, two stores, two schools of thirty to forty children each, and a vigorous church and social life. On virtually every quarter section along a five-mile road, and for several miles in either direction from it, lived a family of five, eight, sometimes ten or twelve persons. Every one of them was completely involved in helping to dig a home and a living from the poplar-, spruce-, and rock-covered soil. And it was not long before even my infant comprehension knew that this work was very hard for all, and impossible for many.

The first settlers in the area did take up homesteads more sensibly than the one-family-to-each-quarter-section pattern. These first were Mennonites from North and South Dakota, Minnesota, and Kansas who came north in 1925 and 1926 looking for inexpensive, sheltered land. Their homesteads were well scattered to allow a good deal of individual expansion. But the main influx of homesteaders, the Russian Mennonites who began to arrive in Speedwell about 1928, disrupted all this. Having always lived in close-knit villages which farmed the surrounding area intensively, these new Canadians felt that 160 acres per family a half mile from the nearest neighbour was surely enough land, and surely enough isolation.

It was not the inadequacy of the land but rather its loneliness that first made life hard for the European settlers. Russia had been vast; but Canada was not merely vast; it was impassively empty and lonely. My mother still recounts how in those early years she would start out early in the afternoon to look for our few cows on the "free range" that stretched endlessly to the west of our homestead, listening for the clear tone of the lead cow's bell to guide her. Having wandered far in their grazing, the cattle would often stand motionless among the thick willows to escape the flies and mosquitoes, and no sound would stir the air. Walking, listening, looking, mother would lose all sense of where in the endless bush our small home clearing was. The search for the cows became somewhat desperate then, because they had to be found to lead her home. In the meantime we small children would be waiting at home, laughing and chasing each other in glee when we heard the bell coming nearer, but frightened when we saw that the cows had come home by themselves without mother driving them. Then father would come from work and, without pausing to eat, go in search of mother. Standing on a hillock, he would send his high, thin "Halloooo—" into the silent evening. And mother would say when they came home together, father waving a poplar branch around her to chase the mosquitoes, that there never was a finer sound in all the world.

So despite a few warnings to give themselves more "living" room, the Mennonites settling in the Speedwell district in the early thirties were happy to take up every quarter of land. The bush was too huge to face except from a central community. Each step of mastery over it was dependent not only on the iron nerve of the settler but also on the steel stake of the surveyor which, with an impassivity quite equal to that of the vast land itself, stated its cold official statistic impartially in a spruce muskeg or on a stony hilltop. When, as a youngster, my elder brother first made me aware that the surveyors had been all over the country long before we arrived, my imagination could not quite grasp the daring of such exploration. Yet there stood the stake. And beneath its statistic was the inevitable warning, cut deep in the iron: "It is unlawful to remove this marker. Maximum sentence: 7 years imprisonment." It was almost as if the imperturbable surveyor, whoever he was, defied the very wilderness itself to swallow the alien organization he had imposed upon it.

The centre of the community was, quite naturally for the Mennonites, the church. It is the church records that give the statistics of Speedwell-Jackpine community growth. The existence of the church was first noted in the 1928 annual Canadian Mennonite Brethren conference minutes. The 1930 minutes indicate 30 members; with the Russian Mennonite influx, this grew to 47 in 1933, 95 in 1935, and reached a peak of 114 in 1936. These figures represent about twenty-five families in the church. Add to them the twelve to fifteen families living in the district but not directly connected with the church, and there was a total of forty families or, conservatively, 250 persons living on twenty square miles of north Saskatchewan bushland in the process of being cleared for farming.

The church record indicates that even in the distress of the 1936 depression, permanent settlement on this scale proved impossible. In two years membership dropped by one third—to about seventy members. The families that remained of course took over the claims of those who had left and so they had the advantage of what clearing and breaking had been done before. For about eight years until the end of World War Two in 1945, the Speedwell-Jackpine community enjoyed its only relatively stable period, supporting about twenty-five families, that is, some 150 persons.

My parents with their six children arrived in Speedwell in 1933. They had lived in south Saskatchewan for a year on relief; that was more than enough. I was born the year after they took up their homestead, and the world which year after year began slowly to register on my comprehension was the world of pioneer work: the production of necessary food and shelter. To live in a compact log house carefully plastered with mud against the fury of winter and sun of summer; to trudge three miles of trails to a single-room school where the first graders clustered about a long table and doodled with Valet razor blades on their bench while the harassed teacher was "straightening out" the sixth graders on the opposite side of the school; to carry a snack of thick bread and cold tea to your father and brothers where they were scrubbing, with axes and a team of horses, the poplar- and birch-choked land: that was the world to me. Towns and cities, with their paved streets, department stores, motor vehicles, electric lights and spacious bedrooms, when I learned of them, inhabited the segment of my imagination reserved for Grimm's fairy tales and the Greek myths. And certainly the myths and fairy tales were the more easily understood of the three.

Ours was a world of labour. It was done by all, men, women and children alike, for the family worked and lived as a unit. With small fields wrested inch by inch from the clutch of the bush, the easy life of grain growing, and harvesting and selling was out of the question. Each member of the family had work to do: in the summer the smaller children fed the chickens, hoed the garden, herded the cattle if the fences (after they had been put up) were insufficient; the older girls and mother cooked, washed, canned, took the children on berry-picking and Seneca-root-digging trips, expeditions which took place every fine day as long as the season for either lasted; the older boys and father cleared land, hayed, broke sod, picked stones and built sod-covered barns. What grain we grew was used to feed chickens, hogs, stock, milk cows and horses. The source of cash income, besides occasional "working out," was the cream cheque which came each week with our returning empty cans. These cheques were never large because poor cows fed largely on slough hay rarely produce either quantity or quality. In winter the children went to school (to grade eight—after that it was correspondence school if one were interested in higher education) and the women took care of the stock while the men, with as many horses as they could employ, cut and hauled timber for any one of several small mills operating in the bush north of us.

Often when the new spring with its demand for seed and absolutely essential, if elementary, equipment strained the slim family resources too far, my two older brothers, then in their late teens, would walk to Fairholme, the nearest railroad stop, and "ride the rods" six hundred miles to southern Alberta. There they would thin and hoe sugar beets for the summer. The money they earned—sometimes as much as two dollars a day—was brought home in fall to help us through the winter. And on Christmas morning when my Santa Claus plate, as was fitting for the youngest and most inevitably spoiled child of the family, would contain a game that shot glass marbles into tiny pockets of varying scores, my brothers' plates would hold such useful gifts as a package of razor blades each and a bottle of after-shave lotion between them.

It did not matter much that in the last days of the thirties we lived from one year to the next without travelling more than ten miles from home, without seeing either a car or a train. It did not much matter that in a rainstorm the only dry spot in the house was under the kitchen table; that is, if the oilcloth was not entirely worn out. We could work and we had something to eat; that was miracle enough to my parents who had almost starved to death in Russia during the early 1920s. What they told us of these experiences made Canada a miracle even to me, who had never known another land.

Though the hard work remained, during the war years it did become more comfortable in certain areas of life. Social activities centred around the two public schools, Speedwell and Jackpine, and the Speedwell Mennonite Brethren Church. Friendly sports competition in summer was replaced in winter by Christmas concerts and school bazaars. The church had a full weekly program, and for several years two qualified teachers taught a winter Bible school which attracted about thirty young people. We younger children snared rabbits and trapped squirrels and weasels in winter; we thought prices were really very good. Financially things improved so much that we even had an extra horse, which could be used to haul my sister and me to school in the cutter during winter. Well, the youngest children of even a pioneer family invariably grow up weaklings!

But the community showed signs of uneasiness. Despite the difficulties of wartime moving, occasional families, beckoned by the greener fields of the South, would leave. Young people were growing up; some of them had spent ten or twelve years working hard to give their families a bare existence; the leavening experience of younger men returning from the war, loud with stories of travel and world wonders, had profound effects on Speedwell and its people.

Yet these more or less ideological forces cannot explain the abrupt dying out of the entire community. In early 1946 there were still forty-seven members in the Speedwell Mennonite Brethren Church; it had a lay pastor, three young lay ministers and two deacons. By 1948 there were twelve members left, and a year later one family alone remained. By 1950 the church, and with it the community, had ceased to exist. For several years there was literally no one living in the entire Speedwell district.

I remember well those years of leaving. Only my sister and myself remained at home in our family; the older children had grown up, married local young people, and had moved away to make their living. There was "moving" in the air. You drove to church on Sunday and were almost surprised to meet your neighbour there. He had, apparently, not yet moved that week.

The younger people obviously did not want to stay. There was no way of getting educated beyond eighth grade in the district; life was so much easier elsewhere. Even if they wanted to stay and farm, they would have to begin as their parents—pioneering in the bush, away from the land that was now at least partially cleared. By working in Speedwell there was no prospect of ever having enough money to buy a tractor to do such clearing, and they had no ambition to do it by hand. The prosperity of post-war Canada beckoned everywhere. And if the young people went, why should the now aging parents and the last of the children stay, labouring at the old work with little prospect of more than a subsistence living?

The land, of course, was the root cause for moving. There was little room to expand in the community itself, and the very best wheat one could ever expect, in the very best of years, was a bare No. 2 Northern. Though one need never starve on his farm, one would also never have many comforts. For example, after twenty years of laborious work, only two or three farmers could afford to own and operate an ancient lug tractor, and only one drove a recent model car. Our family never did own either a tractor or car in Speedwell. We drove into the district in 1933 with what equipment we had on a rented truck and we left fourteen years later in exactly the same way.

Tax problems intensified the situation. For many years no one had the money to pay taxes. The government knew enough not to make itself ridiculous by insisting on taxes on homesteads during the 1930s. But by 1946 tax notices were getting clamorous, and so rather than work out to earn money to pay taxes on land that they were not too convinced of anyway, a good number of farmers simply left. Not that the back taxes even ten years later were very high. Our family quarter was bought from the municipality in 1957 by a farmer who paid exactly the price of the back taxes—$400. In the first winter after he bought that land he cut $500 worth of spruce on it, but he did it with a chain saw and a tractor.

Caught in the moving fever, drawn by the hope for better land and an easier livelihood, the Speedwell farm owners left their log houses and their laboriously cleared fields to revert to the government (there were few, if any, buyers for them) and moved south—to Manitoba, Alberta, British Columbia. In the easier, car-transported life they have found in these areas, they often visit one or the other of their old neighbours and reminisce about those hard, yet happy, pioneer years. Time easily erases the greatest hardships, and the romance of having taken part in such pioneering colours all their memories, so that many, if they ever return, will find Speedwell unrecognizable.

Only two families remained living on the periphery of the district in the early 1950s. They lived by farming and trapping. During a wet year beaver appeared from nowhere, dammed up several sloughs which had been fine hay meadows in our time, and the country become known as good hunting territory. Then, about 1955, several of the younger men who had left in the forties and made a bit of capital in southern cities were drawn by the need for land and returned to Speedwell. Using modern mass-farming techniques, they are now doing what the first farmers could not do: making a good living under fairly comfortable circumstances. The grubbing pioneer life is gone now; town is only twenty miles away on a good road, the church has been torn down, the two schools have been closed (the children go to elementary or high school by bus to Glaslyn), and the world is no farther away than the TV screen or the telephone in the living room.

We left Speedwell in 1947; I returned for a visit in the summer of 1963. The poplars grow much taller and straighter than I remember them; there are no spruce left now. The house where we lived seems so much smaller than I thought. It stands tilted, its windows gaping. The three miles I trudged to school seem no distance whatever; the school itself and the hill where we used to slide and ski in winter seem shrinking into themselves. The narrow fields still stretch over the hills, but the poplars and the willows are quickly reclaiming the territory they once lost, very briefly, to axe and plough. Already they grow young and thick in the church cemetery, almost hiding the small tombstone of my sister's grave. And on every quarter section we pass in our car—sometimes too we have to walk because all but the main road is overgrown—there sag the shells of houses that once heard the laughter of families. No one sees them now, from one year end to the next. Their rotting floors will soon crash into their shallow cellars, and no one except wild animals will hear.

But for some years yet these decaying little cabins—for that is really all they are—with their collapsed barns will stand as individual letters on the face of this tombstone community of Speedwell and the homestead idea that once lived, and now is buried, there.

Harvest Moon

HARVEY WALKER

The glamour of childish days is upon me
my manhood is cast
down in the flood of remembrance,
I weep like a child for the past.
        —D. H. Lawrence, "Piano"

THE CALL OF a meadowlark, the cry of a killdeer. These sounds resonate within me, triggering memories of the past. Autumn is particularly poignant. In the days surrounding the autumnal equinox, I stand in my front yard to listen to the thrum of the engines of post-modern combines—the Case-Internationals, the John Deeres, the Whites—emanating from the fields of wheat, barley, and canola that surround our acreage. I sense the urgency of farmers, past and present, casting their eyes to the sky, attempting to reckon the changing countenances of Mother Nature. When I hear the powerful roar of a combine engine, the "glamour of childish days is upon me." The air is laden with dust that turns the moon blood-red. I sift through distant memories for shards.

One fragment dominates: The image of a boy, aged eight or ten, standing on a toolbox and leaning on the shoulders of his father, who is seated at the controls of a 1940s wine-coloured, self-propelled Massey

Harvey (middle, age 5) with his brother Doug (left) and G.B. (right, playing outrider) re-enacting the Calgary Stampede chuckwagon race, 1946

Ferguson combine. Running ahead of the machine is a dog, a tri-coloured collie, a darting, snapping, whirling canine dervish, bringing death to terror-stricken mice as they flee the protection of the swath disappearing into the mouth of the mechanical behemoth. Neither boy nor man knows what the future holds. In just a few years, the father will be dead, of a failed heart. The boy, also with a broken heart, will move off the farm into town with the rest of his family, forever separated from his dog, his constant boyhood companion.

◆

A farmer's very existence depends on the harvest. In the autumn, there was constant talk at our kitchen table about yields, quotas, bins, breakdowns, parts, hired help, and weather. Harvest was a race against time. However, as a child, I viewed harvest as anything but a serious matter. Each year

I begged to be allowed to stay home to "help." Each year, I was allowed one day off school. And what a joyful day it was! Much of it was spent in my mother's kitchen, command central, the hub of activity away from the fields. Such bounty! Such smells! Fried chicken. Roast beef. Gravy. Produce from the garden: corn, peas, carrots, beets, and potatoes. *Young man, there's potatoes yet to be dug, peas to be shelled. And see that you keep the woodbox filled: I can't risk losing the fire.* Fresh bread, enough for dozens of sandwiches. Cinnamon buns. Pies. Coffee, brewed by the gallon.

Then, mid-morning, a temporary escape—a chance to leave the heat of the kitchen. Out to the wheat fields—likely the north section by now—to transport hampers of food and drink to hungry workers, hired help mostly, an army of bottomless stomachs. I sit on the running board and listen to conversations as the men consume every morsel—except a solitary cinnamon bun, an offering of thanks to me, the young helper. What fortune!

More good luck—a trip to Claresholm in our grey Dodge sedan, with one of the men: *We need some parts, more supplies.* Next, a ride in our red Fargo grain truck to the Wheat Pool elevator in Woodhouse: *There's a partial quota on.* Dad drives inside, onto the weigh scales. I am allowed to stay in the cab as the front wheels are lifted high to empty the grain from the box. Back to the field. A ride on the combine, too! My neck itches with chaff.

Back to the kitchen—*Mom, I got to steer!* We take the men their noon meal. Then, more potatoes and carrots to peel. More bread and buns to bake. My mother exclaims as she holds a rooster by the neck in one hand, an axe in the other, *Lordy, you'd think the hired help were starvin'!* Chickens to scald and pluck. Supper. Father's edict: *Time's a-wasting. We're givin' 'er tonight.* He returns to the field. A huge blood-red moon. Midnight cool. Men and machines stop. Mother sets more bread to rise.

Gracious, are you still up? Off to bed with you. There's school tomorrow, young man. Father's intercession. *Son, there'll be no school for you tomorrow. There's no more room in the bins for wheat. It'll have to go on the ground. You'll help your uncle set up the snow fence and tarpaper.* Darn it!

———◆———

For the past fifty years, I have lived a more urban existence, although for the past twenty I have lived with my wife on a small acreage a short drive from St. Albert, a medium-sized city in central Alberta. As an adult, I've returned to visit that small farming community in southern Alberta. I've stopped by the cemetery in town to pay my respects at the family plot. But Thomas Wolfe was right: "You can't go home again." At the old farmstead, I don't turn into the driveway. The house is lived in by strangers. On my last visit, I could see no livestock. The barn appeared to be empty and in poor repair. I stared down the drive, looking in vain for a collie dog that I finally accept is no longer, looking in vain for my father, whose death it took me many years to come to terms with.

For the most part, I have good memories of those years on the farm. When I hear geese honking above me as they course their way south in the fall, or when I hear blue jays shrieking their return to the bird feeder in spring, I know that I am richer because of my rural upbringing.

The Storm

Wayne Curtis

ONE OF THOSE trips to Cains River stands out from the others. Papa was going to bring home a cookstove that had been left in his old camp on Salmon Brook and which he wanted to get before winter set in. With the fall's work mostly cleaned up, I figured the day away would be a break. Plus we'd be in good partridge country, so I wanted to go in the worst way. Still, I had to coax the old man to take me along, as he kept insisting I stay home to look after the barn.

After an early breakfast of buckwheat porridge and raw tea with molasses, we bundled up and went to the barn. By the light of a lantern, we harnessed the horses, led them into the yard, and hitched them to the truck wagon. We climbed into the wagon's rough plank box and sat on sacks of hay. Papa stood the old .45-70 rifle between us on the seat. He clucked his tongue and whipped the ends of the reins on the mares' rumps to start them trotting. The traces jingled, and the iron-shod wheels rattled and banged on the frozen mud as we crossed the ploughed fields. We forded the big river a half mile upstream from home and headed up South Cains Road, past Taylor Mountain, and on toward the old mill site. I planted my hands firmly on the creaking planks to keep from falling over the side as the big spoked wheels dropped into holes and climbed over rocks and bits of timber, making the wagon tilt and sway. I was cold, but I didn't say anything. As the horses trotted along in the semi-darkness,

Wayne (right, age 4) and his brother Winston (age 6)
at their family farm, 1947

I kept looking into the woods for a deer. This made the trip seem like a dream, one I had been nurturing—the dream of hunting with Papa, away back when he was a fighter and a marksman, when trophy caribou lived in the barrens.

As daylight overtook us, a halo-ringed sun peeked through the drab grey sky. Papa said the sun dog meant a big storm was coming. He brought my attention to the desperate cries of ravens and blue jays as further proof. He cracked the whip, and steam rose from the horses' backs.

We got to the camp just before noon, and tied the mares to a tree and fed them oats in nose baskets. Papa's old camp was built of unpeeled poles. Inside, broken glass and porcupine droppings littered the floor. After we cleaned the ashes from the stove, we dismantled the rusty pipes and haywired them to the wagon. Then we used planks and pries to slide the range out the door and onto the wagon bed. "Jesus Christ, get the lead out of your arse!" Papa puffed as he lifted his side of the range to knock the cover off. "Together now, heave!" We tied it into place with chains.

It was almost midday when we finished, our faces smeared with black ash. While Papa built a fire on the ground, I went to the brook for tea water. I had my slingshot at the ready and kept my eyes open for partridge down on the alder flat. A thin layer of ice covered the edges of the brook,

The Storm

and I broke it to scoop a pail of amber water. I noticed that a deer had recently broken through the ice and riled the water slightly.

Back at the camp yard, Papa was adding sticks to the blaze, stopping now and then to have a sip of brandy. I handed him the bucket and told him about the deer. He fixed the pail to hang over the blaze and when the water began to boil, he said, "Now she's talkin'," and tossed in a handful of tea leaves. We ate our bologna sandwiches and canned beans, and then we tossed the empty cans into the trees. The tea was thick as gun oil, and Papa blew at the rim of his enamel mug, after which he lit his pipe using a brand from the fire. The tobacco smoke that drifted past me carried the sweet scent of farmhouse kitchens on winter nights.

"The country's all gone to hell," Papa said. "She'll never be the same as it used to be!" Then he took to coughing. He stood bent, with his hands on his knees. Tears filled his eyes. He wiped his mouth with his handkerchief. "Jesus, I'm sore all through," he said. "This old damp weather chills me to the bone!" He contemplated the ashes for a long time, sucking on the pipe. His breath popped and whistled. "Hell and damnation, it's an awful thing ta get so old." He coughed again and spit into the fire.

Papa scattered the ashes with a stick, stuck a juniper twig between his teeth, and grabbed his gun. We made our way down toward the brook. I picked my way behind him as he stole among the trees in a crouch, the rifle at full cock pointing ahead of him. Leaves rustled ahead of us, although I couldn't see anything. When I stepped on a dry twig, Papa pointed at my feet and shook his head.

As the noon sun dissolved little frost-pearls on the bracken, Papa put up a hand. I stopped. I did not see the deer. I only saw the old man throw the Winchester to his shoulder and heard the shots bark short in the dampness. The rifle's stock bucked against his shoulder. He worked the lever-action to upend the smoking brass shells into the moss, and the echoes repeated through the hollow woods. I smelled gun smoke and gun oil and the distant blood. There was the rattled breathing of a frantic getaway. Then I saw an eight-point buck cantering off, no longer alive, but not yet knowing that it was running dead. There was a crash like that of a falling stub as the deer collapsed into a brush pile beneath a double pine tree. Specks of blood spattered the fall leaves surrounding the motionless buck.

Papa jabbed the carcass with the barrel of the gun. He passed the rifle to me. "Here, young fella, hold that, will ya?" That he trusted me with the loaded gun made me feel like a grown man. I stood the rifle against a tree. Papa took off his coat and rolled up his shirt sleeves. I did what he told me to do—run for the axe, fetch the rope, hold this or that like a good boy. I had seen all this many times and knew what he wanted me to do.

The deer was heavy. We each grabbed a horn and dragged it up the hill. The horses lifted their heads and chuckled at the smell of the dead animal. We loaded our buck onto the wagon bed, with its head toward the back for all to see. "Yer a great lad ta work, all together," he said. "Keep it up and you'll maker the very best in life."

I said nothing. I couldn't find the right words. I felt proud of Papa because he had shot this big deer and also because he had been doing the work of a young man all fall while Daddy was laid up with the bad arm. Papa could still carry a good load in spite of having ruptured himself years before lifting pit-props. He had refused surgery and was now forced to wear a rubber girdle.

That afternoon as we came out of the woods, I sat on the back of the wagon bed on top of the deer. I held the rifle upright, the butt stock between my legs like I was a shotgun rider on a movie house wagon. Papa cracked the whip and sipped from his flask of brandy. As the horses trotted and the traces jingled, a bracing wind came out of the ash-coloured sky. The black birch limbs seemed to whisper, *Move along, now, it's getting late. There's a storm coming on.* The deer swayed beneath me, its stiff legs moving with every jolt.

Papa sat on the sack of hay, clutching the reins in his leather gloves. He spit over his shoulder and sang "Peter Emberley." I knew he was as happy as he dared to be without fear of bad luck following. It started to snow, small wet flakes that struck my face and melted. I wished I had put on my warmer coat like Papa, who was wearing his sheepskin jumper.

A half-ton truck came up behind, horn honking, and someone shouted at us as it sped past.

As we approached the settlement, the shabbily dressed women, the women-faced boys, the thin girls in their too-small clothes, and the bone-weary old men wearing mackinaws wrongly buttoned stood in their stovewood-strewn dooryards and waved at us. They shouted to praise Papa for bringing out a deer. I stood up and clamped my hands around the deer's horns, lifting the head with its frozen blue eyes, the better for them to see.

At one of those homes, an old man in bib overalls beckoned. Papa stopped the horses. Frank McAfferty came to the wagon and stood with one gum-rubber resting on the hub, talking to Papa as if to suggest a friendship that had never existed. Papa always said that Frank McAfferty was not an easy lad to swallow because he had no word. The man grinned, revealing his one brown tooth. Grabbing the side of the box, he lifted himself to look into the wagon. "'E's a big one too, ain't 'e, Tom?" He took a brown flask from his coat pocket and passed it to treat. "Here's a little warmer upper fer 'e, Tom." He winked at me as Papa took the flask and guzzled from it.

Papa swallowed and screwed up his face. "A little warmer upper, 'tis, by God." Papa spit into the sand and passed the bottle back. "Thank ya ever sa much, Frankie." Without another word, he slapped the reins on the horses' rumps. Old Frank stood on the road, his legs spread, his hands deep down inside his bib overalls like the straw men we sat on verandas for Halloween. He watched, I suspect, until we were out of view. Papa said, "That foolish son of a whore got a different face for every day of the week! I pity the poor soul who got mixed up with him. He trades with his own kind, and those kids of his are twice damned."

Darkness was coming down fast, nightfall and snowfall, cold and damp. When we got to Howards, we found that the big river had risen and was too deep for the horses to wade through. We would have to go all the way to Blackville, a good five miles, and cross the bridge and come up the north side. Papa sang:

> I landed in New Brunswick
> In a lumbering country,
> I hired to work in the lumber woods
> On the Sou' west Miramichi

It was as if the horse and wagon sounds, the bumping of wheels, the jingle of traces, were music to him. And when the horses slowed on the hills, Papa stood up and cracked the reins over their rumps. Still, it seemed like he was more interested in sipping brandy and practising his skills as a teamster than he was in getting home in time for supper. But I was hungry, wet, and cold. At the foot of Campbell Hill, a moose ran across the road, "a great big old son of a whore of a swamp bull." I could have jumped off the wagon right there, crossed the wire bridge and been home in a few minutes. But I wanted to be a part of coming home with a deer. Plus, I knew that Papa was drinking and might need me to drive the horses before we got there. In a way, I was hoping this would happen because I wanted to get my hands on the reins, especially as we passed our neighbours' houses.

As we approached McCormack Hill, which overlooked the village, I heard dogs barking. We crossed the bridge and the railway, and the horses slowed on the hill that went up to the village. Being in Blackville was as big a thing for me as being in Newcastle or Chatham would have been for Papa. As we hurried up Main Street, he sipped his drink and coughed in his homely way and spit out over the wagon wheels. Sitting on the back with the deer and the stove and the rusted smoke pipes, I felt all the eyes of the world upon me, and I was uncertain if I should have been proud or ashamed. I put the rifle down out of sight.

The horses' shoes clomped and sparked as horns honked and cars sped past on the black glistening pavement, sending sprays of slush against our wagon wheels. We passed parked cars that had fox tails fixed to their hood ornaments, and even though it was a dirty night, teenage boys and girls walked hand in hand up and down the sidewalk. I pulled the old hat down on my forehead as we drove past Bean's Billiard Parlour and the Public Hall, past Ross's Canteen in front of which teens stood smoking and from which Hank Williams crooned from a juke box, past Archie Donald's filling station where a crowd of men gathered 'round the gas pumps. Papa hollered "Gee" and "Haw!"

"Get them Jesusless shitting donkeys off the street!" someone hollered from an alley.

I was glad Papa was hard of hearing.

"We'll hurry right along home," he said. "By the Lord Jesus, we're not loved here!"

Maybe he was too old and tired to give a damn. I don't know. But I'd like to see that lad when Papa got finished with him, the son of a bitch. I knew Papa's reputation in the community had won him less affection than he deserved. But I was relieved that no one else along the way shouted at us, because Papa was drinking, and I knew he would take sauce from no one in Blackville or Howards.

Still, if a fight broke out just then, would I be on Papa's side? For some reason, I suddenly hated the old man. Maybe it was because I was wet and cold and hungry and not liking myself for always trying to please him. I didn't even have the backbone to speak up when I should. When I thought of my grandfather in this way, I could see why my mother and grandmother were always arguing. Gram had always been content to follow Papa's ways, but my mother had a different view of things. Mum's way included books and music and fancy dishes, the touch of class she had witnessed as a girl while working as a chambermaid in the village.

Strangely, I wanted to see Papa brought down a peg or two, if only to justify getting even with him for the hard workload he had pushed on me that fall. Because I had given up my own education and restricted my future to save him from running his face. Still I said nothing. But it was not out of respect that I kept silent just then.

Papa slapped the horses' rumps. They quickened their pace as we climbed the long hill through the Mersereau pastures. Wind tugged the mares' tails and manes slantwise. Snow whipped up from the fields on both sides of the wagon, and in that light it was hard to tell earth from sky, where one ended and the other began. Then some hydro poles on the river side rose up to make the separation. They positioned themselves in the ditch like black crosses. And beyond them the crippled fence posts marched in single file toward home. As we rode through a stand of poplars where my father had once seen a ghost, Papa sang:

> *I hired to work in the lumber woods*
> *Where they cut the tall spruce down.*
> *When loading teams with yarded logs*
> *I received a deadly wound*

Passing Keenan's School, where I knew in my heart of hearts I should have been spending my days, I felt a sense of regret. For a brief moment I could imagine myself standing by the side of my desk, reciting

"The Highwayman" for Mrs. Jardine. But all this was subtle and quite overpowered by the events of the day. After all, I had hated school, hadn't I? Or had even that been my idea? The old man was overpowering. Everyone knew that.

Papa believed that a certain amount of hardship and a bit of adventure built character in a man, that a wise man knows how much he doesn't know and so doesn't make a fool of himself. He also believed that happiness was, sooner or later, paid for with pain. Certainly, as a young boy I had never tired of hearing about the drama of my grandfather's early years, adventures such as drinking with gypsies in their caravan in the Underwood fields where they did card tricks and told fortunes for a nickel. But I was starting to doubt him. After all, no one else I knew had seen road gypsies in New Brunswick.

Looking at Papa from behind as he rode through the storm, I thought, *Just like a ghost!* His shoulders were hunched and narrowed, and his hat and coat were heavy with snow. There was not much of the old fighter left in him. For a moment I was sorry I'd had bad thoughts about Papa, who had done a young man's work since early October. Now again, as though driving and singing were meant to be done together, he crooned:

Frank McAfferty humped his mule

He stopped to cough and spit, and I could smell his tobacco smoke strong in the dampness.

And then he got up and danced.

Because, I suspect, he'd had a day in which he was proud, and because he had, no doubt, surprised himself with his stamina, he talked about when he was young and how he had travelled as far away as Campbellton where he worked on the Restigouche Boom and turned handsprings on the big floating logs for the amusement of fellow rivermen. He talked about the caribou and the moose he had shot and the fighting he had done up in Weaver Siding and the bigger men he had beaten and the smaller men who feared him, but for the wrong reasons. For he was not a fight starter, he said, "But by Chrise, let me tell ya, boys, I'd finish one awful quick." He rambled on as though he wanted to hear himself speak. I had heard all this before—every time he had a few drinks. "When I hit that big son of a whore, he went down like a bag of flour! Yes sir, boys. Broke his jaw in two places!"

It was only then that I began to realize that his mind had reached something near dementia. He was repeating himself, and some of his stories were being intertwined and were making no sense at all. Maybe it took a few drinks to stir the anger deep inside and have him expose his true self. But as bits and pieces of the dangerous spirit of his youth resurfaced, I could not help but see my mother's side of things. I became less certain I wanted to go in any direction that would comply with his wishes. It was like I had to look real deep to see past him. And I tried as hard as I could to put him back the way he used to be, keep the old dream positive and moving forward. But it would not happen. And I guessed, down deep, I didn't want it to happen, not then.

I wished Papa would stop talking so foolish, because he was spoiling the spirit of what had been a good day, especially the early part. But then, I thought, that's the price you pay for the kind of day I'd just had, and that kind of talk is all a part of it. And who am I to try to separate the grain from the chaff? His past is my past and a big part of who I am. For the time being, I'd either have to love the whole man or not love him at all.

The old man fell silent. He swayed as if he were going to fall off the wagon. I jumped forward and took the reins from his slack grip. We were in sight of home by then. Papa had dozed off, sitting upright like a tired old workhorse that was afraid to lie down for fear he wouldn't find the strength to stand again. I had seen him do this often in the rocking chair at home. It was the time in his life when no night's sleep could bring him enough rest. He hiccupped and mumbled, "That son of a whore shoulda been horsewhipped." He slumped down like an overtired child, folding his hands upon his chest, like he was in prayer.

Grandpa and Me

Chris Beingessner

THE OLD LEATHER recliner had grown cracks in the seat, and stuffing escaped from its seams. Originally black, it had faded nearly brown after twenty years of frequent use. The two knobs on the right-hand side, near the bottom, still worked, though; one adjusted the heater, and the other controlled the massager. This was my grandfather's chair. His every movement required great effort and caused terrible pain, so he remained motionless in his chair for hours. Then when his dilapidated old body screamed in agony because of stiffness, he gingerly shifted positions. Though his face betrayed the anguish his body endured, he never spoke of it. He slept only in his chair. He hadn't been in his bed for weeks; it hurt too much when he lay down.

———◆———

"Grandpa! Grandpa!" I hollered as he poked his head into the house, back from the field for the day. Even though he spent six days of every week on the farm with us, seeing him was never any less of a treat. He set down his Thermos and lunch box, washed up, and sat down at the table to a late supper. I grabbed the Princess Auto catalogue that had come with the day's mail and, grinning from ear to ear, launched myself onto his lap. He smiled, ruffled my hair, and pushed his supper aside, opening the flyer.

Chris (age 4) with his grandfather, Herbert, and father, Paul, 1983

We studied it in detail, scanning each item on every page, and I showed him which tools I needed. His smile stretched, revealing the origin of his wrinkles, and he agreed that a four-year-old surely needed a palm sander. Whether studying the new Peavey Mart catalogue or a flyer from the Co-op in Avonlea, we sat like this almost every day when Grandpa came home from the field—"talking business," we called it. One Sunday when Grandpa was at his home in Regina, I innocently told my father, "You know, Dad, I love Grandpa more than I love you."

———————◆———————

He was admitted to the hospital. They said he had osteoporosis, that his bones were weak. He seemed to be smaller, but I thought maybe it was just that I was growing. The morphine made him hard to reach, but I could still make him smile. I told him of my plans to break him out of the hospital using a crane or, failing that, a clever disguise and pure brute force. He didn't want to be there and I knew that. In a surprisingly lucid moment one day, he said to my father, "That Chrissy will land himself in jail one day!" I smiled when Dad told me what Gramps had said. I knew that behind the morphine haze, he was thinking of me.

———•———

"The raspberries are ripe," Grandpa told me before I went to school one morning. At four o'clock I exploded out the doors of the school bus and hurried down the lane. I called to him, and he called back, "I'm in the garden!" I tossed my school bag at the house, my metal lunch box objecting loudly, and ran to the raspberry patch at full speed. Grandpa was there picking raspberries, and I joined him, picking the ripe red berries straight into my mouth. "Hey Gramps, any luck?" I asked. "Well, just this pail here, and that one there," he said, motioning toward a pail sitting in the shade of a tree. "But I'm worried." He looked at me, frowning. "That bucket under the tree might spoil. Maybe you'd better eat some of those berries to keep them from going bad." I smiled big and sat under the tree with the pail between my legs, shoving huge handfuls of raspberries into my mouth as Grandpa worked. I told Grandpa about my day at school: how we played baseball all noon hour, how I had smacked a home run, and then how when Jeff hit the ball into the middle of a big mud puddle he had to go in after it. He got so dirty the teacher wouldn't let him back into the school. When my bucket started to get low, Grandpa came over and dumped the contents of his bucket into mine so I could keep eating.

———•———

After two weeks in the hospital, the doctor decided that bone cancer, not osteoporosis, was killing Grandpa. He wouldn't be going home soon, if ever. Lying in his recliner was but a distant memory. He started chemotherapy. He was on an IV. He rarely talked; when he did, he wasn't always coherent. Now the hospital, rather than my best friend's house, became my hangout. I gave him sips of water, then watched him while he dozed. On the days I managed to attend school, I was a nervous wreck. Grandpa got worse. My aunt and uncle from Saskatoon arrived, and we all kept vigil in his hospital room. The doctors gave him two weeks to live. I cried.

———•———

"Chuck one in there, Chrissy," Grandpa cheered from the cab of his 1981 Ford F100 half-ton. I dug in and threw an extra-hard fastball, and the side was retired. While our team batted, I snuck away from the dugout to talk to him. He beamed, and so did I. We shared a love for the sport—no surprise after childhood stories of Dizzy Dean, Satchel Paige, and Josh Gibson narrated by my Gramps. He patted me on the back. "Good job! He didn't even see that last one—swinging at the breeze it left behind!" He winced as he shifted positions on the bench seat; his back was bothering him again. He seemed so small in the cab of his truck. The years of sitting on a tractor had taken their toll.

"You go home to bed, Gramps. I'll finish cleaning up here," I said, motioning towards the diamond. He smiled proudly—letting me know my confidence was justified—and then drove away. I returned to the mound filled with renewed enthusiasm.

◆

He was still holding on. The two weeks had passed; his heart was still strong. I was thankful—but he no longer looked like the Grandpa I knew. He was small, frail. They didn't think he was going to pull through. My grandma had faith; I wasn't sure. I wanted the pain to be over for him, but I still wanted Grandpa in my life. I still had so much to learn.

◆

"That farm there used to belong to Old Jake Pancratz. He was a great guy—a bit crazy, but who wasn't back in the thirties?" Grandpa told me on the way to Regina one day. We were on a parts run; the combine had broken down again. He told me a story about the time Old Jake butchered all the chickens as a birthday present for his wife. He started at midnight, after his wife went to bed, and was finished at five in the morning, just in time for breakfast. No one told a story like my grandpa. I sat spellbound. He had a funny anecdote for every farm we passed and for every curve in the road. I tried hard to remember each story he told, but I forgot most of them.

◆

After Grandpa died, I didn't care about anything. Schoolwork seemed inconsequential. Everything seemed trivial. My uncle told me how lucky

I was to have grown up with Grandpa always there. We passed around stories about Grandpa's generosity, his selflessness. We realized how he'd downplayed his pain. We remembered how adamant he was that my aunt quit fussing over him, and get her income tax filed on time. We were reminded of all the reasons we loved him.

———◆———

"So, you watch the front wheel of the tractor and line it up with the furrow," Grandpa explained to me. He was teaching me how to use the diskers to plough down clover. We were crammed into the tractor cab of the Allis-Chalmers 7000 like hay bales in a loft. It was the same tractor I used to ride in when I was much younger, banging my head on the window whenever he drove over rough terrain, drinking my Grandpa's sweet coffee.

"Pay attention now," he returned me to the moment. "I won't be here forever, you know," he warned.

I laughed and gave him a big hug. "Sure, Gramps," I said, smiling. "Whatever you say." He grinned back.

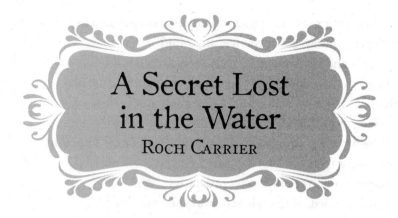

A Secret Lost in the Water

ROCH CARRIER

AFTER I STARTED going to school my father scarcely talked any more. I was very intoxicated by the new game of spelling; my father had little skill for it (it was my mother who wrote our letters) and was convinced I was no longer interested in hearing him tell of his adventures during the long weeks when he was far away from the house.

One day, however, he said to me, "The time's come to show you something."

He asked me to follow him. I walked behind him, not talking, as we had got in the habit of doing. He stopped in the field before a clump of leafy bushes.

"These are called alders," he said.

"I know."

"You have to learn how to choose," my father pointed out.

I didn't understand. He touched each branch of the bush, one at a time, with religious care.

"You have to choose one that's very fine, a perfect one, like this."

I looked; it seemed exactly like the others.

My father opened his pocket knife and cut the branch he'd selected with pious care. He stripped off the leaves and showed me the branch, which formed a perfect Y.

"You see," he said, "the branch has two arms. Now take one in each hand. And squeeze them."

I did as he asked and took in each hand one fork of the Y, which was thinner than a pencil.

"Close your eyes," my father ordered, "and squeeze a little harder… Don't open your eyes! Do you feel anything?"

"The branch is moving!" I exclaimed, astonished.

Beneath my clenched fingers the alder was wriggling like a small, frightened snake. My father saw that I was about to drop it.

"Hang onto it!"

"The branch is squirming," I repeated. "And I hear something that sounds like a river."

"Open your eyes," my father ordered.

I was stunned, as though he'd awakened me while I was dreaming.

"What does it mean?" I asked my father.

"It means that underneath us, right here, there's a little fresh-water spring. If we dig, we could drink from it. I've just taught you how to find a spring. It's something my own father taught me. It isn't something you learn in school. And it isn't useless: a man can get along without writing and arithmetic, but he can never get along without water."

Much later, I discovered that my father was famous in the region because of what the people called his "gift": before digging a well they always consulted him; they would watch him prospecting the fields or the hills, eyes closed, hands clenched on the fork of an alder bough. Wherever my father stopped, they marked the ground; there they would dig; and from there water would gush forth.

Years passed; I went to other schools, saw other countries, I had children, I wrote some books and my poor father is lying in the earth where so many times he had found fresh water.

One day someone began to make a film about my village and its inhabitants, from whom I've stolen so many of the stories that I tell. With the film crew we went to see a farmer to capture the image of a sad man: his children didn't want to receive the inheritance he'd spent his whole life preparing for them—the finest farm in the area. While the technicians were getting cameras and microphones ready the farmer put his arm around my shoulder, saying: "I knew your father well."

"Ah! I know. Everybody in the village knows each other…No one feels like an outsider."

"You know what's under your feet?"

"Hell?" I asked, laughing.

"Under you feet there's a well. Before I dug I called in specialists from the Department of Agriculture; they did research, they analyzed shovelfuls of dirt; and they made a report where they said there wasn't any water on my land. With the family, the animal, the crops, I need water. When I saw that those specialists hadn't found any I thought of your father and I asked him to come over. He didn't want to; I think he was pretty fed up with me because I'd asked those specialists instead of him. But finally he came; he went and cut off a little branch, then he walked around for a while with his eyes shut; he stopped, he listened to something we couldn't hear and then he said to me: "Dig right here, there's enough water to get your whole flock drunk and drown your specialists besides." We dug and found water. Fine water that's never heard of pollution."

The film people were ready; they called to me to take my place.

"I'm gonna show you something," said the farmer, keeping me back. "You wait right here."

He disappeared into a shack which he must have used to store things, then came back with a branch which he held out to me.

"I never throw nothing away; I kept the alder branch your father cut to find my water. I don't understand, it hasn't dried out."

Moved as I touched the branch, kept out of I don't know what sense of piety—and which really wasn't dry—I had the feeling that my father was watching me over my shoulder; I closed my eyes and, standing above the spring my father had discovered, I waited for the branch to writhe, I hoped the sound of gushing water would rise to my ears.

The alder stayed motionless in my hands and the water beneath the earth refused to sing.

Somewhere along the roads I'd taken since the village of my childhood I had forgotten my father's knowledge.

"Don't feel sorry," said the man, thinking no doubt of his farm and his childhood, "nowadays fathers can't pass anything on to the next generation."

And he took the alder branch from my hands.

The Apple Branch

Leah Benvie Hamilton

FALL HAD MOVED a little closer day by day, its hot days clearer and sharper than those of summer, the cool nights making them seem much hotter by comparison. The big white-grape apple tree beside what was once my grandparents' house and was now my uncle's had passed its prime, the ground beneath the tree offering a banquet of ripe, pastel-green fruit to worms and wasps, beetles and hornets, and whatever four-legged creatures might happen upon it in the quiet of the night.

The house had stood there for over a hundred years, strong and white against the rolling hills and hardwood forest that surround the yard. Below it, a green glen, complete with a winding brook, and the road, cutting across the open field, the road that twists and turns until it makes a clean, straight break over the bridge and up the steep hill to the house. My grandparents raised their nine children in that house. My mother and her siblings coasted on the hill beside it and swam in the brook below it. In the fall, each wise, old apple tree bore its special variety of fruit, each with its particular balance of sweet and sour. It is here that *Anne of Green Gables* and *Pat of Silver Bush* came alive for me, here that the novels I've read struggled to find their settings. It is the place my heart is tied to, the most beautiful place on earth.

I'd been invited two weeks before to help myself to the apples, and it was only in mid-September, on a Sunday afternoon, that I finally got

Leah (age 4) with Aunt Bernice in front of her
grandparents' house in Pembroke, Nova Scotia, 1958

around to making the trip to Pembroke. I'd only been to the farm a handful
of times during my adult years even though the distance was twenty miles
shorter than it was when I was a child. The journey felt simultaneously
foreign and familiar as I drove past the site of what had once been the
Crocker family's small mill. The cone-shaped sawdust piles—that had once
sat so close along the road I felt I could reach out through the car window
and grab a handful of golden dust—had long ago rotted and disintegrated,
the buildings and equipment fallen into the ground. But the road was as
it had been in my memory: the enveloping canopy of maple leaves that
accompanied that mysterious turn, and then that long sweep across the
wide open field after the second great turn, followed by the little white
brook bridge and finally the climb up and around and into the yard.

Of course, things were different now. It was no longer the busy,
welcoming barnyard of my childhood where we climbed trees, swam in
the brook, found toads in the sawdust pile, and played with the latest batch
of fluffy barn kittens. The farm, like many small family farms, was defunct,
the barn empty and the tractor shed replaced by a large, dome-shaped
metal structure that housed massive pieces of woods machinery. The long
woodhouse and kitchen that had been attached to the main house and

given it its homey, rambling appearance had been torn off years before. But with all these changes, the old, faithful apple trees remained in their places—the big old white-grape tree to the side, and the orchard behind, a good trek across the field in the back. There stood the tree that bore the Duchess apples, now at its peak and heavy with medium-sized, mottled green and red-cheeked fruit. The tree that had the deepest-red apples, I remembered Granny telling me, was not to be harvested until later in the fall, for in spite of their picture-book beauty the apples were hard and sour, winter apples to be stored until the snow lay deep upon the ground.

I stopped the car in the parking place near the back doorstep where my grandmother's Rhode Island Reds once pecked and scratched for grubs among the plantain and the sweet-smelling chamomile weeds. Three wooden lawn chairs and a picnic table sat with their feet in newly mowed grass close to where the small coupled henhouse and outhouse had once been. To my four children, who piled out of the car carrying plastic buckets and grocery bags, this was just another apple-gathering excursion with Mom. But for me, when I saw that we were alone here, my uncle and aunt having gone away for the day, it was a chance to breathe deeply the sweetly appled air, and to be transported to hot, sunny September Sundays of my childhood: squirming under the barbed-wire fence behind the house with my siblings, buckets in hand, heading across the pasture to the orchard. We would try not to step on the dry cow patties dotting the field or, worse, the fresh patties, soiling our shoes or oozing up between our toes forcing us to wipe our bare feet on the grass before we could bear to take another step toward the small group of apple trees nestled up against the woods at the back of the pasture.

Once we were through the fence, I took the hand of my youngest to help him wade through the grass that used to be cropped by red-and-white Guernseys, while the other three children ran ahead, shouting back and forth, wanting to get to the orchard ahead of us. The cow patties were gone now, having long ago returned to the earth, and the distance to the orchard was shorter than it had seemed when I was young. I wished to give my own children a glimpse of what this spot had meant to me as a youngster, what it meant to me as an adult, but I knew I could not evoke it for them. All I could do was relate a few remembrances as they came to me. Like the one of Pete, the black border collie, who had worn a path along the steep, tree-lined bank between the house and the road. As soon as we crossed the bridge, there he'd be, tearing along that path, smiling and barking and racing the car until, as suddenly as he had appeared he would disappear, and then, as we arrived in the yard, like wizardry, he would be waiting to greet us!

I pointed to the tree we wanted, and the two older boys helped each other clamber up the twisted trunk of the old Duchess. They perched on the sturdy lower limbs, reached up and shook the heavy branches above their heads. Apples rained down, the three of us on the ground scrambling to pick them up while we could still tell which ones had just fallen and which ones were already there, lying in the grass with the inevitable worm and ant holes on the bottom even though the side looking up at the sky appeared perfectly fine.

Probably no one else would have noticed the apple bough lying where it had fallen after being torn from the mother tree seasons ago in a strong, cold northwest wind or in a late-summer gale. It had been weakened, perhaps, by ice and snow and by too many children's feet clambering upon it to shake the apples to the ground, or simply crippled by the sheer weight of its own fruit year after year. Now, what was left of the large bough, a piece of timber three times the length and breadth of a woman's arm, lay half-covered in the grass, at home on the ground, its bark long ago salvaged by insects, its exterior sanded smooth by snow and sun and rain, producing a contour at once as natural and as deliberate as pottery formed by a potter's hand.

My grandmother had picked apples from that very branch. Season after season my mother's bare feet had danced upon it. Her hands had shaken apples from it for her younger siblings to pick up and plunk into their own metal buckets. Each fall the apples had been cut and cooked, sieved and bottled to be eaten as apple sauce when the tree's branches were frozen and laden with snow. They had been cored and sliced and made into pies with the skins left on, a custom I myself had taken from my grandmother who was thrifty with both time and produce. This tree limb was a fragment of the life that had gone on here and was still going on as we carried out the fall ritual of apple-gathering.

Back at home the apple bough rested comfortably amid the pinks and petunias in my flower bed. Another summer had come and gone since I'd wrestled it from its grassy grave beneath my grandmother's Duchess apple tree where it lay anchored, entangled in grass, long strands draped across it like a young woman's hair. I'd wondered at the worlds I was fracturing as I ripped it from the earth. A new world was being created in my own garden, though. At one end creeping thyme made its way up and over the old branch and at the other, groups of Johnny-jump-ups smiled spontaneously from seemingly intentional places, reflecting the amusement I knew my grandmother would have felt at the idea of my uprooting the old limb to adorn my front yard.

In the backyard the kids' paternal great-grandfather puttered in the garden, wrestling with squash and pumpkin vines, trying to create order in the chaotic jungle of vegetables that were still offering themselves in abundance in the warm September sunshine. A few puffs of smoke, greyish white against the crystalline blue sky, wafted lazily up from a forty-five gallon barrel at the far end of the yard. "Uh-oh," I thought wryly. "Gramp is cleaning up again."

The clear hot days of September turned into cooler October ones, with red and gold, wind-rattled leaves warning of impending cold. We cleared the garden produce away, squash and pumpkins sun-cured and stored, ready for pies and jack-o'-lanterns. We set the onions out in the sun until their tops were brown and crisp, and hung them for the winter. We gathered apples and processed them, cooked their gleaming white flesh and sieved and sugared it to make a smooth, sweet sauce. On a cool October day, the smell of freshly baked bread filled the house and wafted from an open window. I removed the last brown loaves from the oven and turned them out of the hot pans, upside down on the racks to cool.

I'll never know what Gramp was thinking when he stepped through the kitchen door that day, windblown and tired, to announce that he had burned the apple bough. I only know that his face wore an expression of triumph, of satisfaction mixed with trepidation, for he must have been suddenly afraid to tell me what he had done. I'm sure he'd wanted to do it for a long time and had never dared, not while all that vigorous life wound its way around and about the old branch. But now that autumn had set in and the blooms had gone to seed, it would have seemed even more ridiculous to him, a rotten, old limb lying in the flower bed where it didn't belong.

I stood motionless as he told me what he had done. I could not speak, for to have done so would have been to reveal the extent of my loss. How would he have lived with himself had he been able to fully understand the value of the life that had existed in that apple branch, life that was as nonexistent to him as the smoke rising from the forty-five gallon barrel, floating up and dissipating into the grey October sky?

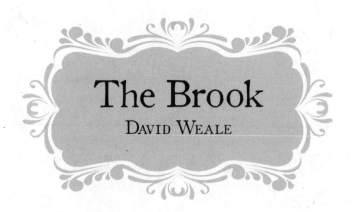

The Brook

David Weale

IN THE LONG, green days of my childhood one of my favourite haunts was along the banks of a merry brook that wound its way through the woods near my home. There, unburdened by purpose and free of adult supervision, I spent countless happy hours. The stream flowed strong and clear between alders and junipers, with quiet deep holes under fallen logs where brown trout waited, and noisy, narrow places where it burbled over rocks and around branches, filling the air with the natural jazz of its tumbling passage. Farther along it flattened out into a little pond, rimmed with watercress, where surface-striders darted in and out of patches of sun, filtered through a low canopy of swamp maple. That little stream was a congenial companion for a boy and his dog, and there was scarcely a summer day we didn't wander there.

According to ancient spiritual lore, a brook or stream was a revered feature of the landscape: a place of spiritual power that represented the two worlds of human experience—the temporal and the eternal—and the importance of being able to cross with a leap from one to the other. I, of course, had no knowledge of that. All I knew was that the brook had the power to draw me to its banks, and that it was for me a place of joy. But looking back it's not difficult for me to believe that when I went there I transmigrated to the timeless world where energy is not broken up into little pieces, and the child is Lord of creation.

David (age 7) teaching Fluffy to beg, Greenmount, PEI, 1950

There seemed to be a brook in everyone's life back then, and just up the road a large one cut across the farm of a neighbouring family where I went often to play. It flowed just one field away from their house, and during the heat of summer they used it as a cooler. In a big, wooden tub, half-submerged over a spring-hole, they kept their butter and cream, and their homemade mayonnaise. Before almost every meal one of the kids would be told to "run to the brook" to get what was needed, and sometimes I ran with them.

There was also a spot, farther downstream, where the cows filed down to drink, leaving deep hoof prints in the cool mud. During early summer the perimeter of that drinking pool was crowded with a bright assembly of waxy, yellow flowers. We called them cowslips. I know that's not the correct botanical name but it seemed perfect, for in my child's mind I always imagined their presence around the pool must have had something to do with the coming and going of the cattle.

A game we played often along the brook was to make little wooden boats—cast-off pieces of board with a V-cut at one end—and launch them together at a place upstream from the wagon bridge. We would release them into the current, then run as fast as our spindly legs would carry us to the bridge and wait to see whose boat would be the first to arrive. It was a simple pastime, but like so many of the other games we played it had the power to engage us utterly and to deliver us out of time. For those few hours, along the banks of that winding stream, we were as free as we would ever be.

It has been more than fifty years since those events occurred, and I find it increasingly difficult to recapture a sense of my existence back then. Occasionally there are openings: tiny, tantalizing intimations, swift as a shutter, when I experience briefly the wonder and immediacy of those boyhood adventures, but mostly it seems a blind has been drawn between who I am today and who I was along the banks of that little brook. It's why I went back, just this past year, on what could only be described as a personal pilgrimage. I'm not exactly sure what I was expecting, but I suppose I was hoping I might somehow become, for an entire afternoon, that boy on his stomach, peering into the clear water, or waiting at the bridge for his little boat to come bobbing around the last turn. Sadly, it was not to be. All that remained was a meandering dry bed, but no water, and no sound of splashing. The brook was gone. Vanished.

I wanted very much to have someone explain to me how such a thing could have happened, or to be able to blame someone. But there was no one to ask, or accuse, so I just stood there, filled with disappointment and a sense of loss. Something eager and precious had gone out of the world, and I was a witness.

I have accepted most of the changes of the past half-century, in Greenmount and in myself, and try not to sentimentalize the world I viewed through a boy's eyes. I understand, and am resigned to, the disappearance of familiar landmarks, the dilapidation of old houses and barns, the straightening and improving of the crooked little roads, and how the entire landscape seems more stripped and less magical than I remember it. But the disappearance of that little brook is another matter. It speaks to me, not just of change, but of diminishment, and of a dryness that has invaded our world. And though I could never prove it, I know in my bones there is a connection between the drying up of that little brook and our society's neglect of the deep-down freshness of the inner life.

I don't wish to resign myself to that.

A Country Song Played Backward

Jill Sexsmith

AT THE EDGE of a town called Somewhere, there's a dirt road that leads to my childhood home. In the background, there's a red barn where my black horse waits for me. My dog is somewhere, probably swimming in the river that runs through it all. All of this, the people and animals, exists now only in memory. It's a slow curve down a back road I seldom revisit, and when I do it's always in a pickup truck driven in reverse. Isn't that how you get back all of the things you've lost? Or is that a country song played backward?

My last months there, years ago, were spent with my grandmother and saw me quitting school, my job, my life, to keep her there as long as possible. I knew her death was the end of more than her life. It was the end of all of this—a century of farming and routine and furrows of land that must have known us all by name or footprint.

Her death was a predictable cancerous one. After years of chimney action, her lungs turned in on her, filled her small body with a plume of chemicals, and painted her insides black. There was the silent elevator ride after news of being beyond treatment, beyond therapy, beyond hope.

My grandmother was an atheist, though I suspect a believer in the odd after-school special in which the shadow sent to escort a person to the other side meets them, squares off eye-to-eye, then turns around and floats the other way, as if to say, not yet. She never acknowledged her death

Jill (age 4) with Nick, 1978

except to say she would never get a chance to wear her new sundress. I helped her hem it, before it was time for open-backed gowns.

"Am I too old to be wearing this?"

"I think it's perfect."

She looked twelve, but I wanted to remember her standing in the doorway, with light and life surrounding her and a blanket of flowers covering her.

For a while, her blue-haired friends stopped by with raisin-laden dainties to say their awkward goodbyes. I was in the kitchen eavesdropping and sweeping prairie dirt under the rug.

When the stairs became too much to navigate, we replaced the dining room table with a hospital bed. She complained it was too hot. In the dining room where we once ate turkey dinners, I listened to her morphine confessions. On highs, she asked me to make sure my grandfather wasn't wearing his rubber boots into town. On lows, she wanted to rewrite her will. On plateaus, there were certain pieces of china to be left to particular people, though the order was always changing and in the end seven people were left sharing the same broken teacup.

Eventually, she required tubes for water, air, earth, and fire. She ate nothing and remained remarkably lucid, though every time she woke up, she scolded me for not having visited her for years. All in all, we were a tight-lipped family, circling her bed, not knowing what to say but doing all the right things.

She died in a hospital room with her daughter and son at her side. I was not there, but I can picture her squaring off with the darkness, searching its eyes and knowing it was time. I can see her changing into her dress before she walked away, shadow by her side. There is one stoplight in Somewhere; it changed from green to amber to red and back to green again. The road to our farm disappeared, and no one seemed to notice.

My family went through her belongings. I wanted to keep the most ridiculous things to save them from Goodwill and to keep my cousins from having them. I wanted all of her lasts. Her last unfinished knitting projects, the last apple pie she baked, her toothbrush, her misshapen ceramic pots.

We cleared out the house, and it seemed like an empty container, too small to have ever held life. I walked up and down the stairs avoiding the loudest creaks—we had mapped them all out like crude cartographers when we were kids, practising our Christmas Eve Santa ambush. Somewhere in all of this, my dog nibbled on rat poison in a nook or cranny of the farmhouse. Between attempts to hoard a dead woman's belongings, there was a flight to a veterinary hospital and a dog whose eyes welcomed her into the darkness.

Somewhere in all of this, my black horse broke out of his pen and went for a midnight snack. He was my steady four-beat friend for over ten years, and I can imagine him in all his glory stuffing his face with food, loving every grain of it. But that kind of eating was no good for an old horse's bones; he bloated and ended up with a bullet in his head, and I was not there for that last breath either.

Somewhere in all of this, I had a boyfriend. We had come to the end of our relationship long ago, though we agreed to stay together until my grandmother died. Once she was gone, we waited a few more weeks to not make it completely obvious. And when the body turned cold, I bought a plane ticket across an ocean and found myself trying to forget where I had come from. While I was gone, Somewhere didn't wait for me. The house was moved. The barn imploded. The land sold out, went commercial, and became a golf course, a flood diversion, a greenhouse, a traitor. And I walked on foreign lands and felt the ground crumbling beneath my feet, and felt my grandmother's breath pushing me along, forcing me not to look back to see if the ground was still there.

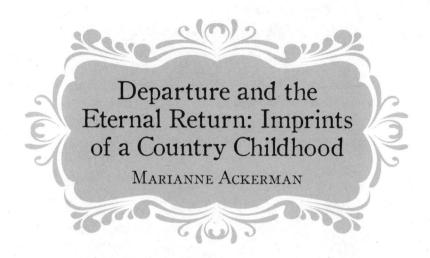

Departure and the Eternal Return: Imprints of a Country Childhood

Marianne Ackerman

AS A CHILD of the sixties, I never imagined the time would come when my past would seem quaint or even faintly exotic. I grew up on a farm in Prince Edward County near the shores of Lake Ontario and, like so many of my generation, left for university determined to establish myself permanently in a city.

Four of my five siblings married and built houses along the crest of 120 acres our father inherited from his parents. Twenty nieces and nephews have spent or are spending childhoods with roughly the same view we had growing up. A savvy lot, they have high-speed Internet, satellite TV, and schoolmates from many countries. I can still sometimes surprise them with an exotic delicacy from Montreal, but it's easier to get their attention with tales of life when we were kids, back when heading to the toilet meant a freezing trek to the outhouse and the neighbours could pick up their telephone receivers and listen in on our conversations. We walked five miles to school over crusty snow, bicycled home in the rain, and worked— of course we were all slaves to the chores, with hardly the strength to flop in front of a black-and-white TV on Sunday night for an episode of *Bonanza* or *The Ed Sullivan Show*.

Stripped of embellishment, though, the fundamentals of being young in a rural environment haven't changed much at all. A country childhood is still often idyllic and sometimes insufferable. My nieces and nephews

Marianne (left, age 4) with sister Maureen (right) in the washtub, 1956

seem both as happy and as obsessed as I was with the one geographical feature that distinguishes city living from its opposite: a clear view of the horizon. That distant line is a powerful force. Airports and trains don't seem to hold the same fascination for urban youth. More than a question of being bored or dissatisfied, it's something about the existence of space, the natural convergence of land and sky above ploughed ground and woods that makes the road seem so important. And I suspect they'll find as I did that behind their escape plan lies in waiting an equally powerful yearning for return.

This past summer, my three preteen nephews watched as a backhoe scraped loads of topsoil from a fence line, and they wondered out loud whether the seasonal creek might turn into a river. Assured they could expect white water rapids any day (shame on the old boys!), Elliotte, John, and Jake embarked upon a three-week effort to build a raft, complete with a steering shaft and a strong box for food. After an arid fall, the ditch is still bone dry, and the barge is in the township dump. But I'm sure their Huckleberry Finn fantasy left indelible marks. The idea of changing their world by making something out of scraps will resurface. It's only a matter of time until the urge to sail away fixes around a new scheme. They will probably leave the farm, and if so, they will hanker to return. These two contradictory compulsions have propelled my life, providing both momentum and a lingering sense of displacement.

———————◆———————

When I complained of boredom growing up, my mother's consoling words seemed calculated to sting: "Thank your lucky stars you're not stuck in downtown Toronto." I secretly swore I'd make the curse come true. I imagined myself in a poison ivy–free environment with movie theatres on every corner, newspapers delivered to the door, and plenty of cafés where I could linger writing in my diary without fear my sister would read it and tell other people, as she had. (Maybe I secretly enjoyed the publicity; what else is a novel but a story whose deepest truths seem like secrets?)

Even for someone who loved school, the end of the year was delicious. On the last school day of June at S. S. No. 6 Massassaga, I'd point my bicycle toward home with a parcel carrier full of notebooks and art, a ride that marked the end of the year more surely than the noisy adult party following Christmas. Summer was so long you were another person by fall. Late August was the highlight, when my mother and a friend picked a few acres of field tomatoes and packed them in baskets for the local supermarket to pay for our new school clothes. We kids were all expected to help out in one way or another. Disdainful of the heat and dirt involved in field labour, I happily chose the kitchen, where I could be left alone and in charge. I made meals and perfected my signature recipe: the Queen Elizabeth cake, a dark spicy loaf of crushed dates, coconut, and brown sugar icing. Between meals, I lay in the hammock reading novels and dreaming of living a writer's life.

In my mind's eye, all of those days run together into one gloriously sunny afternoon leavened by a perpetual breeze from the west. This is not just rosy nostalgia. At the time I was conscious of being happy, and it worried me. What writer has a happy childhood? What would I write about? The dark side of this self-conscious idyll was a disturbing sense that I was missing out on something important—information, experience. There were no magazines or metropolitan newspapers in our house; the few books belonged to my mother, thick tomes on religious themes. Once we inherited boxes of old *Time* magazines. I was stunned by the avalanche of news and set about cutting out all the important stories, placing them in carefully labelled files.

High school was a revelation, a solid academic environment dominated by well-educated nuns whose mission it was to impress upon us the need to forge a "philosophy of life" and pay attention to one's immortal soul. Still, I wondered about the middle ground between birth and death. In my senior year, I worked on the student newspaper and got a taste of how powerful words could be: when we printed a recipe for homemade wine, the nuns shut the publication down.

That same winter, I landed a part-time job at the *Kingston Whig-Standard* with a by-line as "district correspondent" for Prince Edward County. My mother got me in the door through a friend. Naturally, she was eager to point out that such an opportunity would never have presented itself on the streets of Toronto.

In the early seventies, the *Whig* was a lively, family-owned daily run by Robertson Davies's brother, Michael, an elegant man who wore a three-piece suit and kept a substantial library in his office. Despite having only five hundred subscribers in the county, the *Whig* took coverage of the area seriously, employing a full-time reporter and a weekend stringer. I earned five dollars for a feature, three dollars for a news story or a usable picture taken with the company's Yoshika B box camera, plus a mileage allowance. Since my father's ancient Fiat was full of gas when I set out for Picton on Saturday mornings, the car often netted more than my reporting.

Waiting for life to begin, I'd wasted precious little time on what my father called "the business end of a hoe," yet a scrapbook of my first stories reveals an eager farm crusader with a tendency to meddle. When the Mountain View canning factory spurned local farmers in favour of processing imported beans—obscure crops destined mainly (I claimed) for the "ethnic neighbourhoods of Toronto"—I was shamelessly on the farmers' side. I wrote about West Indian workers who'd come up from the Caribbean to pick apples in Lyle Van Clief's orchard, quoting the pickers as saying "the pay could be better." When I told Van Clief they wanted to stay on, he said they'd probably change their minds after the first snowfall. In a piece about a pick-your-own strawberry farm near Bloomfield, I noted that "although the plants are extremely large, they do not provide shade, and at one point during the recent heat wave, all pickers fled the field." Including this reporter, no doubt.

First jobs are like first loves: they have a lasting impact on one's personality. I was a loner, full of self-doubt, excruciatingly self-conscious and accident-prone. But being "from the *Whig*" offered a handy mask for adolescent angst. It forced me out of introversion, rescued me from a dream state induced by reading novels, and provided an instant persona, or at least the veneer of confidence. Faced with deadlines, I learned to value task completion over perfection. I acquired skills that would prove useful in other fields: how to find people and convince them talk, how to avoid taking no for an answer. At the same time, it confirmed my stinging sense of knowing nothing.

Had there been more books in our home, I might have lost myself in literature, turned further inward and taken another route to becoming a writer. Instead I became convinced it was essential to know how the world worked, to grasp the larger forces that shape existence. So I headed for Ottawa and political science at Carleton University. After graduation, I followed in the footsteps of my favourite writers and went to Paris.

———◆———

For the first two decades of my adult life, I pretty well spurned nature. In Montreal, I bought an eight-room house (the third and fourth storeys of a row house on the Plateau) without acquiring land. My daughter grew up without a pet (I convinced her that a dog or a cat would be unhappy in the city and prevent us from travelling). We went back to the farm at Easter and Christmas, and I stayed long enough one summer to write my first play in an abandoned chicken coop. But the lure of the land was mainly convenience. It saved my sanity, in absentia. As soon as Fiona was old enough to inveigle her way into my siblings' growing broods, I took to dropping her off after *la fête St-Jean* and staying away until Labour Day, when it was time to bring her back for school. It's not that I actively disliked the country, but my real life was elsewhere.

As for the European fantasy, it flared up once again as soon as Fiona left home. I sold the house, ditched my impecunious theatre company, and on little more than an enchanted dare, went to live with a Welshman in the south of France. Forty-four and deep in the throes of a mid-life crisis, I closed my eyes to implausibility, feigned enthusiasm for his dream of restoring a three-hundred-year-old ruin, and plunged into writing my first novel, *Jump*, about a single mother in Montreal who throws away everything and…

Living in France, I was obsessed with getting a place in the county—a cabin on my father's land, a drive-shed with a loft above the farm machinery. If not on the farm, then a few rough acres somewhere closer to Picton, with building possibilities. Sitting in a perfectly beautiful house in Provence, I would look out over the vineyards and picture a dilapidated cottage on the shores of Lake Ontario, a lighthouse maybe, or an abandoned canning factory. But the time I spent roaming county real estate websites came to nothing.

By the time *Jump* was published, I'd gone from intrigued bystander to helpmate and was careening toward marriage. Meanwhile, I discovered gardening. Compared with Ontario, everything in Provence is small-scale and intensive. The French word closest to garden is *jardin*, which always includes flowers; a spot for vegetables is called a *potager*, which conjures up soup. Our garden was no more than a scrap of hard dirt bordering a high stone wall, hardly enough ground for paths to the kitchen entrance and the cellar door. The centrepiece was a large acacia tree, probably fifty years old, with persistent shoots sprouting up wherever there was a crack in the stone. The whole mess was fenced in with chicken wire and a creaky gate that wouldn't have kept out a shy child.

I had hardly noticed the garden for the first few years, so preoccupied were we with interior concepts such as plumbing, electricity, tiles, and wooden beams. Eventually, though, I realized things were coming up year after year, blooming gloriously and settling into a sad brown sulk until the mistral came along and cleaned out the dead leaves. Miraculously, the whole colourful cycle started back up again towards the middle of February.

One day, when the typing wasn't going well, I decided to take a break and pull a few dead leaves off the crocuses. On the next trip to town, I bought a box of herbs, and I was hooked. Second novels are usually much harder to write than the first, which is, of necessity, an act of blind bravado. In the years I spent struggling to finish *Piers' Desire*, my garden went from abandoned eyesore to popular landmark for hoards of camera-toting tourists, who eagerly snapped shots of spectacular roses, colourful annuals, and perennials—more than a hundred varieties ranging from hardy little nothings prepared to flower in the crevices of stone walls to a full-fledged mimosa tree that did so well I was forced to sacrifice a delicate flowering sage—all carefully nurtured with horse manure, which shocked even the locals.

Begun as a respite from the head work of fiction, my garden soon took over. Finally, while a season of digital images flew back to Japan with the string of tourists that snapped them, my hobby reached a climax, and I was forced to admit my novel had stalled. The truth came by way of a backhanded compliment from an eighty-year-old neighbour who had grown up in our house. "When you first moved here, you never gardened," she declared. "Now that's all you do."

Friends published their second and third novels; I had the satisfaction of knowing I had popularized the butterfly gaura in La Roque Alric, a hamlet of fifty-six people that figures on few regional maps. Impressed by its delicate blooms, two or three other women rushed out to get pots. My most stunning accomplishment was a bearded hot-pink succulent started in a corner of cement-like lime-based soil, which quickly spread to a surface of four square metres, coincident with the trouble in Afghanistan, which prompted us to call it the Taliban.

Gardeners will go on ad nauseam if allowed. I was worse. I kept a series of maps documenting the many growth phases and flower coverings. I approached the task like an Ontario farm girl, impatient for results and betting on a ten-week growing season.

In 2004, Gwyn got a job at McGill, and we moved to Montreal. By the time we left La Roque, the folly of my over-planting had become a scandal. Referred to politely as "an English garden" by the French, my project had become a jungle. The young tenant who now presides over my monument to writer's block has let half of it die, and there are still blooms galore. By the time we returned after the first winter, it was too late to do much more than bag up the dried leaves and water the survivors. I didn't care. I'd broken the cycle.

Since settling back in Montreal, I have written and published a third novel. We live in a house with an enclosed yard, and so far I've stayed on the literary side of the fence. As the geographical distance between me and the county, past and present, shrank, my desire to own a bit of it seemed to disappear, although I fully expect the urge to nail down a piece of the physical, territorial past will return.

Meanwhile, I go back to the landscape of my childhood for the latest stories, tales of rafts built to face the open sea, and a chance to watch young lives unfolding amid a familiar landscape. The last time I was there, Elliotte, John, and Jake were busy transforming a push lawn mower into a hybrid rough-terrain vehicle. They figured the first trip into the woods might be rough going, but by the second time out, they'd have forged a path. The perfect invention from the minds of rural children: a mode of transportation made for doubling back.

Acknowledgements

I am grateful to the Alberta Foundation for the Arts for providing funding that made this anthology possible. Dennis Johnson, Nik Burton, Myrna Kostash, and Jeananne Kirwin provided helpful advice on particular aspects the project. Many thanks to the staff at Nimbus Publishing, particularly editor and fellow former country kid Patrick Murphy, who was enthusiastic, conscientious, and respectful in his work on the anthology. I couldn't have asked for more. Above all, I am grateful to the authors who so willingly shared their stories. Thank you for your generosity, patience, and grace.

—Pam Chamberlain

Publication Credits

Pamela Banting's "Believe It or Not" was first published in *Alberta Views* 5.3 (2002): 46–49. Reprinted with permission of the author.

NJ Brown's "Wave Riders" was first published in *WestWord* 27.4 (2007): 24–28. Reprinted with permission of the author. "Wave Riders" contains quotations from *Jon Whyte: Mind Over Mountains* (Ed. Harry Vandervlist. Calgary: Red Deer Press, 2000) and the unpublished autobiography of Thomas N. Wood, *Memories of an Old Prairie Rancher* (1983).

Roch Carrier's "A Secret Lost in the Water" is from *The Hockey Sweater and Other Stories*, by Roch Carrier © 1979 House of Anansi Press. Reprinted with permission of the publisher. www.anansi.ca

Pam Chamberlain's introduction includes quotations from Warren Cariou's *Lake of the Prairies: A Story of Belonging* (Toronto: Doubleday Canada, 2002, 12), Timothy Findley's *Inside Memory: Pages from a Writer's Notebook* (Toronto: HarperCollins, 1990, 88), and Wes Jackson's *Becoming Native to this Place* (Berkeley, CA: Counterpoint, 1996, 3).

Catherine R. Fenwick's "Guardian Angels" contains a quotation from Warren Cariou's *Lake of the Prairies: A Story of Belonging* (Toronto: Doubleday Canada, 2002, 13).

George Fox's "Section 29" was first published in *My First Cow: Ranch Stories* by George Fox (Trail of the Fox Inc., 2001). Reprinted with permission of the author.

Betty Howatt's "The Outhouse Affair" was first published in *Tales from Willowshade Farm: An Island Woman's Notebook* by Betty Howatt (Charlottetown: Acorn Press, 2003). Reprinted with permission of the author.

Wayne Johnston's "The Goulds" is excerpted from *Baltimore's Mansion* by Wayne Johnston. Copyright © 1999 1310945 Ontario Inc. Reprinted by permission of Knopf Canada.

Ruth Latta's "Fargo, North Dakota" was first published in *The Grist Mill* 7 (1998–1999): 69-72. Reprinted with permission of the author.

Shelley A. Leedahl's "Road Trip: Why I Write About Saskatchewan" was first published in *NeWest Review* 21.6 (1996): 6–8. Reprinted with permission of the author.

Shirlee Smith Matheson's "Valley Girl" was first published in the September 6, 1984 edition of *Western People*, a supplement to the *Western Producer*. Reprinted with permission of the publisher and the author.

Habeeb Salloum's "Our Family's Homesteading Days" is excerpted from *Arab Cooking on a Saskatchewan Homestead: Recipes and Recollections* by Habeeb Salloum (Regina: Canadian Plains Research Center, 2005). Reprinted with permission of the author and the Canadian Plains Research Center at the University of Regina.

Jill Sexsmith's "A Country Song Played Backward" was first published in *PRISM International* 44.3 (2006): 52–54. Reprinted with permission of the author.

Pamela Wallin's "The Centre of the Universe" is excerpted from *Since You Asked* by Pamela Wallin (Toronto: Random House, 1998). Reprinted with permission of the author.

David Weale's "The Brook" was first published in *Chasing the Shore: Little Stories about Spirit and Landscape* by David Weale (Charlottetown: Tangle Lane, 2007). Reprinted with permission of the author.

Rudy Wiebe's "Tombstone Community" is extracted from *River of Stone: Fictions and Memories* by Rudy Wiebe. Copyright © 1995 Jackpine House Ltd. Reprinted by permission of Knopf Canada.

About the Contributors

Marianne Ackerman was born and raised on a farm in Prince Edward County, Ontario, where she returns whenever possible. She studied French at the Sorbonne, political science at Carleton University, and has an MA in drama from the University of Toronto. A journalist, playwright, and novelist, she is publisher and founder of the online arts magazine *Rover*. Her most recent novel, *Piers' Desire*, is set in the south of France where she and her husband Gwyn Campbell spent six years. They currently live in Montreal.

Janice Acton was born in 1948 on South View Farm, a small mixed farm located north of Saskatchewan's Qu'Appelle Valley. In the 1950s, she and her family embarked on a series of seasonal moves off the farm, first to the nearby town of Lemberg and later to Saskatoon. In 1972, following graduation from the University of Saskatchewan, Acton moved to Toronto. She has lived in Halifax since 1994, working as a writer and researcher.

Luanne Armstrong, MFA, PhD, is an award-winning writer of novels, children's books, and non-fiction. Her memoir, *Blue Valley: An Ecological Memoir*, is about her lifelong relationship with her family's farm. She is an adjunct professor of creative writing for the University of British Columbia and lives on the family farm in the Kootenay region where she grew up.

Pamela Banting grew up in Birch River in northwestern Manitoba. She has since lived in Winnipeg, Gimli, Calgary, Edmonton, and London, Ontario, and currently lives in Cochrane, Alberta. She is a professor of Canadian and environmental literature at the University of Calgary. Her courses on animals and the rural have attracted the attention of the Humane Society of the United States, the *Western Producer*, and CBC Radio. In addition to dozens of articles, poems, and essays, she is the author of *Body Inc.: A Theory of Translation Poetics* and editor of the anthology *Fresh Tracks: Writing the Western Landscape*.

Andrew Beattie was raised on a farm near Hay Lakes, Alberta, alongside chickens, pigs, goats, sheep, and the odd llama. After earning an English degree from the University of Alberta, he spent six years in Towada, in mountainous northern Japan, where he taught English to Japanese children during the day and played in an old-timers' hockey league in the evenings. In 2009, he returned to

Canada with his wife, Rie. His writing has been published in *Horizon, Crows' Toes Quarterly*, and *Alberta Anthology 2007*.

Chris Beingessner was born in 1979 and raised on a small mixed farm near Truax, Saskatchewan, fifty miles southwest of Regina. After his grandfather's death in 1995, Beingessner farmed while attending high school and university. He then taught in rural Saskatchewan for four years before he and his wife Brenda moved to Cambodia to teach. In 2007 they returned to Regina and in 2009 welcomed their daughter, Norah, to the world. Beingessner was awarded the Gary Hyland Award for Excellence in Teaching English and the Lieutenant Governor's Award for Arts and Learning for his innovative work in the classroom.

Laura Best was born in 1960 and raised in the community of East Dalhousie, Nova Scotia, where she has lived her entire life. Her writing has been published in *The Antigonish Review* and *Grain* and in the anthologies *Christmas in the Maritimes* and *A Maritime Christmas*. Her young adult novel *Bitter, Sweet* was published in 2009. In addition to writing, Best works in the Christmas tree industry, shearing trees and making wreaths, and she volunteers for the local church and museum.

NJ Brown was born in 1964 in Empress, Alberta, and raised in Burstall, Saskatchewan, where her father worked for the Pacific Gas Plant. She has lived in small towns across the prairie provinces, including Leader, Fort McMurray, Wandering River, Athabasca, and Plamondon. She now lives in Edmonton where she works as a freelance writer and editor and teaches at Grant MacEwan University. Her writing has appeared in *Legacy, Rags, WestWord, Edmontonians*, and various MacEwan publications. She won the 2007 Jon Whyte Memorial Essay Prize for "Wave Riders."

Sharon Butala has lived nearly all her life in Saskatchewan, including thirty-three years on a ranch in the Frenchman River Valley. She has published sixteen books, including the bestselling memoir, *The Perfection of the Morning*, and has received the Marian Engel Award among other prizes and awards, five of which, with her late husband, were for conservation. She is an Officer of the Order of Canada and was invested into the Saskatchewan Order of Merit in 2009. Her latest book, *The Girl in Saskatoon: A Meditation on Friendship, Memory, and Murder*, was released in 2008.

Roch Carrier was born in the small town of Sainte-Justine, Quebec, in 1937. He received a BA at the Université Saint-Louis in Edmunston, New Brunswick, a master's degree at the Université de Montréal, and a doctorate at the Université de Paris. He published his first book, *La Guerre, Yes Sir!*, in 1968. He was secretary-general of the Théâtre du Nouveau Monde in Montreal, the director of the Canada Council from 1994 to 1997, and the National Librarian from 1999 to 2004. An Officer of the Order of Canada, Carrier lives in Ottawa and Montreal.

Pam Chamberlain was born in 1970 to grandchildren of Ukrainian and English homesteaders. She grew up on a mixed farm in the agricultural community of Tulliby Lake, in east-central Alberta. She has lived across Alberta—in Athabasca, Camrose, Lloydminster, Edmonton, and Calgary—and in Whitehorse, Yukon, and Freising, Germany. She has a BEd and an MA from the University of Alberta and has been teaching English literature and writing for more than a decade.

Keith Collier grew up in the tiny town of St. Joseph's Cove, in Bay D'Espoir on Newfoundland's south coast. He moved to St. John's to study at Memorial University, and he now works there as a historian and writer. He enjoys hiking, camping, sea kayaking, and other activities that let him explore the beauty of Newfoundland and Labrador.

Wayne Curtis was born and raised on a family farm near Blackville, New Brunswick. He has published twelve books, including *Wild Apples*, a collection of essays, and *Night Train to Havana*, a novel. His memoir *Long Ago and Far Away* will be published in 2010. Curtis has been awarded the George Woodcock Award and the David Adams Richards Award for Fiction. In 2005, he received an Honorary Doctorate of Letters from St. Thomas University. He has lived in Ontario, Yukon, and Cuba, and now divides his time between Fredericton and the Miramichi River in New Brunswick.

Laurie Elmquist was raised in rural Ontario near the town of Wiarton. She left at the age of nineteen to attend university in Hamilton. Elmquist, who holds an MA in English and creative writing from the University of Windsor, now lives in Victoria, where she teaches creative writing and composition at Camosun College. Her short stories, poetry, and essays have appeared in several periodicals and anthologies, including *My Wedding Dress* and *Wrestling with the Angel*.

Catherine R. Fenwick was born in 1945 in Indian Head, Saskatchewan, and raised on a mixed farm nearby. She has since lived in several Saskatchewan towns and cities, including Kendal, Estevan, Humboldt, and Saskatoon, and she now calls Regina home. An educator for more than thirty years, Fenwick holds a master's degree in clinical psychology and gives workshops across Canada. She has published two books, *Healing with Humour* and *Love and Laughter*, and one poetry chapbook, *Telling My Sister's Story*.

Darlene Foster was raised on a mixed farm near Medicine Hat, Alberta. After living in Calgary, she moved to British Columbia, and has settled in Tsawwassen with her husband and their two cats. She loves the mild weather of the west coast but will always call the prairies her home. Foster is an ESL teacher and a youth employment counsellor. She enjoys travelling, reading, walking on the beach, and telling stories. She has won prizes for her short stories, has published travel articles, and has recently e-published a travel/adventure novel for young readers called *Amanda in Arabia: The Perfume Flask*.

George Fox grew up on a cattle ranch in the foothills near Cochrane, Alberta. A popular musician, singer, and songwriter, he has released eleven albums and twenty-seven singles and hosted television specials such as *A George Fox Christmas*. He won the Juno Award for Country Male Vocalist of the Year and the Canadian Country Music Awards' Male Vocalist of the Year three times each, as well as many honours from the RPM Big Country Awards. Fox's hometown honoured him in 1995 by naming a new street George Fox Trail. Fox lives with his wife and daughters in southern Ontario.

Joyce Glasner was born in Germany, raised on a small farm in Ontario, and currently calls Halifax, Nova Scotia, home. She is an editor, author, and freelance writer whose articles have appeared in publications such as *Canadian Gardening, Canadian Geographic, Harrowsmith Country Life*, and *The Beaver*. She is the author of three non-fiction books, including *The Halifax Explosion: Surviving the Blast that Shook a Nation* and *Pirates and Privateers: Swashbuckling Stories from the East Coast*.

Leah Benvie Hamilton was raised in Brookfield, Nova Scotia, and spent much time on the farms of relatives in the Stewiacke Valley. After completing one year of a BA program, she and her husband spent five years in a log cabin overlooking the Stewiacke Valley. Two of four children were home-birthed there, and a car battery-powered radio provided her lifeline, CBC Radio. Hamilton now lives in the village of Upper Stewiacke and is a gardener and a voracious reader of novels, poetry, and short stories. "The Apple Branch" is her first published text.

Betty (King) Howatt was born and brought up in Charlottetown. She spent school holidays in the rural community of Forest Hill in eastern Prince Edward Island, on a farm that her ancestors established in the 1800s. She taught for six years before becoming a full-time fruit and vegetable farmer with her husband, Everett. She has a weekly column on CBC Radio's *Mainstreet*, which was the source of her book *Tales from Willowshade Farm*. She lives beside the Tryon River in central PEI, where her husband's ancestors settled in 1783.

Wayne Johnston was born and raised in the Goulds, Newfoundland. He earned a BA in English from Memorial University and an MA in creative writing from the University of New Brunswick. He worked as a reporter for the *St. John's Daily News* before devoting himself full-time to writing. His novel *The Story of Bobby O'Malley* won the W. H. Smith First Novel Award for the best English-language book in Canada. *Colony of Unrequited Dreams* made the *Globe and Mail's* list of one hundred most important Canadian books, and his memoir *Baltimore's Mansion* won the prestigious Charles Taylor Prize. Johnston lives in Toronto.

Ruth (Olson) Latta was raised on a 160-acre mixed farm in the Timiskaming district in northern Ontario. She earned a teacher's certificate from North Bay Teachers' College, a BA and an MA in history from Queen's University, and a BA in English from the University of Waterloo. Latta is the author of twelve books, including short story collections, two historical books, a biography, four Delia Cornford mysteries, and the novels *An Amethyst Remembrance* (2008) and *Spelling Bee* (2009). She also writes a monthly books column for the Ottawa magazine *Forever Young*.

Shelley A. Leedahl was born in Kyle, Saskatchewan, in 1963, and grew up in Turtleford, Wilkie, and Meadow Lake. She participated in a Canada-Mexico Writing/Photography Exchange and has received fellowships to international residencies including Fundación Valparaíso (Spain), Hawthornden Castle (Scotland), and the Hambidge Center (Georgia, US). Her titles include *The House of the Easily Amused*, *Orchestra of the Lost Steps*, *Talking Down the Northern Lights*, *Riding Planet Earth*, and *The Bone Talker*. Leedahl lives and writes in scenic Middle Lake, Saskatchewan.

Andrew Leitch was born in Edmonton, Alberta, and has lived in Toronto, Ontario; Yarmouth, Nova Scotia; and Hinton, Alberta. He has degrees in English from the University of Alberta and journalism from Ryerson University and currently works as a communications professional in Edmonton. Leitch's writing has been published in magazines and newspapers as well as corporate, non-profit, government, and university publications. Like most of the boys in his neighbourhood, he grew up watching *Hockey Night in Canada* on Saturday nights and playing on a local team.

Rose-Marie Lohnes was born in Upper Northfield in 1941. She worked for thirty-seven years as an educator, volunteered with CUSO in Barbados and Bolivia, and won the US Department of Education's Adult Literacy Award. She graduated with a Master of Education degree from Mount Saint Vincent University at the age of 48. Since her retirement, she was elected to the local school board, became part of a writing group, The Scribblers, and joined the South Shore Ukulele Players. She has just completed a manuscript about volunteering in Bolivia and now lives in Bridgewater, Nova Scotia.

Shirlee Smith Matheson was born in Winnipeg and raised on farms near Riding Mountains in Manitoba and Sylvan Lake in Alberta. She currently lives in Calgary, where she is employed at the Aero Space Museum. Her sixteen books include *Flying the Frontiers, Volumes I, II, and III; Lost: True Stories of Canadian Aviation Tragedies; Maverick in the Sky;* and, most recently, *Amazing Flights and Flyers.* Her titles for young readers include *Fastback Beach, Keeper of the Mountain, Flying Ghosts, The Gambler's Daughter,* and *Jailbird Kid.* Her short stories have been published in numerous magazines and anthologies.

Kay Parley was born in 1923 and raised on a mixed farm in the community of Moffat, Saskatchewan. She holds degrees in sociology and education and has worked as a commercial artist, teacher, secretary, and psychiatric nurse. She retired in 1987 after eighteen years of teaching at the Kelsey Institute in Saskatoon. She has published stories in *Western People*, the *Western Producer*, *Transition*, and *Folklore*, and she self-published *They Cast a Long Shadow: The Story of Moffat, Saskatchewan*, and *Lady with a Lantern*, an inside look at the Weyburn psychiatric hospital in the 1950s. She lives in Saskatoon.

Habeeb Salloum grew up in southern Saskatchewan, joined the RCAF during World War Two, and worked for the Canadian Department of National Revenue for thirty-six years. As a full-time freelance writer specializing in food, history, culture, and travel, his publications include *Classic Vegetarian Cooking from the Middle East and North Africa*, *Arabic Contributions to the English Vocabulary*, *From the Lands of Figs and Olives*, *Journeys Back to Arab Spain*, and *Arab Cooking on a Saskatchewan Homestead: Recipes and Recollections*. Salloum's articles have appeared in the *Toronto Star*, the *Globe and Mail*, the *Western Producer*, *Vegetarian Journal*, and *Saveur*.

Jill Sexsmith grew up in Manitoba and has lived and worked in Australia and Japan. She has a BA in sociology from the University of Winnipeg, a diploma in communications from Red River College, and is now an MFA student in the University of British Columbia's optional-residency creative writing program. Her writing has appeared in literary journals such as *PRISM International*, *The Fiddlehead*, and *The New Quarterly*. She lives in Winnipeg, where she works as an editor.

Marianne Stamm was born in 1958 on a small mixed farm in Switzerland. Her family immigrated to Fort St. John, British Columbia, to pioneer a dairy farm. Marriage took her back to Switzerland before she and husband Robert bought a grain farm near Westlock, Alberta, which they operated together for many years. They spend several months each year working on agricultural projects in Zambia. Marianne writes regularly for the *Westlock News*, *Grainews*, and Swiss and Zambian farm newspapers. She also writes a weekly blog for the *Western Producer* online.

Brent Sutter was born in Viking, Alberta, and raised on a mixed farm nearby. He played NHL hockey for eighteen seasons, winning the Stanley Cup twice and the Canada Cup three times. As a coach, he led the Canada National Junior Team to World Junior Championship gold medals in 2005 and 2006 and to the Canada-Russia Super Series gold medal in 2007. He is the owner of the Red Deer Rebels and the head coach of the Calgary Flames. He lives with his family on a farm near Sylvan Lake, Alberta.

Gordon Tootoosis, great-grandnephew of the Cree leader Chief Poundmaker and son of political activist John Tootoosis, is a painter, sculptor, singer, dancer, and actor. His films include *Legends of the Fall*, *Big Bear*, *Reindeer Games*, and *Hank Williams First Nation*. A champion of Aboriginal rights, he has served as chief of Poundmaker Cree Nation, vice-chief of the Federation of Saskatchewan

Indian Nations, and a member of the board of directors for the Saskatchewan Communications Network and the Saskatchewan Native Theatre Company. A Member of the Order of Canada, he lives with his wife and four grandchildren at Poundmaker Cree Nation.

Harvey Walker grew up on a mixed farm near Claresholm, Alberta, in the 1940s. After teaching high school English for thirty years, he now occasionally teaches English to francophone soldiers at the Edmonton garrison. Walker has written travel articles for the *Calgary Herald* and the *Edmonton Journal*. His short stories have appeared in *Freefall*, *On Spec*, and *Prairie Journal for Canadian Literature*. Two of his stories have been nominated for the Journey Prize. His first novel, *Bananarchy,* was an Alberta bestseller. *Monkeywrench* is its sequel. He lives on an acreage near St. Albert, Alberta.

The Honourable **Pamela Wallin** was born in Moose Jaw and raised in Wadena, Saskatchewan. After thirty years as a popular journalist and broadcaster, in 2008 she was appointed to the Senate of Canada. She is also the chancellor of the University of Guelph and the senior advisor on Canada-U.S. Relations at the Americas Society and the Council of the Americas in New York. An Officer of the Order of Canada and recipient of fourteen honorary doctorates, Wallin has written three books: *Speaking of Success, The Comfort of Cats*, and the bestselling memoir *Since You Asked*. She lives in Toronto.

David Weale, a self-described mystic, was born in Calgary, but moved to Prince Edward Island as a child. He has authored eleven books, including four for children and the memoir, *Chasing the Shore: Little Stories about Spirit and Landscape*. Well known on the Island as a story-teller, Weale hosted an award-winning radio program called *Them Times* for CBC Charlottetown and has been featured frequently as a guest contributor on CBC Radio's *Tapestry*. He lives in Charlottetown.

Rudy Wiebe was born in 1934 in an isolated farm community near Fairholme, Saskatchewan. For thirty years, he taught literature and creative writing at colleges and universities in Canada, the United States, and Germany. He is the winner of numerous awards, including two Governor General's Literary Awards for the novels *The Temptations of Big Bear* and *A Discovery of Strangers* and the 2007 Charles Taylor Award for the memoir *Of This Earth: A Mennonite Boyhood in the Boreal Forest*. An Officer of the Order of Canada, Wiebe lives in Edmonton.